THE
TELEVISION
PROGRAM

Its Direction and

Production

THE TELEVISION PROGRAM

Its Direction and Production

FIFTH EDITION

Edward Stasheff / *Rudy Bretz*
John Gartley / *Lynn Gartley*

HILL AND WANG / NEW YORK
A division of Farrar, Straus and Giroux

This edition copyright © 1976 by Farrar, Straus and Giroux, Inc.
Prior editions copyright © 1951, 1953, 1956, 1962, 1968
by Hill and Wang (now Farrar, Straus and Giroux, Inc.)
All rights reserved
Printed in the United States of America
Published simultaneously in Canada
by McGraw-Hill Ryerson Ltd., Toronto
ISBN (clothbound edition): 0–8090–9181–X
ISBN (paperback edition): 0–8090–1378–9
Illustrations, except where otherwise credited, by Rudy Bretz
Fifth edition, 1976
Designed by Marion Hess

Sixth printing, 1982

Library of Congress Cataloging in Publication Data
Main entry under title:
The Television program.
    First–4th ed. by E. Stasheff and R. Bretz.
    Includes index.
    1. Television programs. 2. Television—Pro-
duction and direction. I. Stasheff, Edward.
II. Stasheff, Edward. The television program.
PN1992.5.T37 1976   791.45′023   75–29333
ISBN 0–8090–9181–X
ISBN 0–8090–1378–9 pbk.

Acknowledgments

As we have said in earlier editions, no book on television could ever be written without the help of many people, just as no television program can be produced without the cooperation of nearly the same number. We express our gratitude to the many organizations and individuals who have contributed to this volume.

The organizations include the following: the ABC, NBC, and NHK (Japan Broadcasting Corporation) networks; Stations KTLA, WMSB, and WBBM; Michigan State University, Northwestern University, the University of Michigan Television Center, and the University of Southern California; and Desilu Productions.

The individuals to whom we are most indebted are Henry R. Austin; Alfred Bester; Guy de Vry; George Finkel; Garnet R. Garrison; the late Albert McCleery; Thomas Pincu; Hazen J. Schumacher, Jr.; Hal F. Schulte, Jr.; Alfred H. Slote; and Shozo Usami.

Contents

Illustrations

Plates

Figures

Scripts (*excerpts*)

Charts

THE
TELEVISION
PROGRAM

Its Direction and
Production

1 / Introduction

THE NATURE OF TELEVISION

Television, the child of three parents—theatre, film, and radio—found it hard to establish its own identity in its early days. While television experimented with its potential and strived to determine its own creative identity, practitioners from its parent arts gave it unkind names. Some theatre actors who had fared poorly before the electronic cameras called television drama "summer stock in an iron lung." Film people who feared the rapidly growing infant contemptuously named it "grade-Z movies with the fluffs left in." A few radio producers who foresaw the end of radio as an art whistled past the graveyard by referring to television as "bad audio with pictures."

Actually, many of the programs of television's younger days were almost literally transplants of material from the theatre, the vaudeville stage, or the radio studio. Some took hold and flourished; others could not make the adjustment to the new medium and faded away. Live television made possible the transmission of other forms of entertainment at the moment of, and from the place of, their original presentation. Examples of this type of broadcast include telecasts of sporting events such as the Rose Bowl and other imitators and events such as variety shows, the Oscar presentations, and some situation comedies.

Television variety programs were often produced on the stage of a studio theatre. The performers, especially comedians, were mainly from stage and vaudeville and depended on the reactions of a live audience in order to gauge their timing. In addition, the viewer derives added enjoyment from hearing (and occasionally seeing) the laughter and applause of spectators. This consideration led many producers to dub recorded laughter into the sound tracks of filmed comedies, or to "augment electronically," by skillful use of microphone, amplifier, and echo chamber, the less than thunderous applause of an actual audience. Within certain

3

limits a poor joke seems better if you hear others laughing at it; a good joke is sure to sound funnier. The viewer-listener is subconsciously carried along by the crowd.

Besides being an electronic means of transmitting older art forms, television soon began to be seen as a new art form in itself. As radio and film had done in their early development many years before, television first borrowed techniques from other media and later developed traditions and techniques peculiar to itself.

Perhaps the most distinctive function of television is its ability to show distant events at the moment when they are taking place. The Kefauver hearings with a close-up of the hands of Frank Costello; the Army-McCarthy hearings; the complete coverage of manned exploration of the moon; the presidential nominating conventions; the Watergate hearings; the funerals of the Kennedys and Martin Luther King; the live transmissions from around the world via satellite—this is television doing what no other medium can do.

THE NATURE OF TELEVISION PRODUCTION

It is important to distinguish *live* television production from tape or film production *for* television—which is *also* called "television production" today. In general, the public uses the term "television" for whatever is finally seen on the home screen. A film made for television in 35mm or 16mm may be in contention for a television Emmy Award, not a film Oscar; a film made originally on video tape, transferred to film, and shown in theatres, may use television production techniques but would not be called television.

The most striking characteristic of television production, either live or on tape, is its speed. Even allowing for differences between large and small stations and the types of programming in each, there is a tremendous quantity of product that must be, can be, and usually is turned out in a minimum length of time. The producer or director of a major-network program may concentrate on an hour of air time every week. In smaller stations, a combination producer-director may grind out as many as five hours a week, although much of this programming consists of "format shows"—that is, productions in which the sets, talent, even basic camera shots are the same day after day, as in the case of newscasts, interview programs, and audience-participation shows. The amount of material developed in individual stations has, of course, increased dramatically in those stations that have taken full advantage of the half hour of additional time made available with the advent of the Prime

Time Access Rule.* Producer-directors in the active Public Broadcasting Service (P.B.S.) and cable-television operations, of course, have even greater responsibility for programs that they originate.

In addition to full programs, the small-station director is often assigned to "residue," a polite name for the odds and ends of station breaks, local commercials, "cut-ins" on network programs, and "sign-on" and "sign-off." Or this individual may put on the air half a dozen locally produced videotaped commercials or as many film spots in the course of an hour of syndicated film—all this on top of full responsibility for some full-length programs. Yet, while the flow of program product cannot hope to achieve the artistry or even the sheer surface "slickness" of a film production which has consumed several weeks or months, television programming must still meet at least minimum standards of smoothness, to say nothing of entertainment value.

The Television Craftsman

The preceding discussion of the responsibilities of the director-producer is not intended to intimidate the neophyte, but simply to point out the conditions of terrific pressure and speed under which television personnel work. The video director takes part in the performance while it is on the air or being taped and the quality of his performance definitely and immediately affects the production. Accordingly, the director must be quick to react, must make immediate decisions, must be able to coordinate a great many elements and tie them into a consistent and effective whole.

The need for an individual who can maintain absolute control over himself, his crew, and his assistants, under the most adverse and trying circumstances, has led most stations in the country to restrict the actual directing of the show to their staff directors or to outside directors of established reputation. The program may be produced or written by an outsider, it may be conceived by persons not connected with the station, and even require preliminary rehearsal elsewhere, but when the show comes into the studio, it must be placed in the hands of individuals who have complete mastery of the tools of their trade.

The limited opportunity to rehearse in the studio compels all concerned, but particularly the director, to do a great deal of planning and rehearsing. The director of a one-hour dramatic program or musical variety show that is to be taped will have ten or more hours in the studio for full technical rehearsal and taping, preceded by two or more weeks'

* A Federal Communications Commission ruling that restricted network broadcasts on any local station to three hours, during the 7:00 to 11:00 P.M. period.

work in an outside rehearsal hall. During the rehearsal period, the director will have planned his action in relation to camera shots, visualizing every camera move and position, so that when the cast comes into the studio, the fewest number of changes will have to be made. This method of operation requires a very close familiarity with just what the studio facilities can and cannot do.

Whether the prospective worker in television is to operate as a writer, as a director, as a producer, or in one of the many other capacities associated with production, a knowledge of the limitations and possibilities of the television studio is essential.

Plate 1.   Large TV studio of station KTLA, Los Angeles independent station. Dramatic production, *Moon for the Misbegotten*, in progress. (Courtesy of KTLA)

Television Studios

By 1960, only about half the stations in the country were operating in buildings specifically designed for television production. While the situation has dramatically improved in commercial stations, many P.B.S. and CATV studios and studios utilized by educational institutions for training, instruction, or both, are often located in facilities inadequate for the needs of television. As a result, the favorite complaint of production personnel often is concerned with the lack of space.

In a complex production facility (such as WBBM–TV in Chicago) lack of space around the studio is as serious as lack of space on the studio floor. As a rule, the complex production studio should have three or four times as many square feet of service space outside the studio as in the studio itself. This area is needed for storage and production needs—including set building and painting, furniture and prop storage, storage of completed and temporarily unused sets, maintenance and storage of costumes, dressing and make-up rooms, facilities for the production of graphics, and, finally, empty rooms for rehearsal. So regularly have stations supplied insufficient space for these services that one gen-

Plate 2.   Typical small TV studio. Theta Cable, Los Angeles. (Courtesy of Berkey Colortran, Division of Berkey Photo)

erally finds a pile of miscellaneous props, special effects, and assorted equipment—stored, or at least "placed temporarily," in the halls or in the studio itself. In buildings specifically designed for television production, with adequate construction and storage space, such crowding is less common.

The average studio at a small station rarely exceeds 30 by 50 feet. It is equipped with two or three cameras mounted on wheeled supports capable of quick repositioning in any direction. Each camera is connected by a long flexible cable to its own monitor and control unit, which is placed in the control room.

Television Control Rooms

The process of directing a show utilizing two or more cameras requires switching between them. While one studio camera is in use, the other(s) may be repositioned and lined up on shots that are to follow.

Switching originally was done by an engineer, sometimes called the "switcher"; sometimes—as in situations in which the individual also served as a supervisor of the entire engineering crew assigned to a given production—he was called the "technical director" or T.D. In England, the job is known as "vision mixer" and is generally performed by women. In more recent years, many of the smaller commercial stations and some of the educational stations have evolved a system whereby the director does his own switching. Some directors find the manipulation of the controls during a complicated program an added burden and a source of potential error; others prefer it for the added precision of timing it allows. (See Plate 20.)

Under either system, the person doing the switching operates a battery of push buttons, levers, and dials which control the transitions from one camera's picture to another's. Usually each camera or other picture source is displayed on a separate screen. The result of this switching—the air program as the audience sees it—is viewed by the director on a screen called the master program or line monitor.

Not all the images that make up the show will come from the cameras in the studio. Projection units called "film chains" or "telecine" may supply slides, stills, and/or motion-picture film, all of which must also be previewed in the studio's control room. Usually this projection equipment is located in a projection room, but in smaller stations it may be found in the control room itself.

In order for the director to preview what is being projected, each film chain usually has its own monitor in the control room, as does each videotape recorder (VTR), but in some systems a preview monitor is provided for added convenience, and on it the picture of any source—

Plate 3. Three control rooms. *Top:* Example of an elaborate control room, NHK TV Studio CT-106, Tokyo, used primarily for dramatic programs. Front row from left: audio operator, production director, technical director, lighting director, and two lighting operators. In back row, foreground: sound-effects operator. (Courtesy of NHK [Japan Broadcasting Corp.]) *Center:* News Center Control Room, NHK. Monitors display various picture sources, such as videotape, film chains, and studio cameras locally, plus incoming pictures from remote pick-up trucks, helicopters, and international transmissions via satellite. News-program run-down (script outline) is displayed for the control-room crew on the large monitor at their right. (Courtesy of NHK [Japan Broadcasting Corp.]) *Bottom:* General-purpose control room, Channel 34, Los Angeles. Video-camera controls at left, director and audio operator center, videotape operator standing at back. In foreground agency representative watches production. (Courtesy of Berkey Colortran, Division of Berkey Photo)

live camera, film chain, or VTR—may be "punched up" at the director's request. Such a preview monitor may be used, with proper auxiliary equipment, to preview special effects, such as superimpositions, keys, or special montages (all of which will be discussed in later chapters). In short, even in a modestly equipped station, the director must often keep his eyes roving over the screens of two camera monitors, two film-chain monitors, a preview monitor, and a line monitor.

Many control rooms are built on two levels—one level behind and slightly above the other, both facing a window into the studio or a wall of monitors (this second type of arrangement is called a "blind" control room). On the lower level are placed the monitors described above, the camera control units, and the video engineers who operate them. The production staff—the director and his assistant(s)—sit at a desk on the upper level. The switcher may operate on either level, depending on where the switching equipment has been located. Since switching is a production function and is frequently done by the director or his assistant, it really belongs on the production desk at the top level. Many stations have worked out their own variations on this basic plan determined by their own particular production needs.

Completely separate from the video or picture system, and usually with its own operator, is the audio or sound system. The studio console that controls the various microphones and sound production equipment is similar to that found in most radio stations. Some television stations still use turntables as an audio source, but greater use is made today of taped sound, utilizing a tape deck or cartridge (cart) system. Carts are most often found in master control,* where they are used for quick messages behind station identification (I.D.) slides.

The television control room contains a loudspeaker through which the personnel involved may monitor the audio portion of the program, which then goes out of the studio on a separate line. In many modern studios where complex production is done, the audio operator is placed in a small adjoining control room, with glass partitions separating him from the confused mumble of sound generated by other crew members in the control room. This permits greater concentration on the audio engineer's part, and closer attention, for example, to the subtleties of balance between an orchestra and a vocalist.

The audio console controls various microphones—which may be of different types or may be identical—some of which may hang from overhead, some, like radio mikes, may be mounted on stands or on tables, some on long booms to follow performers, and some may be placed on

---

* Stations with two or more studios commonly have a master control room into which all studios feed and from which transmissions emanate.

the performers themselves. Small lavalier (around the neck) and "tie-clip" mikes are used by many newsmen and other performers. Cordless microphones that transmit by radio are often preferred because of the greater mobility they allow the performer.

The Television Crew

We have so far described, in addition to the director and his assistant or associate director, the following control-room engineers: a technical director, one or more video engineers, and an audio engineer, who sometimes has an assistant. In the studio there will be a cameraman for each camera (some of the more sophisticated dolly and crane cameras—discussed in Chapter 2—require at least two operators), and possibly a microphone-boom operator or two, depending on the size of the studio and the number of boom mikes in use. Also working in the studio is another assistant of the director's, usually called the floor manager, floor director, or stage manager. In addition to transmitting the director's instructions to performers on the set, the floor manager carries on whatever activities the director would if the director were able to be in the studio as well as in the control room. The floor manager cues the cast and controls the floor crew, which may include persons who shift the scenery, move props and furniture, change lights, and produce sound effects. Sometimes this floor work is done by the camera crew, sometimes by specially assigned personnel, engaged for that specific purpose, who in larger stations are union stagehands, drawn from the same union (IATSE) which supplies the legitimate theatres.

The floor manager and cameramen wear telephone headsets that connect with similar apparatus used by the director and T.D. The mike-boom operator wears earphones through at least one of which he can hear the instructions of the director; when necessary, the audio engineer may come in with his own instructions.

It should be pointed out, however, that we have been discussing the maximum, rather than the typical, television crew. It is to be found chiefly in the network studios in New York and Los Angeles. Many variations are common. For example, one network-owned station places the assistant director in the studio, where he also performs the duties of a floor manager, and we have mentioned that in some stations the director does his own switching. In others, video control and the video engineers for all studios are centralized in the master control room. Thus one may walk into a smoothly functioning local station and find in the control room only the director and one engineer. On the studio floor will

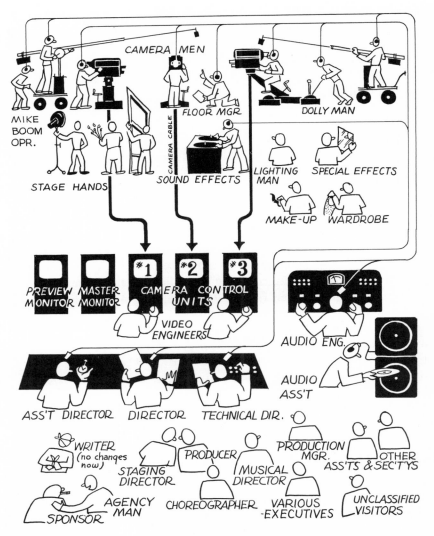

Figure 1. Studio and control-room personnel involved in a large-studio production. Musicians and performers are not shown. Observers at the rear of the control room are rarely all present at the same time, but all can have access to the control room. It is common practice for the video engineers and the audio engineers each to have their own control room, or glassed-in cubicle adjacent to the production control room.

be one cameraman at each camera and possibly, though not inevitably, a floor manager who is also the complete floor crew.

Going even further toward the end of the "limited personnel" spec-

Figure 2.   Studio and control-room personnel involved in a typical small-station local program. One performer is shown, indicating an educational program or a news show. The director is simultaneously following the script, watching monitors, and doing his own switching. He may also control projectors, watch timing, and make simple video adjustments.

trum, some instructional television centers have simplified production to the point where they can operate with a one-man crew. By the mid-1970's, a number of universities, including Southern Methodist, Stanford, the University of Michigan, and the University of Pennsylvania, had begun operating "classroom studios." In these facilities, professors teach on-campus classes of twenty to thirty students while simultaneously reaching hundreds more in special receiving classrooms at distant points. Many of these distant installations were set up for their employees by industrial organizations such as Bell Telephone, Bendix, Chrysler, General Motors, RCA, and many others, to permit employees to work for advanced degrees, usually in engineering and business administration, on company time. Classrooms in participating company buildings are frequently linked to the campus classroom studio by telephone lines, thus permitting two-way radio communication during *live* presentations.

A typical originating classroom of this type is equipped with three

Plate 4. Typical classroom studios. *Top, center right,* and *bottom:* Norman Topping Instructional TV Center, University of Southern California. (Courtesy of University of Southern California) *Center left:* College of Engineering, University of Michigan. (Courtesy of Mr. Hal F. Schulte, Jr.)

remote-control cameras: one at the back of the room covering the instructor and the chalkboards at the front of the room; one overhead covering a predetermined area on the instructor's desk, on which he may write notes, diagrams, or formulas on a fixed pad; and a third, mounted at the front of the room, covering the on-campus students during a discussion, and ready to zoom in on an individual student as he asks a question.

In the control room, a single operator (call him/her director and engineer combined, if you like) points each of the cameras by remote pan, tilt, and zoom mechanisms, cuts from camera to camera as the situation requires, handles the audio inputs from the instructor's microphone or from the hanging mikes that pick up the responses of the in-studio class, and in addition must still be alert to questions or comments from the distant students who may join in by using the telephones or hanging microphones in the remote classrooms. Student responses are heard in the studio and in all connected locations. Occasionally, students at remote locations carry on discussions with students in the studio.

When necessary, the operator also starts a videotape recorder, if the lesson is to be preserved for future study, and in some installations changes slides or inserts film segments as the instructor calls for them. While it has been said facetiously that the ideal individual for this job would be an octopus with a major in television production and a minor in electrical engineering, the number of such one-man operations is increasing.

Lest it be assumed that remote-control cameras are limited to instructional uses, it should be pointed out that many broadcasting studios have used such systems in localities where labor contracts did not specifically forbid it. For instance, the BBC news room, the setting for nightly newscasts, is equipped with five plumbicon* color cameras, each capable of panning, tilting, or zooming from fixed positions with never a camera operator in sight. At the BBC, presumably, the attempt is not to save salaries but to save space. Camera operators are located in the control room; one man can handle two or three cameras.

Initiating a Program

The particular production procedures commonly used in producing

---

* Video cameras are generally classed according to the pick-up tube they employ. The plumbicon tube, like the vidicon, is about one inch in diameter and six inches long, but has greater sensitivity to light, among other advantages. The name derives from the Latin *plumbum* (for lead, a compound of which is used in its light-sensitive plate).

a given show will depend on the size of the station and its staff, the extent of its facilities, and the type of program. It is obvious, for example, that the production procedure required to produce a half-hour situation comedy will differ radically from that involved in a fifteen-minute (host-guest) interview.

A program begins with an original conception in someone's mind—station producer, outside producer, independent writer, or, more often, the station's program director. Very often other members of a station's staff will submit ideas which the program producer may decide are salable. The concept is then embodied in what is called a "presentation," which may vary from a few typewritten paragraphs, summarizing the program and its advantages, to an elaborate folder illustrated with photographs of the proposed performers or story-board drawings visualizing the program. In most stations no further progress will be made until this presentation has attracted a sponsor. In some cases, the program actually may be produced and presented on a sustaining basis (i.e., paid for by the broadcaster) for a limited number of weeks in the hope of building up an audience and attracting a sponsor.

A station may even completely produce the initial program of a series without broadcasting it. This is standard procedure with independent production companies involved in production either for eventual network programming or for syndication. Such sample programs are known as "pilots." They may be produced on film, videotape, or videotape transferred to film so that they can be shown to numerous groups at different times. Occasionally a potential commercial message advertising the product manufactured by a prospective sponsor is included in the pilot, or spliced in for the occasion, so that the client may see how his commercial will look within the framework of the program.

Once the new program has received the green light, the executive will assign the series to a producer, to a writer if scripting is indicated, or, in a smaller organization, to a producer-director who may also be given the responsibility of writing the script. Sometimes the person who originated the program idea will continue to supervise its production for the length of its run; sometimes the originator will take active control of the series for the first few broadcasts, then turn it over to another person after the production policies have been set. In any event, *someone* will be assigned the task of putting the various elements of the program together, either for live broadcast or for recording in advance of broadcast date.

Program Personnel

Our discussion so far has been concerned with those workers most immediately associated with actually putting the show on the air. On the staff of a network-originating station we are likely to find several producers. One producer will supervise a number of programs, each of which will have its own director. The producer will be held responsible for the quality of his programs, will make sure the show stays within its budget, will select scripts or commission writers, and will advise the director on many matters.

Other specialized workers employed by network-originating stations include dance and musical directors, scenic designers, carpenters and painters, lighting supervisors (lighting directors), sound-effects and special-effects technicians, property men, wardrobe supervisors, make-up personnel, and a host of others. Since the smaller stations cannot afford these many specialists, the program and engineering staffs pitch in and do everything. An intermediate position is taken by other stations, which have one or two individuals who design and execute settings and graphics and whose cameramen and floor managers put up the sets, do the lighting, and generally take over where the set designer leaves off.

BACKGROUND FOR A TELEVISION CAREER

In view of both the derivative and unique nature of television, the student may well wonder what background and training would be best to bring into the field. While there is no one answer, the accompanying chart shows how the production techniques of radio, film, and theatre have contributed to the techniques of television. As can be seen, television owes a great deal to its parent media. There are many other fields that can provide background for a television career. In addition to expertise with studio equipment, the potential psychological impact of the medium demands an understanding of the techniques involved in production. A student who is seriously involved in the educational aspect of the medium should have some teaching experience, know something about the theories of learning and how to specify learning objectives, and be familiar with instructional television utilization techniques, methods of testing and evaluation, and educational television experiments and programs throughout the world.

This short discussion can do no more than barely suggest the complex skills that are involved in television production. The newcomer to the field needs to have some awareness of all that is involved, a reasonable competence in several areas, and the potential for developing great skill in some specialized subdivision of the many television arts.

A beginner, embarking upon his first job in television, may get the

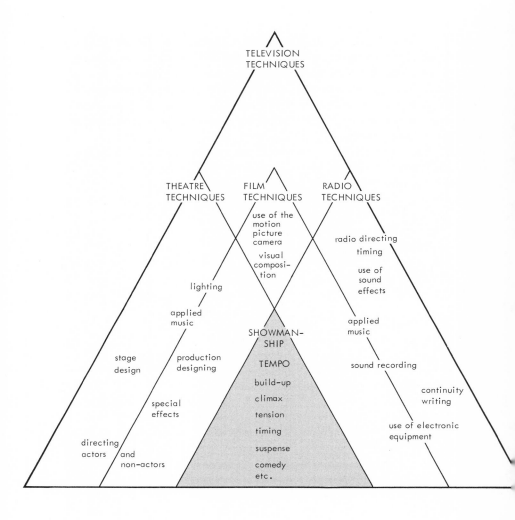

Figure 3.   Production techniques of television in relation to those of three parent media. The three inner pyramids, representing theatre, film, and radio, overlap in large areas, as indicated by lower-case labels. Television is represented by the larger, overall pyramid, not because it is the highest medium, but because it incorporates most of the production techniques of the other three.

feeling that ways of doing things are set and that innovations are no longer welcomed. This is true only to the extent that innovations, whether technical or aesthetic, must be practicable, and if he is working in a commercial station, this means commercial. In many stations of all sizes and types, experimentation in production methods is still going on. The discussion of production techniques, program types, and directing methods in the following pages is meant to introduce the reader to the standard techniques and a few recent innovations as a point of departure from which he may later devise some techniques of his own.

2 / Camera Concepts: Shots and Lenses

Television's basic unit is the *shot*. Except in sequences utilizing only one camera, any television show consists of one shot after another, building up to a unified whole whose total effect is generally greater than the sum of its individual parts.

What is a shot? Generally speaking, it is what appears on the television screen at any given instant. A shot may change imperceptibly or abruptly, for example, when either the camera or the subject moves. It may last for a very few seconds, or it may be held for a minute or even for the entire program if that is the best way to show what is going on. But anyone who works in television must learn to think in terms of shots and must master the basic shots that have been taken over by television from the film medium.

In television a shot is what is seen on the screen from the moment one camera is put on the air until it is replaced by another. In motion pictures it can be defined as one continuous series of frames (usually one piece of film), representing a continuous operation of the camera. In either medium, then, a shot is the image (series of images, actually) created by one camera, during one discrete length of time.

Programs usually consist of a large number of shots; sometimes as many as a hundred or more in a half hour. Over the years of television and film for television, certain sequence patterns have been established. These patterns or conventions have been guided by what information the audience wants to see. This text is based on the accepted conventions of television, with the realization that there are situations which require breaking these rules or conventions. The television director may follow the conventions of shot sequence or follow his own inclinations if he believes it will enhance the artistry of the program. The director should be cautioned, however, that an unfamiliar pattern of shots may make an audience overly aware of technique.

CAMERAS, MOUNTS, AND LENSES
MAKE THE SHOT

The shots to be discussed in this chapter can be conceived by the director, and realized in production, only within the limitations of the television cameras, mounts, and lenses with which he works. The lighting, the set design, and even the shot selection are, at least in part, all affected by the electronic characteristics of the particular camera that is used. The three electronic camera types (*vidicon, plumbicon,* and *image-orthicon*) are discussed in more detail in the section on lenses. The type of camera movement within a shot and the speed of repositioning between shots are determined by the camera-mounting devices.

Camera Mounts

The tripod dolly is the typical camera mounting used in small stations and in many industrial production studios. Originally a heavy-duty photographic tripod was attached to a simple triangular dolly with three caster wheels. Once the camera had been mounted on tripod and dolly its height could not be changed. Later designs combined tripod and dolly into one piece and added a means whereby camera height could be changed while the camera was not on the air. The tripod-dolly design is

Plate 5.   Tripod dolly, *left*, in training studio in Denver Police Academy. Shibaden color camera is shown, mounted on a cradle head. At *right*, students at Pitzer College, California, operate a light pedestal dolly which has a hand crank for off-the-air vertical adjustment. (Courtesy of Berkey Colortran, Division of Berkey Photo)

excellent for quick repositioning of the camera, since the casters will swivel in any direction and the camera can be moved directly without backing and steering. Some skill is needed, however, to achieve smooth on-the-air movement.

The studio pedestal, especially designed for television, is the most flexible all-around camera mount in the television studio. Typical equipment in a complex production facility and often preferred by cameramen to two-man boom dollies, it can be repositioned quickly in any direction.

Plate 6. Typical camera pedestals. *Left:* Innovative Television Equipment pedestal (Model ITE-P4) with mechanically counterbalanced vertical adjustment. (Courtesy of Innovative Television Equipment) *Right:* Vinten pedestal (English manufacturer) with pneumatically counterbalanced vertical adjustment. The Norelco camera shown is mounted on a cam head. (Courtesy of KTLA)

Its three wheels are connected by a bicycle chain and may be steered synchronously by the large circular wheel around the pedestal. Skilled cameramen use this consistently for on-the-air dolly shots. On the simpler mechanical pedestals, a large crank on the side raises and lowers the camera. The better pedestals are counterbalanced, pneumatic, or hydraulic, so it is only necessary to lift the camera gently to raise it.

The panoram dolly (or two-man dolly) contains a turntable bearing a six-foot boom which can be placed at any angle, and can raise the lens of the camera to seven feet or lower it to about eighteen inches. Use of this machine allows for more complex camera movement than the pedestal will normally provide, but it takes up considerable room in a small studio. The panoram dolly is used with greatest flexibility when space allows it to be placed crossways to the set. The cameraman then releases the turntable so it spins readily and, standing on the floor behind the camera, dollies in or out by walking forward or back. Vertical movements ("boom up" or "boom down") can be made on the air if the cameraman-dollyman team is highly skilled.

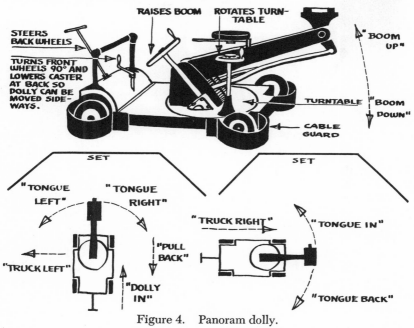

Figure 4. Panoram dolly.

The camera crane requires two and sometimes three operators. When the operation is manual, a cameraman, dolly pusher, and boom operator are necessary for full utilization of the device. Some cranes are provided with electrical controls so that the cameraman can operate the boom. This reduces the required crew and simplifies production, since coordination among fewer operators means less rehearsal time required. NHK, the Japanese broadcasting service, developed a crane on which the cameraman does not ride the boom, but sits instead on the wheeled base, watching an electronic viewfinder and manipulating both camera and boom by remote controls.

Camera Mounting Heads

The camera mounting head fits between the camera mount and the camera, allowing the camera to be rotated left and right or up and down. There are three common types of camera mounting heads, each with a different means to prevent the camera from becoming top-heavy

Plate 7.   Elaborate crane dolly in use at the NHK studios, Tokyo. As with all crane dollies, effective operation requires three operators. Left to right: the car driver, the boom operator, the cameraman. In this unique design the cameraman operates remotely with an electronic viewfinder, instead of riding the crane, thus allowing a lighter boom construction with less counterbalancing. The cameraman's platform rotates with the boom. Note that each operator is provided with his own electronic viewfinder, a necessity for accurate work. (Courtesy of NHK [Japan Broadcasting Corp.])

when it is tilted. Each of these has locking devices and drag controls to adjust tension on both the pan and tilt mechanisms.

The *torsion head* uses a strong spring to counterbalance the camera weight when it is tilted. The farther the camera tilts, the greater the resistance of the spring. The spring is adjustable to fit the weight of various cameras, but is rarely exactly matched, and a cameraman cannot take his hands off a camera on such a mount without having to first lock the tilting mechanism.

The *cradle head* has the effect of rolling the base of the camera back as its top is tilted forward, thus rotating it about its center of gravity and preventing it from becoming top-heavy. (See Plate 7.) Cradle heads are often used with particularly heavy cameras. They must be constructed for the specific cameras with which they are to be used, however; cameras with differently located centers of gravity require different cradle heads.

The *cam head* supports the camera in a tilt by a much simpler process, which is difficult to explain without the aid of a motion demonstration. The part of the head that is attached to the camera rests against the base of the head by means of two curved pieces called cams. When the camera is level, the center (highest part) of each cam rests on its roller support. (See Figure 5.) When tilted forward, the camera rises while the end of the cam comes to press against the roller from the front, thus opposing the tendency of the camera to tilt farther forward. To tilt further the camera must rise further; thus it is actually counterbalanced

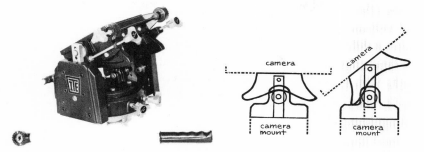

Figure 5. Cam head. Drawings illustrate how the cam forces the camera to rise as it is tilted forward. A different cam is required for each camera model because weight and location of center of gravity vary between cameras, and the cams are designed to balance top-heaviness with camera weight at every degree of tilt. Cams may be changed easily when the head is used for another camera. (Photograph courtesy of Innovative Television Equipment)

by its own weight. The cam head may be easily adapted to cameras of different size and weight simply by changing to cams of a different shape.

The Lens

Each television camera is usually equipped with one zoom lens or, if a turret camera is still in use, three to five lenses. Occasionally, a director will leave it to the cameraman to choose which focal length to use on a given shot, as though it were some mysterious technical function about which he could be as legitimately innocent as he is about electronic tubes and circuits. This is actually not the case, however. The choice and application of the right lens are dependent on the content of the shot and the position of the camera in the studio; a director cannot plan either of these without taking the lens into consideration.

Focal Length and Field of View

The core and center of the television camera is the camera tube. Television cameras are built around camera tubes of several types, the most common of which are the plumbicon, vidicon, and image-orthicon.

The director who works in a studio equipped with plumbicon or vidicon cameras, as in most school studios, uses a zoom or two standard lenses (the one-inch and two-inch) most of the time. The plumbicon and vidicon tubes utilize the same lenses, but the image-orthicon requires a different set of lenses (approximately twice the focal length for the same angle of view). The director in a studio using image-orthicons works with the zoom lens or the 50mm, the 90mm, and the 135mm lenses. These numbers refer to the "focal length" of the lens, its most distinguishing characteristic. Yet the *result* of the focal length is actually the most important factor, and that is the field of view.

Technically, focal length may be defined as "the distance between the optical center of the lens and the face of the television tube when the

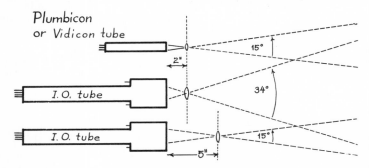

Figure 6.   Comparison of the plumbicon and vidicon with image-orthicon tubes. Due to the larger image area on the face of the I.O. tube, a 2-inch focal length results in a wider angle of view. For a 15-degree angle of view the I.O. camera requires a 5-inch focal length.

lens is focused at infinity." In nontechnical terms, the focal length of a lens determines how much of the subject and its background will be taken in, as well as certain other factors which are discussed later.

At first, it might seem tempting to keep the cameras a good distance from the subject and use the longer focal length to view the subject. The problem with this procedure is that the longer the focal length, the shallower the depth of field; the flatter the picture; the more difficult the problems of focus and smooth movement.

The other extreme is the wide-angle lens or an equivalent position on the zoom. The shorter the focal length, the greater the exaggeration of depth, and the easier the problems of focus and camera movement. When the camera is on a wide-angle lens, however, it must work much closer to the subject. It may intrude into the field of view of other cameras, run up against risers or platforms, or cast shadows on the set. A short focal length also may distort the image at the sides of the picture, and if a performer extends an arm toward the camera, the hand looms very large and the fingers may take on the appearance of a bunch of bananas.

Both long and short focal length have a marked effect on depth of field. Depth of field may be defined as the area within which objects are held in sharp focus without adjusting the camera. It is described in terms of the distance from the nearest sharp object to the farthest sharp object. If the depth of field is great, a subject may move toward or away from the camera a considerable amount without requiring the cameraman to adjust focus; if the depth of field is shallow, the cameraman will be constantly focusing even for relatively slight forward and backward movement. It is in the optical nature of lenses that lenses of short focal length have a greater depth of field, and lenses of long focal length have a shallower depth of field. The shorter, the deeper; and of course, the longer, the shallower.

TYPES OF SHOTS

We may classify and discuss the most commonly used shots in six different ways: (1) field of view; (2) area of subject visible; (3) number of subjects included; (4) camera angle; (5) camera movement; (6) purpose or function of the shot.

1. Field of View

This is the most convenient way, in most instances, for a director to describe a shot to the cameraman who must get it for him. The widest possible shot would be the

Extreme Long Shot, or ELS

As we move closer, we get the more familiar

Long shot,   or LS

Moving steadily in, we come to

Medium Long Shot, or MLS
Medium Shot,   or MS
Medium Close-up, or MCU
Close-up,   or CU

The long shot shows us as much of the subject as possible, but is long only in relation to the other shots associated with it. For example, if one is shooting a sequence involving objects on a tabletop, a shot covering the entire table would be a long shot. But if the sequence involved an entire room, this same tabletop shot might be a close-up. The major purpose of the long shot is to acquaint the audience with the overall appearance of the whole subject and with the relationship of each of its parts. This type of shot is often called the orientation, or establishing, shot.

The close-up is one of the best compensations for the small size of the television screen. It is most essential in creating intimacy and in getting the viewer to see clearly what is transpiring. Dramatic effect is due as much to what is not shown as to what is. When the attention of the audience is limited to a small area of the scene, a particular detail can be pointed up and emphasized in a way that would be impossible if it were seen only as one among many objects in a wider shot. An important number on the door of a hotel room; a telling expression on an actor's face; an incriminating bit of evidence left behind by the criminal, later to be found by the great detective—each of these can be shown exclusively. The entire meaning of a scene can be changed by the details which the director may choose to emphasize in close-ups.

The term "tight close-up" (TCU) is used to describe a shot that includes an even more limited area than the close-up. A common example is an actor's head which more than fills the screen. When the camera approaches even closer to the subject and we see, for example, only a portion of the face, the shot is usually called an "extreme close-up" (ECU).

An interesting shot that probably had its genesis in television drama

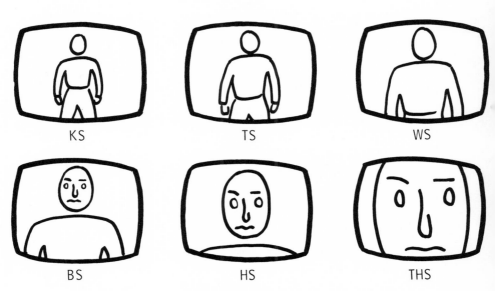

KS   TS   WS

BS   HS   THS

Figure 7.   Shots classified according to area of subject visible.

is the combination of a close-up with a long shot. This "combo" shot places one person close to the camera while another is seen beyond him in the distance. This type of shot lends itself to interesting composition, since there is depth in the scene and the figures of people are of different sizes and different heights.

2. Area of Subject Visible

Since the subject most often on the screen is a person, it is often convenient to identify a shot in terms of the portion of the figure included in the frame. Since the top of the actor's head is usually near the top of the picture, shots will vary according to the lowest part of the actor shown at the bottom of the picture. Thus we have a series of identifying terms like this:

Full-Figure Shot	FF
Knee Shot	KS
Thigh Shot	TS
Waist Shot	WS
Bust Shot	BS
Head Shot	HS
Tight Head Shot	THS

Each director will develop his own abbreviations and often his own special shot categories. John Frankenheimer, for example, started a new trend, at least among Frankenheimer admirers, by calling an extremely tight shot cutting off part of the subject's head a "slash."

Some directors, for example, refer to a "pocket shot," one whose bottom frame line just barely includes the gentleman's pocket handkerchief. Again, two heads in close proximity and tightly framed supply a shot sometimes known as a "tight two-shot."

There are no hard-and-fast rules about the use of these terms or any of the others in the four categories that follow. The terms all serve to help a director tell a cameraman as quickly as possible the type of shot he wants, or help the cameraman make notes to himself on his cue sheet.

3. Number of Subjects Included

This is undoubtedly the simplest, most easily memorized set of shot designations and accompanying shorthand symbols. If only one person is included in a given shot, we call it a "one-shot" and abbreviate it as "1-sh." Obviously, then, a shot that includes two persons is a "two-shot," or "2-sh"; one with three people is a "three-shot," or "3-sh"; and four people give us a "four-shot," or "4-sh." But as we move on up to five or six people, we find a tendency to refer to such a composition as a "group shot," or "GP-SH."

4. Camera Angle*

The Low-Angle and High-Angle Shots. While "low" and "high" are relative terms, we may use a rough general rule: If we assume that the eye-level shot with the taking lens at four or five feet from the studio floor is normal, then any shot in which the lens is less than three feet from the floor is a "low-angle" shot. On the other hand, the lens may be

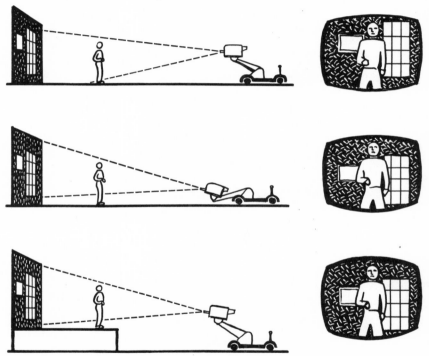

Figure 8.   Low-angle shot: two ways to achieve it. *Top:* normal, about shoulder level; *center* and *bottom:* camera at level of thigh. This can be achieved either by lowering camera or raising subject.

kept at any given height, but if the subject is elevated by means of a platform, a stairway, or even a ladder, we would still have a "low-angle" shot. (See Figures 8 and 9.)

* "Camera angle" refers to the placement of the camera in relation to the subject and should not be confused with "angle of view" of the lens.

By the same token, any shot in which the camera is above the eye level of the subject would be called a "high-angle" shot. This can be achieved by raising the camera or, if more practical, by lowering the subject.

The ends of better composition are often served by proper choice of vertical angle. When the camera is raised to a higher position, foreground objects go lower in the frame. More floor is seen, more of whatever horizontal planes may be present, such as table and piano tops. The difference in apparent height between foreground and background figures usually improves the composition when the camera is either lower or higher than eye level.

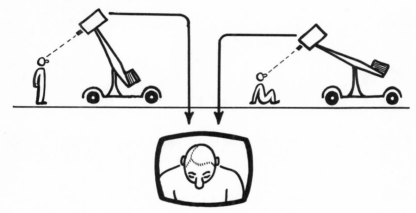

Figure 9.   High-angle shot: two ways to achieve it. *Left:* raise camera; *right:* lower subject.

When the limitations of the budget or of the studio prevent the scenery from being built high enough, the cameraman is severely hampered in obtaining good long shots. When he pulls back to take in a width of, say, thirty feet, he finds that his entire subject matter is then confined to a strip thirty feet wide and usually only nine feet high.

Since the height of the television picture is always three-quarters of its width, the camera in this case must show large floor areas if it is to avoid shooting above the sets. Television designers solve this problem in one way by decorating the floor so that if large areas of it must be seen, they will not be entirely uninteresting.

In some cases, a high camera angle will enable the camera to get better long shots, or at least make the shots more interesting in design. Although the higher camera illustrated in Figure 10 is shooting with the same lens, the shot it is taking is entirely different. The horizontal planes of the scene cover more area in the high-angle shot, and the musicians

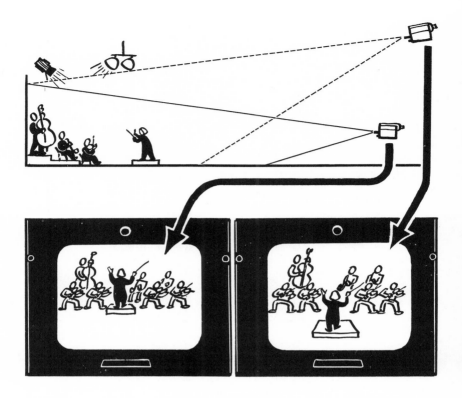

Figure 10. Improved composition as a result of changing vertical angle.

are filling a lower area of the picture, which in the low shot is occupied by bare floor.

The significance of being able to vary the height of the camera often lies in the dramatic effect that the shot can convey. An object seen from below is "looked up to" and the same object seen from above is "looked down upon."

The Reverse-Angle Shot. A camera taking a reverse-angle shot looks at the subject from the opposite direction from which it has just been seen. If a number of shots are taken from the front, front right, and front left of a subject, a shot from the back will be called a reverse-angle. In film, where only one camera set-up is used at a time and the camera is reset to shoot other angles of the same scene, a reverse-angle can be a full 180 degrees from the first shot. In live television or video tape production, this would not be possible unless the program format would allow the second camera to be seen; some news programs, round-table discussions, and interview formats benefit from the studio

Figure 11. Typical pair of reverse-angle shots. The conversation line between the two subjects is shown.

lights, cameras, and other equipment being visible. Other programs, such as dramatic shows, would have illusions spoiled by the intrusion of studio equipment. Thus in television, reverse-angles are generally somewhat less than 180 degrees apart, so one camera will not show the other.

Reverse-angles are most commonly used in pairs. Such a pair of shots should be similar or even identical in composition, but they will be opposite, of course, in emphasis. It is important that they be matched, however, or they will not cut smoothly together. It is important to:

1. use lenses at the same focal length (or matched zoom lenses at the same zoom position);
2. position the cameras at the same *angle* from an imaginary line drawn between the two characters;
3. position the cameras at the same *distance* from this "center line" or axis.

The Over-the-Shoulder Shot. The best example of a pair of reverse-angle shots is the matched over-the-shoulder (OS) shots that are commonly used in covering a conversation between two people. These shots are effective because they allow the audience to see both people, while giving the person speaking a full-face exposure to the camera. An OS shot can quickly be changed to a CU by changing the lens or zooming in. The director must be careful to match these shots in terms of focal length used, or the distance between the two people may seem to change when cutting from one shot to the other. Over-the-shoulder shots are popular in dramas and interviews, since they permit us to concentrate the viewer's attention on one person while still reminding him of the existence of the second.

The Overhead Shot. Sometimes called a "top shot," this shot is obtained by placing a camera almost directly over the subject. This angle can be very effectively used for dramatic effect in a scene with people seated or standing in a circle, playing cards, or engaged in other activity that can best be seen from above. A completely different purpose is served by the camera shooting a football stadium from a blimp or helicopter. This camera is used to show the whole stadium and its surroundings; the camera is usually equipped with a powerful zoom lens so the cameraman can zoom in from a shot of the entire stadium to a shot of the offense just before the ball is snapped. The overhead shot is almost always a costly process in or out of the studio and it almost always necessitates tying up a camera throughout a whole program for a very few shots.

5. Camera Movement

So far we have considered shots (and the names of those shots) in which any movement would come from the actors; we have presumed that the camera in each case was motionless, or that if it was moving, such movement would not affect the designation of the shot. At this point, let us turn to the *moving* shot, whose designations derive from the manner in which the camera is moving. That in turn depends on the camera mount.

The Pan. The pan is a horizontal twist of the camera on its mount, either left to right or right to left, effected by turning the camera head with the panning handle. Many film and television people also include a vertical or tilting movement under this designation. Thus, the director may give his cameraman the command "Pan up" or "Pan down," as well as "Pan right" or "Pan left." The important point to remember is that in a pan shot only the *camera* moves; the base upon which it is mounted does not move.

It may be helpful at this point to clarify "right" and "left" as used in television: "right" is always the camera's right, which makes it also the right of the cameraman, of the director, and of the viewer; similarly, "left" is always "camera left" (left on the camera viewfinder, the control-room monitor, and the home set). This can be confusing to the stage actor, who is used to stage right and stage left being *his* right and left as he faces the audience.

The Tilt. Vertical movement (or nodding) of the camera on its mount is called a "tilt." "Tilt up" requires the cameraman to move the lens up (by pushing the panning handle down), bringing into view the space

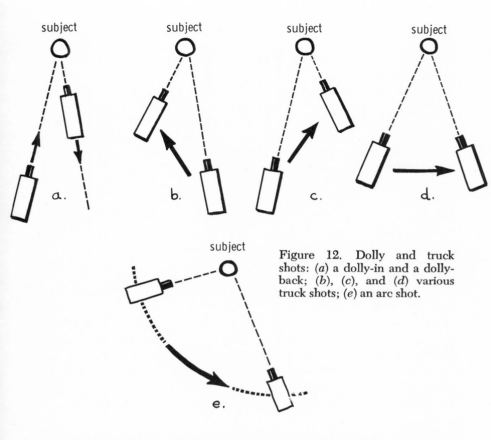

Figure 12. Dolly and truck shots: (*a*) a dolly-in and a dolly-back; (*b*), (*c*), and (*d*) various truck shots; (*e*) an arc shot.

above the original shot. When the lens is dipped below a horizontal position (by lifting the panning handle), in response to the command "Tilt down," more is seen below the original shot. The director will often use these commands to have the cameraman adjust the head space (space above the subject's head).

The Dolly. This operation involves movement of the entire camera either *toward* or *away from* the subject. The director's command for this movement is "Dolly in," to get the camera closer to the subject, and either "Dolly back," "Dolly out," or even "Pull out," for the reverse.

The Truck. A movement of the entire camera mount in any line which is not toward or away from the subject is called "trucking," and the resultant shot is, therefore, a "truck shot." It is difficult to visualize trucking past a single person, but if we will think of a line of people and of the camera rolling from left to right or from right to left past them, at an equal distance from each one, we can see the effect of the command "Truck left" or "Truck right."

The Arc. A truck shot which follows a curved path is known as an "arc shot." The command may be any one of a number of directions, so long as director and cameraman understand each other. Thus, a director may command, "Arc around to the left," or "Arc in to the right," as circumstances may suggest. In operating a camera pedestal for the execution of this shot, it is not enough for the cameraman merely to set the dolly wheels in the specified direction and push. He must guide the movement of the camera in a smooth and steady curve, constantly changing the direction of the dolly wheels. Dollies that can be set for a curve and hold it without constant steering are better adapted for achieving arc shots than are pedestals.

The Zoom. The term "zoom" refers most commonly to the effect created by the operation of a "zoom lens," or varifocal lens, a lens specially designed to permit variations in focal length (the distance between the optical center of the lens and the face of the television tube; determining the angle of view) during a shot. (Even if it is not a term for camera movement, it does refer to an effect that is similar to moving.) With a zoom lens this is accomplished by movement of a handle, lever, or crank either on the lens itself or linked to the lens and more conveniently

SHOT	MOTIVATING ACTION	CAMERA MOVEMENT
Medium shot (four-shot)	Actor C walks camera right behind A and B and out of the frame. The action is reduced to include only two people, and the audience wants a better view.	Camera dollies in during action of C.
Two-shot	Actor A walks to other side of B and leans in a little closer.	Camera pans left with action of A and pushes in slightly to hold a tighter shot.
Tight two-shot	Actor C comes into frame again from camera right behind A and B, crosses to camera left, and comes down stage.	Camera pulls back as he crosses, so as not to lose A and B from the picture.
Combination close-up and medium shot		

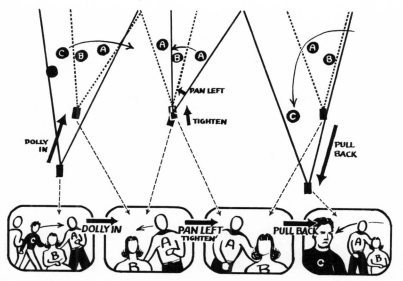

Figure 13.   Typical example of camera movement coordinated with actor movement.

located at the back of the camera. Some zoom lenses are equipped with small electric motors so the zoom effect, as well as other lens adjustments, can be executed even from a point considerably remote from the camera.

There are visual differences between the result of a camera dollying and the result of a zoom. The dolly changes the relationship of foreground and background while the zoom does not. When the camera dollies through a doorway, the sides of the doorjamb appear to move apart and the interior of the room beyond gradually becomes visible; the zoom merely brings the whole scene closer to the viewer without revealing anything more within the room beyond.

Choice of Camera Movement

It is easier to direct a show with cameras that never move on the air than to plan and rehearse camera movement, but this type of coverage often has a "static look" and limited visual appeal. Conversely, programs may also suffer if excess of camera movement makes the audience aware of technique instead of program content. In general, no camera should move except for a definite purpose. A camera should be moved only if the movement enhances the value of the shot (1) by showing us something we were not able to see without the movement or (2) by creating an emotional impact that strengthens the effect that writer and actor desire.

Most directors think first of moving their actors, but actors cannot take the place of all camera movement. The combined action of actor and camera must be well integrated and well rehearsed. It is only when sufficient rehearsal time is available that a director can combine actor movement and camera movement so that a long shot becomes a medium shot, then a close-up, then a medium shot again, smoothly and with constantly balanced composition. Notice in Figure 13 how each camera move is motivated.

This last dolly-back is a motivated move throughout its duration since it is made in coordination with the forward movement of the actor. The shot widens as the action widens. An attempt to pull the camera back to this shot without the actor's movement motivating the pull-back might easily have called attention to the camera movement. If the last actor, for example, had merely been discovered in the final position after the camera pulled back, there would have been no initial reason for the camera move. The audience might have felt dragged away from something in which it was very much interested. A cut to this final composition would even have been better than an unmotivated movement of the camera.

Earlier in this chapter, we examined the most common movements: the pan and the tilt, the dolly and the truck, the arc and the zoom. These are all interesting movements in themselves, but they must be used with purpose. Therefore, let us examine the various ways in which television directors have learned to use these basic camera techniques.

Reasons for Panning and Tilting. The most common reason for panning is to follow a subject as it moves. The viewer is watching someone, wants to continue to watch that person, and is given exactly what he wants when the camera keeps the subject in the frame.

Sometimes a pan, a tilt, or both will be used when the shot is a close-up. When the camera shows first one small detail then moves to another, the viewer can discover things for himself. The "subjective camera," when the camera takes the actor's place, usually calls for much panning and tilting as the character is represented to be looking around. As long as the shot retains interest throughout, and is constantly showing objects meaningful to the story, it will be accepted.

Reasons for Dollying. Sometimes the essential activity of a scene reduces to a smaller area and the viewer's natural urge is to move closer and get a better view. A dolly-in or a zoom-in can do this, but if there is not enough time, as when an important character in the background of the shot suddenly speaks, a cut will be better. When the area of action gradually expands, a dolly-back will satisfy the viewer's desire to see what is going on.

A dolly-back that gradually takes one away from the action he is watching is sometimes useful at the conclusion of a program. If, during the closing announcement, the camera is pulling back from the scene, a nice tapering conclusion is effected. This is often used on a program which began in the opposite manner, starting with a long shot and dollying up close for the start of the essential action. This technique is sometimes called "bookending."

Reasons for Trucking and Arcing. The camera may truck simply to reveal an actor previously covered by another actor in the foreground. Trucking is often used to follow actors across the set, keeping abreast of them, preceding, or following. A camera may truck or arc around a subject (preferably during some action of the subject) in order to bring a different background into the shot. If an entrance is to be made, for example, the director can time the truck or arc to reveal the door just at the moment of entrance.

The most valuable effect of trucking or dollying is the increased feeling of depth it gives to the scene. Since foreground objects move against the background, these camera movements separate foreground from background and reveal the distance between. Dollying and trucking provide a more interesting manner of showing a scene than panning or zooming, but are physically more difficult and require skilled cameramen.

Reasons for Zooming. The zoom or varifocal lens allows the director to quickly and easily adjust composition as well as change the scope of the shot. The zoom provides a faster, steadier, low-risk method of moving in or out of the set because the camera base and tripod do not have to be moved. When properly focused at both extremities of the zoom, a zoom lens will automatically hold its own focus during the action of zooming.

6. Purpose or Function of the Shot

There are a number of shots that are named entirely according to the function they fulfill. Among these are the establishing shot and the reaction shot.

The Establishing or Cover Shot. Earlier in this chapter we stated that the long shot shows us as much of the subject as possible, that the major purpose of the long shot is to acquaint the audience with the overall appearance of the whole subject and with the relationship of each of its parts, and that this type of shot is often called the orientation, or establishing, shot. Since in subsequent shots we will most often see only a small portion of the scene at a time, it is important for the viewer to know early in the sequence that the staircase is to his left, the window is to his right, and the main entrance door is in the center. As the drama goes on, it will be necessary from time to time to remind him of these relationships, and such a shot will be called a "re-establishing shot."

The establishing shot is usually a long shot, although the same purpose may be achieved by a pan, slow enough for the viewer to register the positional relationships of scenic elements and of people. When the action begins to cover a great deal of floor space, however, it is difficult to follow the frantic movement of several characters at once. At such a time the director takes a cover shot—essentially the same long shot used to "establish," but now serving another function, that of "covering the action" no matter what happens. This shot is particularly useful when trouble develops during the production. "When troubles hover, go to cover!" In an emergency when, for instance, your actors suddenly skip two pages of script, you get on a cover shot at once. Then, no matter who speaks or where people may move, you can keep them on the screen until they recover themselves—and you, the director, can recover your camera pattern.

The Reaction Shot. In a drama, an interview, or a panel discussion—to name only a few appropriate types of program—the camera is not always on the person speaking. As Mary breaks a startling piece of news to John, the director frequently cuts to a fairly close shot of John just a second before the news registers on his countenance. We still hear Mary's voice, but we now see John's *reaction.* It is wise to cut to John a second early so that we may take in his expression just before his features begin to show his reactions. It is not common, however, that the audience is more interested in a person who is listening than in a person who is speaking. The student director must be critical of his use of such shots, lest he give the audience the impression that he made the error of putting his camera on the wrong person. A further discussion of the reaction shot will be found in Chapter 3.

SUMMARY

The reader now has been introduced to the basic units of television: the most common shots and the lenses and camera mounts that make these shots possible. It may seem to the reader that despite the differences in lenses he can get any shot he wants on any lens, provided his studio is big enough and he is willing to pay the price of difficulty of focus or of camera movement. Not so! While he can get *approximately* the same shot—can include the same subjects by using a wide-angle lens a short distance away from the subject, or a normal lens a medium distance away, or a long lens a good way off—these three shots will not be the same in such important particulars as apparent depth, relationships between subjects in the foreground and those in the background, and relative size of subjects.

If, however, he is willing to pay the artistic price involved in settling for less appropriate relationships, he can get the shot on a wide-angle lens, for example, and be ready for a fast, smooth dolly. In television, if not always in life, for everything you gain, you have to lose something; for most things you lose, you gain something. Thus much of television becomes the best compromise you can arrange between what you *would like* to get and what you *can* get.

3 / Transitions: Shot to Shot and Scene to Scene

A transition is like a bridge that takes us from one side of a river to another. Sometimes the river runs through a city, and crossing the bridge makes little difference, because we find ourselves still in the same city. Another bridge crosses a river that separates two states, and we find ourselves in a slightly different environment. Some bridges have customs and immigration buildings on each end, and crossing these bridges brings us into another country, sometimes into what seems to be a different world.

So it is with the conventional transitions of television. One type may indicate that one portion of the program is ended and a new one is about to begin, or it may take us into a different realm of reality altogether. A second keeps us in the same time and place and simply shows us a continuing action from another point of view. A third type can indicate the passage of time or a change in place.

In recent years some television directors and producers have begun to question the old theory that a television program, like a film, is a sequence of shots. They are beginning to feel instead that a television show is a continuous flow of events, which the camera picks up and brings to the viewer in the most effective way. In film, each shot is planned separately, lighted and given a camera set-up, rehearsed, and filmed several times over until perfected. In live television or videotape production, on the other hand, all the shots for a live broadcast or even for most taped programs must be planned in advance, the entire area prelighted, and still, invariably, some artistic decisions are made while the program is in progress. (This is true, certainly, of those programs produced at small and even medium-sized stations, even though the productions may be prerecorded for later broadcast. Small stations cannot afford the cost of expensive post-production or videotape editing except for the most serious errors.) However carefully shots are planned, the director is still compelled by the spontaneous nature of the medium to take things as they come. As a result, not all the cuts or other transitions in any given television program can be assured the perfection they have in film, where the editor can spend hours determining the exact point at which to make each cut. Accordingly, some television directors prefer to cut as little as possible, considering it a necessary evil, rather than an advantage. The exception to this is the big-budget taped television special with many artistic special effects, but these programs do not make up the bulk of taped programming.

While there are no rigid rules governing transitions from scene to scene, a number of conventions have been developed in film over the years, and many of these have been taken over by television. In the theatre we may indicate a simple lapse of time (scene change) by fading down, then promptly fading up the stage lights, whereas lowering the curtain and bringing up the house lights indicates the end of an act. These are conventions which have been understood by generations of theatregoers. Similarly, the conventions of film and television, while somewhat more subject to change than those of the theatre, still provide symbols or clues which help the viewer to follow the progress of events. This process of going from shot to shot, and the selection of the shots which adjoin one another, is a very important part of television. The most important concept, whatever conventional or unconventional techniques are used, is that the sequence of shots must provide a flow of continuity. There must be a smooth connection between shots as they carry us along in progression from view to view, always showing us what we want to see, always bringing us further information. Anything that disturbs that flow interferes with our enjoyment of what we are watching, unless the disturbance is a deliberate punctuation that informs us that one train of thought has ended and another is about to begin. The conventional transitional devices, then, may be given new meaning by a director, but the director must devise ways to make sure that the viewers understand the meanings that he intends. Dialogue or narration can often help the visual at times like this. Here are the transitions most commonly encountered by television.

THE FADE

The combination of a *fade-out* with a *fade-in* gives us the feeling of a major change. The fade-out is the process of bringing down the brightness, or "gain," of the picture to zero, leaving the screen blank. A slow fade has the psychological effect of a descending curtain in the theatre.

A fast fade, however, does not necessarily conclude; it may serve to get us from one scene to the next. At the very beginning of a program, for example, the main titles or the commercial may fade out, followed by a blank screen for part of a second, after which the first scene of the show itself fades in.

The fade-in, of course, is the reverse process, beginning with a blank screen and gradually bringing the picture up to normal intensity. The combination of fade-out and fade-in may be used between scenes, especially to denote a lapse of time when two successive scenes take place in the same set. Or the two fades may be employed between two scenes in different sets where there is a definite lapse of time as well as a change in place. In past years, it was quite customary to find the end of each act of a dramatic program indicated by a fade-out, with the commercial fading in after a short instant "in black." While this convention is still used, most commercials currently are produced with the fade-in, if desired, included with the commercial itself. The advertisers then pay for the time utilized by the fade-in. The bookending convention in this case would have a fade-out from one segment or scene followed by a fade-in to the next. Without this convention, say the purists, you get an effect as bothersome as setting off a phrase with a parenthesis at one end and a bracket at the other.

THE TAKE OR CUT

Used as a method for getting from one shot to another, the terms "take," "cut," and "switch" all mean the same thing: an instantaneous change from the picture of one camera to that of another camera. Since in most studios the command to execute this change is "Take One" (for Camera One), this instantaneous change is most commonly called a "take." It is usually used to introduce a shot that is a different look, from a different angle or distance, of the same continuing action going on in the same place.

It is interesting to note that what is commonly called a "take" in television is usually termed a "cut" in film, since in conventional film editing a change from one shot to another is accomplished by literally cutting the film and cementing on another piece of film containing the succeeding shot. In a few television studios, the command for the change from one camera to another is "Cut One." In this situation, care is always taken to insure differentiation between "Cut One" and "Cut" meaning to stop action in the studio.

Cutting Techniques

Cutting is obviously more than going to a new shot when the director feels the audience should be given another view. If the cut is to achieve its primary function of showing the viewer what the director judges he would most like to see, then cutting must be carefully planned and accurately done, to the right shot and at the right time. In addition, the cut should not be obvious. If it distracts or disorients the viewer, the director has not been cutting smoothly.

In cutting, the first decision is whether to cut at all—not only at any given moment but throughout the entire show. Some fine programs have been done entirely on one camera, with a tremendous amount of imagination involved in zooming, dollying, panning, and arcing as well as in having the performers "make the shots" by their movements about the set, nearer and farther from camera. Although they do use more than one camera, television daytime soap operas often employ the idea of moving people instead of cameras and provide an excellent example of letting people make the shots. Even in a show blessed with four cameras or more, an imaginative director may find a sequence of several pages of script in which no purpose will be served by cutting to another camera.

On the other hand, by holding on one camera, the director must sacrifice the advantages of cutting: quick change in camera angle or field of view, a greater variety of shots, the increased tempo produced by new shots; and an increased ability to concentrate attention quickly on a chosen subject, especially in rapid-fire conversation between physically separated persons.

Why to Cut

Fundamentally, the most common reason for cutting is that it is the quickest method of showing the viewer what he wants to see, when the preceding shot cannot include it or cannot show it from an angle where it could be properly seen. The viewer, for example, usually wants to see a facial close-up of an individual speaking, not the back of his head.

Cutting between two shots that are visually quite different may be used to punctuate or emphasize a dramatic moment. Cutting from a long shot to a close-up of a character as he enters a door to deliver some important message, for example, will lend additional importance to what the character is saying because of the abruptness of the shift in emphasis. (A quick zoom-in will also accomplish the same end even more dramatically.) Cutting from a moving shot to one that is static can have the same sort of shock effect.

The cut is also used in capturing a quick reaction. In an interview or discussion situation, the reaction of the listener is often more interesting and telling than that of the speaker. A quick cut to the listener or listeners can often communicate a great deal of information to the home viewer and can also make the shooting pattern more visually interesting —especially when one individual is speaking for an extended period. The quick reaction cut is also often used in a dramatic situation to reveal an actor's feelings about the situation he finds himself in. In a theatrical performance, the audience is often forewarned of possible action to follow or receives a clue to a particular facet of a character by watching the reactions of other actors on stage. Because the television director must focus on the actor delivering lines in a television drama, the quick reaction cut will allow the television viewer to receive this kind of information.

When to Cut

The right moment for cutting depends on the nature of the two shots which are to be joined and also on the timing and rhythm of the production. If the two shots are *both of the same subject* and the second shows nothing new, we are involved in simple continuity cutting. The second shot may be a closer or longer view of the same subject or a view of the subject from a different angle. Care should be taken that you do not cut from one shot of a subject to a second shot of the same subject with practically the same view and the same angle. Not only is this the rankest example of cutting for no purpose at all, but it usually makes it seem that the subject has suddenly jumped a few inches to a new place on the screen. A somewhat similar effect will occur in film if the camera is stopped and started again in the middle of an otherwise continuous shot. Some examples of shots of the same subject that can be cut together are:

Close shot of a person (or persons) to a longer shot of the same (or reverse);

One of a pair of over-the-shoulder shots to the other;

Long shot of several persons to a closer shot of the same group;

Medium shot to a long shot (if new subjects are not introduced);

Any shot of a group (two or more persons) to a shot of part of the group.

When the second of two shots that are to be joined by cutting is *something entirely new or different,* we are talking about the second category of cutting, which film critics have liked to call "montage." Examples of cuts in this category are:

Close-up of one of two people to a close-up of the other;

Any shot of a group of people to a shot of another person or group;

Any two shots between which the visible environment is different, although the subject *theme* may be the same. In a documentary, a train starting to cross a trestle, for instance, followed by a plane taking to the air.

The cutting will be done at different times and will be based on different motivations between the "same subject" and the "different subject" categories. There are some cutting situations which are intermediate—that is, where the second shot contains the same subject *plus* additional subjects. A cut from a close-up of one person to a two-shot containing the first person is a case in point. Cutting from a two-shot to a three-shot is another example. In these cases we can usually use cutting techniques that apply to either of the above categories.

When shall we cut in each case? When cutting between two shots of the same subject, it is always smoothest to choose the moment of some subject action. Sitting, rising, turning, gesturing, and so forth are typical motivations for *cutting on action*. The cut should come in the midst of the action, so that the movement begun in one shot is completed in the second shot—forming a bridge between the two shots. Under these conditions even the expert may not be conscious that a cut has occurred.

When cutting between shots of different subjects, it is usually meaningless to cut on action except for special effect because, obviously, action initiated in one shot will not correspond to action completed in the other. It is usually advisable to wait until the action is completed in the first shot before cutting to the second. The primary motivation for cutting between close-ups of different people in a dramatic scene or an interview situation is *dialogue*. As one individual finishes speaking (to someone not in the shot), we cut to the second person just as he begins to reply. *Cuts on dialogue* in a dramatic scene may be marked on a script, and even the script-bound student director who does not watch the monitors has a chance of cutting accurately when he is cutting on lines. This is not true of cutting on action, however. Describing the action in your script will not give you the precise second in that action at which to cut. Only by watching the monitors and choosing the right instant can this be done.

If an actor's reaction is an important means of advancing the plot, it is usually convenient to agree in rehearsal that the reaction will dawn at a given word in the dialogue, and the cut may be made on that word. If the reaction is late, we simply are on hand to see the dawn break. If the cut is late, however, the reaction has already begun, and part of it will be lost.

Cutting on the direction of attention can apply to a visual or audio stimulus. Visually, this type of situation occurs when someone sets up our attention—by pointing or looking at some object which is out of the frame of the current shot. The attention of the viewer may also be drawn by a sound such as a voice, a breaking window, a shout, or a sob, especially if he also sees heads turn toward it. Whether visual or auditory, the viewer wants immediately to know what is happening that he cannot see. That wish is satisfied by cutting to a shot revealing what is occurring. In many scripts, the feeling of fright can be heightened by *not* showing the viewer what is occurring out of frame, but care must be taken with this technique that the viewer does not become frustrated instead of frightened.

Cutting in rhythm is a technique which can be used in a song or dance number or in a dramatic sequence. In the former, the usual convention is to cut between phrases of music. In a ballet, however, it is often better to cut on action, even when that action is not at the end of a musical phrase, since a visual flow of images and the continuity of action is almost always the most important factor.

In a song number, particularly a popular song whose musical structure is mathematically rigid, the cutting can be done at the end of an eight-measure segment (just before the release or as the vocalist pauses for an instrumental break), in rhythm if the music is contemporary and has a strong beat, or against the beat to create a feeling of "counter rhythm." The type of cutting used is largely dependent on the rhythm of the song.

In commercials, in the introduction to a program, and sometimes in dramatic segments, cutting can be used to show the audience many images very rapidly. There is a quick limit, luckily, to fast cutting in television, since the director after two or three shots simply runs out of cameras, although some apparently do not notice this and use the same shots over and over. Some films have incorporated a technique where a very short shot, probably no more than two frames in length, flashes suddenly in the midst of the shot of an actor, giving an impression of what he is thinking of, or in another context, to present a glimpse into the future. To be effective, this shot must be so short as to be almost subliminal. The viewer should be not really quite sure that he saw anything at all.

Whatever the timing of the desired cut, experimentation during rehearsal can reveal the exact moment at which a cut will be most effective. A good director "knows" when a cut will be right—but this comes with experience.

How to Cut Effectively

Smooth cutting depends not only on the timing of the cut, but even more on the relationship of the two shots between which the cutting is

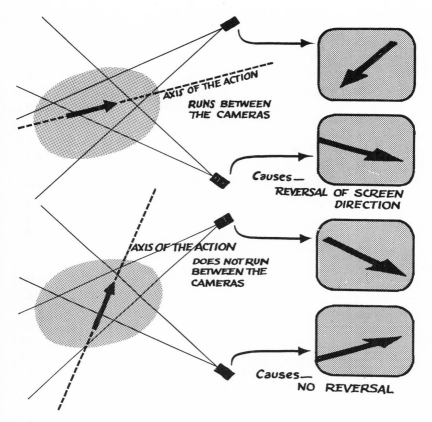

Figure 14. When the axis of the action runs between the cameras, cutting from one to the other will reverse the apparent direction of the action.

done. When possible, too great a discrepancy between the shots is to be avoided or compensated for in some manner. When other factors are inappropriate, such as two camera angles that if juxtaposed will reverse the direction of action or attention, the director may stage an action which will move participants in the studio into a position that will make a smooth cut possible.

Relative Angles. In a two-camera show, the student director is often tempted to place his cameras at opposite edges of the set, shooting inward, in order to get a wide variety of camera angles. Yet cameras placed so widely apart may create problems.

The background may suddenly change drastically as we cut from one shot of a person to another shot of the same person from a widely dif-

ferent angle. Widely different angles can also be a problem when shooting a person who is talking about an object on a table. Generally, we
would want the cameras relatively close so that a close-up of the object
would at least be recognized as the same object. Showing it suddenly
from side view may make it look like something else.

A concept that the director must always keep in mind is the *action
axis,* an imaginary line extending in the direction of an actor's movement or his direction of attention. There are only two screen directions:
left and right. If the actor enters from the left on Camera One and moves
toward the right, cutting to Camera Two should show the actor continuing to move from left to right. If, however, Camera Two is on the

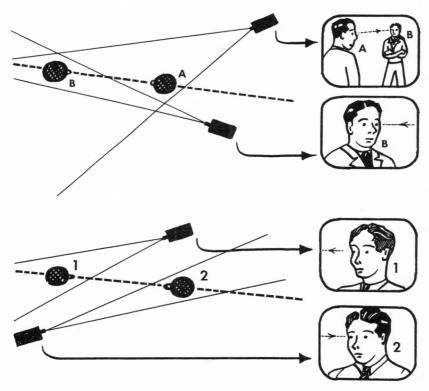

Figure 15.   When cameras are on opposite sides of the conversation line,
screen directions are reversed in cutting. In the first example, actor B can be
mistaken for actor A; in the second, both people seem to be looking in the
same direction, not at each other.

wrong side of the action axis, the actor will reverse direction as the cut to Camera Two is made.

Whenever the action axis runs between two cameras, the direction of the action is reversed on the screen. The screen direction problem crops up again when two people are conversing. Instead of an action axis, we have here a "conversation line" joining the two people. As long as both cameras are on the same side of this conversation line, no screen direction problems will arise. If, however, one of the cameras is placed on the opposite side of the line, a cut to this camera will reverse the apparent direction in which a subject is looking; he will seem to be looking in the same direction—away from—the person to whom he is talking.

Relative Composition. The cut in which a subject seems to jump from one side of the frame to another is, of course, to be avoided. This type of situation occurs when three or more people are side by side and covered in two-shots as illustrated in Figure 16. First we see B on the right of the frame in the shot with A. Then, as we cut, we see B on the left of the frame alongside C.

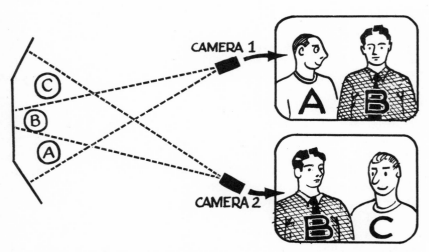

Figure 16.   Cutting between these two shots results in character B appearing to jump from one side of the frame to the other.

Even when there is a total change of subject in two successive shots, it is possible to make a cut smoother and less noticeable by matching composition. Keep the centers of interest of the two successive shots in approximately the same position in the frame. Then, even though the subject changes, the viewer's eye need not jump to a different part of the screen.

THE DISSOLVE

The *dissolve* is an overlap of two shots in which the first shot slowly (or rapidly) disappears as the second appears. It is actually a fade-out superimposed on a fade-in. The dissolve is usually understood to represent a minor discontinuity in time or place or both, although it is also often used only decoratively, as in a song number in which the director dissolves from a medium shot of a singer to a close-up. This decorative use of the dissolve can easily be misused. It is effective if the subject is of a different size in the second shot. One technique is to leave the singer in the center of the frame, then just before dissolving, pan the camera off the subject to a plain background for a "clean dissolve." This is especially important when going from one shot to another of the same performer. A dissolve from a close-up to another close-up will most probably look like a mistake because the two pictures are so similar. If you have not had time to rehearse your dissolves thoroughly, you may be able to "punch up" the two cameras on the preview monitor moments before you make (or decide not to make) the dissolve, to see what it will look like at its midpoint when both pictures are on the air at the same time.

Until quite recently, the convention was to use the dissolve in a dramatic production to indicate a transition to a different time. In a nondramatic production, the dissolve had less fixed meaning; it was commonly used to join two shots that were not clearly part of the same scene, as when going from action in the studio to a film or still picture that was not obviously part of the studio scene. A film sequence that is taking place in the past (a flashback) would usually require a dissolve, or possibly one of the variations on the dissolve which will be discussed in the pages immediately following. A film insert of street traffic, presumably as seen by an actor from his hotel window, would require a cut. News programs involving film, photographs, and videotape inserts usually utilize cuts, partly to maintain the fast-moving pace which we associate with news. Today, the cut is frequently used where dissolves were once mandatory. Transitions through time and space are made more cleanly and quickly by cuts. So that the viewers will not be confused, directors devise ways to make such changes clear from the context of the action. The sound from the scene following may be overlapped onto the end of the preceding sequence, for example, so that although the sound may make no particular sense at first, the viewer shortly encounters and enters the new scene without readjustment, having already been listening to it for a few seconds.

When using the dissolve either as a transition device or for decorative reasons, rhythm is an important factor and will determine the dissolve's timing and even whether it is desirable in the first place. Many production formats, including news shows, have their own inherent rhythm, or as in dramas the rhythm may vary within the production depending on the action or the scene. Obviously, the rhythm for a ballad is quite different from that of a rock number.

VARIATIONS ON THE DISSOLVE

Matched Shots

Two shots may be matched in composition or in action. We may go from the head and shoulders of a man who would be king to a plaster bust of Napoleon or Caesar; from the action of mopping a kitchen counter to erasing a blackboard; from a sledgehammer driving a spike to a judge's gavel banging on his desk. In any case, the last shot of one sequence matched in some way to the first shot of the next creates a bridge. The dissolve is generally used as a transition between the two matched shots, and thus the effect is often called the "matched dissolve." The result, dramatically, could easily seem contrived and gimmicky if the matching of special shots were done just for the sake of creating an effect. It is necessary that there be a dramatic as well as a completely logical reason for each of the matched shots to be there in the first place. The transition from the man who would be king to the bust of Napoleon could imply, more strongly, what his dialogue had been hinting at, but for the sake of logical acceptance, the bust has to be there as part of the scene—it cannot be dragged in just for the dramatic effect. The transition from the kitchen table to the blackboard might contrast the lives of two sisters, one a housewife and the other a teacher, or merely take us from one to the other, or make the time transition from one period to the next in a single person's life.

The Defocus-Refocus

Sometimes the situation in a drama calls for a transition that creates a feeling of unreality. The heroine faints at the end of a scene, and in the next is coming to her senses. An old woman muses on her childhood and suddenly is confronted with a character out of her past. For these or similar situations, the defocus transition used to be quite common. It is accomplished by defocusing the camera at the end of a scene, then dissolving quickly to a second camera, previously defocused, which is quickly brought into focus. Usually the second scene leads us back to the principal actor or object of the first, and we usually use the defocus-refocus device to get back.

The defocus-refocus transition may be used to indicate a time lapse and may be combined with a "matched dissolve" when the situation lends itself to setting up two shots of identical composition on similar objects. The danger lies in reaching too far and in concentrating on subjects that would not normally be featured if the director were not attempting the effect. Timing is the key to doing this transition effectively; it must proceed quickly. The student at first often lingers too long on out-of-focus shots, to the distress of the viewer.

Time-Lapse Transitions

If a transition involves a lapse of time, as many transitions do, it is often not sufficient to simply state, by use of a dissolve or one of its alternatives, that the next scene is "later"—it may be necessary to indicate about *how much* later. Often the writer will handle this problem in the dialogue—"Darling! [they clinch] I didn't know three weeks could seem so long"; or "Ben, is that really you? I haven't seen you in a coon's age." If the two characters have been together in the previous scene, it is immediately evident that exactly the age of one raccoon has intervened. Again, the time lapse may be explained by dialogue which precedes it. "Well, I can tell you one thing, you'll never get *me* to go with you to New York"—transition—and the next picture is a shot of the Empire State Building.

The most common visual means of indicating lapse of time utilizes the matched dissolve. A given shot dissolves to another shot of the same subject, obviously at a later time. Who has not seen the April page of a calendar changing to that of June? The winter landscape dissolving into the same scene in spring? The tall candle blending into a shorter one, or the empty ashtray becoming filled with cigarette butts? They are all too familiar, yet there are endless variations still possible, arising out of the actions or the settings of the scenes involved.

SPECIAL EFFECTS AS TRANSITIONS

Within the means of most television studios are many effects that can enrich a production if they are used with discretion. The effects dis-

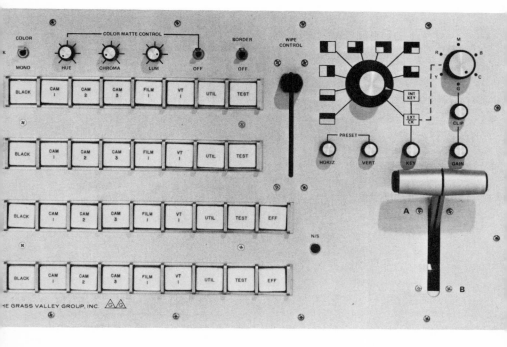

Plate 8.   Typical small-studio switching system: Grass Valley Group 1400-12.
This system provides for eight inputs, eight wipe patterns, and keying and
matte effects (used when a news commentator, for instance, is to appear
against a pictorial background that originates from a film chain). Except when
effects are desired, only the bottom two buses (rows of buttons) are used, plus
the large fading handle at the right, which is the last control before the output
of the system. In the illustration the handle is at the A extremity of its travel,
hence feeding out the output of mixer bus A (second from the bottom). Simple
switching between cameras would be done with the camera buttons on the
A MIX bus. (All buttons on any bus are mechanically interlocked, so that
when a second one is punched, the first is released.) A dissolve is effected by
presetting the camera, or other source to which the dissolve is to be made,
on the lower bus (MIX B), then on cue moving the fading handle from A to B.
(Bus A is actually faded out as bus B is faded in.) At this point bus B is on the
air, so any direct switching between cameras would then be done on bus B.
The next dissolve will be made by presetting on bus A and moving the
handle up.
    Wipes or other effects are set up on the top two buses (Effects A and B).
The output of the effects system is then re-entered into the mixer system by
selecting the effects button on one of the mixer buses. The total effects combination is thus switched or dissolved as though it were a single camera. With
the effects system on the output line, a wipe is effected by using the wipe
control handle at the top. (Courtesy of the Grass Valley Group, Inc.)

cussed below are often utilized as transitional devices to take us from scene to scene. These effects originate from a special-effects generator. Other special effects will be discussed later in the book.

The Wipe

A method somewhat different from the dissolve but which also replaces the picture being made by one camera with that being made by another is the *wipe*. Almost literally, one picture wipes out the other. A vertical line, for instance, may move across the picture from left to right, progressively revealing a new picture as it obscures the old. It may be brought in vertically, from top to bottom or from bottom to top (called a "vertical wipe"); that is to say, the second picture may be "pulled down" over the first like a window shade, or the first may seem to rise from the bottom like a theatre curtain, revealing the second. A clean line separates the two pictures where they touch. The first may also be wiped over the second from any corner of the picture (called a "corner wipe" or a "wedge wipe"). Since these effects are controlled and paced by the movement of a lever, they may be halted at any point, thus giving us a special effect known as a "split screen."

In a split screen, portions of the pictures from two cameras occupy different areas of the frame. A typical example is the phone conversation in which both speakers are shown on the same screen; another is the familiar football situation—the quarterback in the backfield, receiver going downfield to catch the pass—while the viewer of the game may keep his eye on both at the same time.

The wipe and the electronic split screen require special circuits and electronic equipment and depend on the process of *blanking*. Blanking means turning off the scanning beam so it does not transmit an image as it sweeps across certain areas of the picture. If the second half of each scanning line is blanked out, for example, the right-hand half of the entire screen will show black. The pattern generator then proceeds to blank out the first half of each scanning line in the other camera, and superimpose the two in a split screen, with the line of demarcation sharp and clear. Moving the control level varies the amount of blanking signal that goes to each camera, and turns the split screen into the wipe. As the handle is moved, the line of demarcation moves from right to left or from left to right across the screen. (This is also called a "horizontal wipe.")

There are many variations on the simple wipe. One picture may replace another by having a rectangular frame come in from the outside; by having a diamond shape expand from the center; by having what looks like a Venetian blind appear, turn its slats, and exhibit the second picture. These patterns could be used to connect the various segments of, for example, a variety-show program.

Altogether, there are about 150 patterns available in elaborate wipe equipment, but a basic half dozen or so suffice for most purposes. (See Figure 17.) It is probably inevitable that the beginning director will go through a wipe-happy stage in which he is enamored of the effect. This

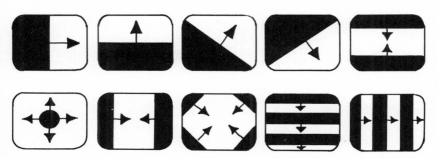

Figure 17.   A selection of standard wipes. White areas represent camera A; black areas represent camera B, which in each diagram is in the process of replacing camera A. Arrows show direction of movement of the wipe line. With most wipe equipment, direction may be easily reversed.

should be abandoned as early in his career as possible, since it is extremely rare that a legitimate dramatic or informational use can be found for these engaging effects.

TRANSITIONS FOR ONE CAMERA

All the transitional devices discussed in this chapter so far have assumed the availability of at least two cameras. It may be necessary to end one sequence and begin the next on the same camera, however. There are times when only one camera is available—as when one is working with a Portapak or Video Rover system—a hand-held camera and portable video recorder. It seems appropriate, therefore, to list briefly some of the devices which may be used to change shots when using only one camera.

To begin with, many of the devices listed above can be used. Of course, you cannot cut or dissolve from Camera One to Camera One, but you can do the following:

1.   Fade to black (or close the iris), quickly change the scene, and fade in again (or open the iris).

2. Fade to black (or close the iris), pan the camera to a new subject, and fade in again (or open the iris).
3. Run the camera completely out of focus to the point at which the camera movement or scene change is almost unnoticeable, change the subject, and refocus on the new scene.

In live television, the defocus transition is particularly difficult to do with one camera, since the cameraman must locate the new subject more by instinct than by recognition of its blurred image on his viewfinder. In videotape productions, the recording may, of course, be stopped after the first fade-out or defocus has been accomplished. The fade-in or refocus may be done later, or on another piece of tape sometime, and the two put together by editing, as it would be done in film production.

In a studio situation, other sources of picture may be at hand, even though only one studio camera is available, and it is possible sometimes to bring these into play. The film chain, for example, with its possibilities of film and slides, may be usable as a source for transitional shots. Each scene could begin with a still picture or period print to set the mood and contribute a little visual exposition concerning where and when.

The best solution for transitions using only one camera is often found in camera movement. The camera merely pans or dollies back from the first scene to reveal, in the foreground, people or props of the second scene. A transition from opening titles to the first live scene can be achieved with one camera simply by placing the camera in the correct spot for the live shot, then putting the title cards on a low easel or music stand before it. At the conclusion of the title sequence the camera merely pans or tilts off the cards, changes focus for the scene beyond, and the story can begin.

In a nondramatic production, such as a musical show, the numbers can be staged so that one ends where another begins. The first act leaves the stage, and the new act enters. (In television, the "stage" is the area that the camera is covering at any given moment.) If a host introduces each number, he can lead the camera to a new area during his introduction.

Another manner in which staging can effect a transition involves the manipulation of the lights. For example, as the host of a variety show finishes an introduction, the lights go up behind him on a singer or a dancer he has introduced, and the camera moves on past the host until he is excluded and the singer or dancer is now the sole subject visible on the screen. Some dramatic productions have used this technique to introduce flashbacks; a light change is used to reveal the new scene in the background of the old. Sometimes the setting for the first scene is painted on scrim, a net-like material from the theatre, sufficiently solid-looking when the lights are on it from the front, but disappearing almost entirely when these lights are dimmed out and a newly illuminated scene is seen through it.

SUMMARY

Clearly, then, the television director has a great number of possibilities available to him as he goes from shot to shot and from scene to scene. There are no hard-and-fast rules, although the most accepted pattern is to use:

A *fade-in* or *fade-out* to indicate a major discontinuity;

A *cut* whenever possible;

A *dissolve* to indicate a minor discontinuity in time, to smooth or decorate camera-to-camera transitions in music, dance, or other nondramatic productions.

Some directors mix their dissolves and cuts indiscriminately; they have no rational pattern to guide them in their choice of transitions, but simply explain their strange patterns by saying, "I dissolved at that point because I liked the feel of it." This is legitimate in the case of pure art, and may be indulged in by the genius. All others will please know what they are doing. In Chapter 5, which deals with pictorial composition, we shall point out the importance of developing a *feeling* for a good picture. In matters of transitions, however, feeling and taste must be based on knowledge of the effect that a transitional pattern or device will have on most viewers.

4 / Television Directing: Terms and Cues

Much of the following information deals with the director of a live or live-on-tape program. Even though much of television is done on film or on tape which is edited, the student director is more likely to get his first experience by directing live laboratory productions. Directing a live or live-on-tape program is a type of activity and showmanship which has never had a real counterpart in any other medium. If the film editor and the director of a motion picture were combined into one person and he were asked to make most of the decisions of timing during the running of the film (cuing in dissolves, camera movements, and all the myriad elements of the production), a general comparison could be made. The film or theatre director is not a real counterpart, because he makes every decision weeks before the running of the show, calmly and with considerable thought. He does not leave any element of the production until he is satisfied that it is as nearly perfect as he can make it. He has ample time for trying everything out and deciding on the basis of trial and error what will be used and what will be changed. If a film director is not going to edit a film himself, he will often shoot a scene in every conceivable way, leaving the final choice of shots to the editor, who can look at the problem in a calmer light and devote more thought at that later stage than the director could have during the shoot-ing. A master of the film director's craft, however, such as Alfred Hitchcock, will rarely shoot anything he does not intend to use, and rarely extend any shot beyond the point at which he intends the editor to cut away from it. Thus there is usually only one way to cut a Hitch-cock film, and the editor will have very few out-takes (unused shots) and very few trims (unused beginnings and ends) left over when the film is complete.

This delegation of authority and decision is even more useful in the making of situation comedies and other films for television use than in films shot for motion-picture theatres. Few directors of films for television can take the time to supervise the editing of the episode they have just shot, since they must go to work immediately on the next. The television director working with special-effects videotape editing is not working in the style of the film director, because the VTR "editor" is generally an engineer, not a creative artist as the film editor must be, and the director must follow the production through its editing; he cannot turn it over to an editor. As an example of the way in which the same footage, shot for *Gunsmoke,* was handled by three different editors, instructors in either film or television classes can profitably screen for their students a film called *Values and Interpretations.**

The old radio director, before the advent of magnetic tape, was another example of a director who worked under great time pressure and could only very rarely achieve perfection. He had to make his decisions quickly, and he could not delegate any of them to specialists in various phases of the production. He had to be the final authority in every aspect. In comparison with television there are really only a few considerations in the production of radio programs. There are the audio elements: voice, sound, and music, and the problems of timing and tempo. Behind the purely production aspects, however, are more basic considerations involved with directing the actors, revising the script, and perfecting such basic factors as characterization, interpretation of the lines, and plot structure, or (if the program is not of the dramatic type) progression of thought and other elements of structure. These are things which might be called basic showmanship. They are fields in which almost any director must become expert; and if he learns to control them in one medium he can control them in another.

In this respect (and this respect only) a good director in one medium is a good director in another. A skilled radio director is not *ipso facto* a skilled television director, although he has certain control-room experience which is an excellent preparation for some aspects of the television director's job. The good film director may be lost in a control room but understands camera shots, and thinks in visual terms. The good theatrical director (from which field many of the first television directors were originally recruited) must learn both control-room procedure and thinking in visual terms. He is usually well grounded in the elements of showmanship, however, since success in the theatre often calls for considerably greater artistic value in the product than either of the two more popular media.

It is interesting to note that half a dozen brilliant young television directors who made their reputations in the early fifties reversed this

* This film can be obtained from the American Cinema Editors, 6722 Hollywood Boulevard, Los Angeles, California.

Plate 9. Television director at work: *Top:* Ralph Nelson stages a scene from *The Man in the Funny Hat* with Ed and Keenan Wynn. *Bottom:* the control room is a tense place when the program goes on the air. Standing behind director Nelson is writer Rod Serling. (Courtesy Desilu Productions, Inc.)

trend and subsequently directed a number of productions on Broadway. It is now quite common for directors in the film, television, and theatre media to move from one medium to another in some creative capacity.

What the Director Must Do

It would be valuable at this point to list the things that the director of a live television program of any type must do during the time the program is on the air.

The director must watch the program on the master or line monitor. It is not easy to take an active part in running a show and to hold an objective point of view toward the program at the same time. If an unrehearsed or ad-lib show gets boring, the director must be able to realize that and take some kind of action to speed it up. In a rehearsed show, this function is most important during rehearsal. Often the control-room staff, cameramen, and other production assistants will be better able to judge the show than the busy director.

The director must watch at least two or three individual camera monitors. In the rehearsed show only one of these monitors carries the next shot at any one time, and the others are less vital. In the unrehearsed program, however, any camera may turn up the best possible shot at any time, and all must be carefully followed.

The director must watch his script or routine sheet. In an unrehearsed show a routine sheet or run-down will list all sections of the program, major actions, and so forth, without carrying any exact words to be spoken. In a fully scripted show, all cues that the director must give during the show, camera takes, directions to cameramen between shots, cumulative timing, and so forth are marked on the script. Many a director finds he has the sequence of shots pretty well memorized by the time the show goes on the air, especially if it is a well-rehearsed dramatic show that he has been working on for a week. There are many items on the script, however, that are not part of the straight-line progression of the show. A cue to move a camera around behind the set, for instance, to shoot through a window, and a cue to open the window blinds for the camera as soon as the interior of the window no longer shows in the other camera shots, must be marked on the script considerably ahead of the point where this reverse-angle shot is to be used. Since these cues are not in the direct line of the show at that early point, it is not easy for the director to have them memorized.

The director must watch the time. Just as in radio production, television shows must begin and end at a definite time, and the progress of the show must be carefully controlled so it will end at the right moment. This requires checking the time frequently and comparing it against notations on the script indicating what the time should be, and either speeding up or slowing down the show when necessary to make the two coincide. This is usually done only near the end of the program. When the director has an assistant in the control room on the network level (usually called the "associate director"), this relatively mechanical operation is taken off his hands, but he still retains primary responsibility. In some stations the floor manager uses a stopwatch out on the studio floor and assists the director with his timing from that position. In either case, if the assistant makes an error, it is generally considered to be the director's fault, and it is the director who must shoulder whatever blame may accrue.

The director must listen to the program sound. He must make certain evaluations too, in this process, cuing the audio engineer to alter the balance between dialogue and music when the music is too loud or too soft, and being conscious of bad quality in the sound. Beyond this basic approach to good audio the director should be careful in mike placement and the overlapping of sound, particularly in recording musical and dramatic presentations. Despite the importance of good audio in virtually all television productions, it is frequently neglected and the networks may be the least careful of all. American television viewers continually see mismatched audio and video, in both filmed and taped programs. This does not, however, justify the frequent total ignoring of audio by student directors.

Advertisers must cringe when they see their taped spots with out-of-sync video and audio—cringe, and demand that the broadcasters make good. The problem is not purely human, however. Audio quality is limited by home reception equipment. Said one network producer: "It wouldn't matter if you had a separate mike for each instrument of the New York Philharmonic and balanced levels for a perfect reproduction of what the audience in the concert hall is hearing. The viewer still hears what comes out of the tiny three-to-four-inch monaural speaker on his set." The criteria for television's audio production should not be determined by present receiving capabilities and must be a concern of the director. It is true that bad lighting may be noticed sooner than bad sound. Certainly, rough camera work will be noticed sooner than a voice which is slightly off-mike. Still, levels, balance, and even perspective are elements which require creative evaluation and fast decisions when changes must be made. Concern with sound cannot be delegated entirely to the audio engineer or the associate director.

The director must talk. In addition to the above considerations, the director must simultaneously converse with several members of the production crew. This conversation is often of a one-way nature, as in the case of camera directions and cues to the floor manager, although most studios use two-way intercom, which makes it possible for the floor crew to reply to the director. This conversation, although it may occasionally take the form of discussion of a singer's personal attributes, is usually devoted to planning and directing what the cameras will do next. Probably 90 percent of a director's words are directed to the cameramen.

The director is concerned first of all with the camera on the air. On the master monitor, he detects weaknesses of composition and camera handling which he is quick to call to the attention of the cameraman. He anticipates action on the set and warns the cameraman what to expect. Then he may also guide camera movement, evaluating the speed of a zoom or a dolly, and speeding it up or slowing it down as he thinks best.

At the same time he has a great deal to say to the camera that is off the air and repositioning for a new shot. The camera angle must be right, the framing correct; the cameraman must be warned if he is to be expected to zoom or dolly after his shot is on the air.

The director is also busy talking to the technical director or switcher, calling takes, giving "ready" cues (warnings) before takes, and setting up dissolves and fades. He talks to the floor manager quite often, cuing performers on the set, and sending word through the floor manager's hand signals, when the last three, two, one, and one-half minutes of time remain. In the control room he warns the audio operator when new mikes are to be opened, when music should be ready, and when it should be brought in. In a complicated show he may also have the following extra persons on earphones as well: projectionists, lighting-control engineer, and live musicians or conductor.

What the Director Must Be

In the light of all this activity, it is understandable why some workers in this field have said that the ideal television director will be hard to find, since he should have six pairs of eyes, several voices, and a few extra hands (the educated octopus mentioned before). A practical solution to this problem has been found in dividing up the directorial chore among a number of people. At a later point in this chapter several methods will be discussed in which this has been done.

Whether the director has assistance, either above or below him, in handling all of these activities, he himself is still the manager, and as such he must have certain managerial abilities if he is to be successful in the work. Some of these qualities are personal; the director must be able to inspire confidence and achieve complete cooperation from his associates. Other attributes are connected with his alertness and clarity of thought. Finally, the need to control many aspects of the production at the same time requires a skill which can be developed only in the television control room in the process of directing more and more complicated shows. Some self-styled geniuses have felt that they could come into a television control room and, without any extended training period, direct the most complicated dramatic or musical shows and keep everything under control. The results have usually been pretty miserable. Although these individuals undoubtedly were good showmen, and endowed with the ability to instill confidence in the minds of their sponsors or superiors, their lack of the skills needed to handle television directing is what caused their failure.

The director must be a master of his medium. Only a television director who is thoroughly familiar with the tools of his trade can be successful in this complicated medium. He must know cameras and lenses, lighting equipment, special-effects techniques, videotape editing, and a hundred other things that implement the production arts of television.

The director must be calm. Throughout all this, the television director must be calm. The nervous tension during a television rehearsal and especially during air time is very great. Although the television director is churning around inside, with all his many responsibilities and worries, and with so much to do and so little time to do it in, he must not let this condition be seen. He must put on a calm and collected front so that everyone else can work calmly and efficiently. The director himself will work better too if he can maintain at least surface calmness. This is true whether the program be a daily soap opera or a news show—in fact, it is probably especially true of directing news.

The director must remember, as he is putting on a show, that each member of the crew working under him does not have nearly the responsibility or the personal stake in the result. In many cases the production crew are only doing a routine job. If the director is irritated at the time it takes to make a camera move, or the stupidity of a cameraman who has misunderstood a direction, he must never let this reaction be known. He must always be on the side of each associate, appreciating his individual problem; he must be firm in his demands, but never criticize or upbraid. Once he has raised his voice, no matter how justified he may be, he has lost ground. Crew members smile at each other; the man being shouted at mutters to himself and resolves to cooperate as little as possible (at least until he calms down); and everything is a little bit harder from then on.

If the hysterics continue (and with some directors this is standard operating mood) the staff may pass beyond tolerant amusement and get jittery themselves. That is when errors begin. And a crew in this condition will multiply each other's errors so badly that the show may actually fall apart on the air. It has happened many times. There have been times when the cameramen simply took their earphones off and ran the show themselves, rather than try to follow a lot of hysterical screaming. It is clear that television directing is no field for the nervous type.

The director must be alert. The television director must always be fully alert and able to transfer his attention from one thing to another at a rapid rate. He must, in other words, be doing many things at the same time. Untrained directors often make errors such as these: The director calls a shot; it is switched onto the air; and then he forgets about it, puts his attention on the script, or on a camera that is not on the air, while the action moves out of range of the air camera, or the camera remains on a shot that is not at all what the audience is wanting to see. Or again, a director may forget which camera is on the air (although the master monitor is always clearly marked) and watch the wrong monitor, thinking he is following the show.

The director must remember also that whereas he can watch the show through several cameras, the audience is seeing through only one, and he must give them the best shot at all times. An observer in the control room can readily evaluate the quality of the director's work in this one aspect. He simply notes how often the picture on the master monitor does not fully satisfy him and he finds himself watching one of the individual camera monitors instead.

The new director may often make the error of not watching the camera monitor just before he calls the take. In television it is axiomatic that nothing is ever put on the air unless it has just been previewed. The director who works with his nose in the script, or his eyes always on the master monitor, may often call a take and then be surprised when the picture that appears on the air is completely different from what he imagined it would be. He may catch the cameraman adjusting his lens, or with the camera pointed at the floor as it is repositioned for another shot. There have been television directors who react to such a situation by shouting at the cameraman, but they eliminate themselves from the profession very quickly.

A frequent error is to confuse such common terms as "left" and "right." It is an easy mistake to make. The director sees an image on the monitor that is not centered. Perhaps it is too far to the right of the screen and he wants to move it over into the center. So he says, "Pan left," and is surprised to see the subject disappear off the right-hand side of the screen. If the director early in his career forms the habit of thinking of the *frame* of the picture rather than its contents when he gives camera directions, this error is less likely to happen.

Even the experienced director must often stop and consider before giving an order. Let's see, he will think to himself. If I want the title a little lower on the screen I will have to say, "Tilt up." The cameraman has no such problem, since he is as aware of the subject in front of the camera as he is of the image on his viewfinder, and he will often save the director from panning off the set by refusing to move when he gets a mistaken order, or, if the intention is obvious, moving in the opposite direction. At some stations it is accepted policy that when a director calls for something wrong, he is saved once, then if he repeats his erroneous instruction he is saved again, but if he still doesn't catch on and calls for it a third time (usually louder now because he has concluded the cameraman is probably dreaming), then, by golly, he gets it. It doesn't take very many such errors to improve a director in this respect, if he has the capacity for improvement at all.

The director must be definite. The director must give his orders clearly and definitely. Even when there are two or more possible courses of action, either one of which may be "best," he must still make a decision, any decision, and announce it as definitely as though it were the only possible thing to do. In giving these orders he must use the accepted terms so that the order can be given and received with as few words as possible. The order "Tilt up" is much simpler than "Get the title lower down in the frame," although that may be what the director has in mind.

The director must be prepared for emergencies. The director must be able to think ahead, to anticipate, with or without a script, what is going to happen, and be prepared for the next action at all times, keeping the entire production crew prepared as well. This is more of a problem on the unrehearsed show than on the scripted one, but applies in some measure to all television directing.

Besides being prepared for the next action in the show, the director must always be prepared for something to go wrong. A great many people are teamed together, and all must function smoothly or the show will jump its trolley. Someone, anywhere, at any time, can fluff, and if the director does not make a quick recovery, other errors can follow in the wake of the first. Some television directors have complained that they are always at the mercy of a large number of people who may or may not know what they are doing, and any mistake that anyone makes will be the fault of the director.

A wise director looks forward early in the planning of the show and anticipates mistakes which might happen (which have no doubt happened to him before) and decides what he will do in each case to make recovery easy. For example, he knows that in glancing back and forth between monitors and script he can easily lose his place; so he marks the script clearly, sometimes in colors—one for each camera—so he can find the place by the camera that is on the air. To avoid a miscue in sound, the director sees that each audio cue is clearly marked in the script. But this is mostly prevention. The real trick is in recovery. Sometimes the script must be abandoned and the show produced ad lib. This is necessary when a camera goes out of commission. Here are some questions to ask yourself before tackling even the simplest television show:

If you are doing a show with still pictures and commentary and you are one picture behind with the visuals, can you skip a cue, give the order to take *two* pictures off an easel instead of *one*, and get back on the track again? What do you do when your talent starts talking and there is not a microphone within earshot? What do you do when you cue the film to start, hit the audio tape, start the announcer, fade hopefully into film, and it comes up backwards or upside down? Assuming that you try to prevent these things from happening in the first place, what do you do if they should happen?

Many times an experienced on-air personality will see the trouble and carry the show away from the error. Experienced personnel in all aspects of the production are very necessary because in many cases the director is left completely helpless. Once, in a discussion conducted around an oblong conference table placed on risers, the table fell off the risers and tumbled out of the shot with a loud crash, leaving the panel feeling exposed and completely unable to pick up any thread of the discussion. The table had been placed too close to the front edge of the riser and when a member of the panel changed his sitting position and pushed the table slightly forward, the inevitable occurred. What happened? There was one of those disastrous pauses, but fortunately the moderator picked up the cue and began to ask another question. A quick-thinking director cut to a tight close-up shot of the moderator, and, while he was speaking, the table was replaced by the floor manager and the panel went on. Since the noise and participant reaction in a case like this can be quite obvious to the viewing audience, it can be very frustrating to them for the moderator to proceed as though nothing had happened. An amused word of explanation would probably be mandatory. Things happen and they are done with; there is nothing anyone can do but laugh it off. You can't do this in a drama, however. An actress in an emotional scene once pulled a gun from her purse and without looking at it pointed it at the heavy. But she was so carried away by her own histrionics she did not know she was holding it by the barrel and pointing the handle at the villain.

Sometimes equipment failure can be very serious. With only two cameras in a studio, the failure of one can mean the suspension of activities in the case of many shows. On some types of programs, however, it is possible to "wing a show" with one camera, even though that one camera must do a lot of panning back and forth.

The most complete foul-up that the authors can remember took place long ago on a news show, which was much more complicated than today's news productions, with still pictures on easels, film segments, a large studio map, and live commentary. Near the start of the show the first mistake occurred. Instead of changing just one card on the easel, the stagehand pulled the whole stack of them off, while the camera was on the air, leaving nothing but the bare easel. Frantically, the director looked to the other camera (One) for something to cut to. Camera One was in transit from one position to another, and there was no help from that quarter. Luckily the next item was a film story. The director hit the film and dissolved to the film channel, knowing he had a minute or so to get things unscrambled on the floor. But a splice broke in the film projector. By this time they had the cards back on the easel in front of Camera Two, but with some totally unrelated picture at the front. Minutes of script went by with this picture on the air.

The director tried to get Camera One in position for the map story, dissolved into it just as the story was ending, and had to go back to the same picture on Camera Two again. By this time the film had been rethreaded and the ready light was on. The script came to the next film story and the director hit the film. But the newscaster was talking about a funeral in New York while the film, which had not been run past the first film story, still showed political demonstrators in Germany. By this time there was only one thing for the director to do—put the camera on the newscaster. It was this newscaster's first news show. The director had been constantly harassing him, through the floor manager, with "stretch it out" cues while he was trying to get a camera on something, and "speed it up" cues when he had no picture on the air. Sometimes a speed-up sign came so soon after a stretch-it cue that the floor manager almost worked them into one gesture. It was all the poor newscaster could do to hold doggedly to the reading of the copy.

At one point in the script he had rehearsed a move where he got up from his desk and moved off the set, where he could watch a floor monitor (in those days, in a small studio, the monitor was not built into the newscaster's desk or placed where he could see it easily) and take his cues for a film story directly from the screen. At the precise moment when the director finally got his camera in position for a shot of the newscaster and got rid of the still picture he had been holding so long, the newscaster came to the point in the script where it said, "Move to floor monitor." Up he got and blurred out of the shot, while the director hastily dissolved back to the same old picture. With so little air time left, it was possible for the director to kill the floor microphone, and have the floor manager speak directly to the newscaster, telling him to pick up the show on the next-to-the-last page at a story which had little visualization. The director was then able to dissolve back to the news-caster seated at his desk and take the last section of the show—meanwhile setting up the slides for the closing credits.

There are steps the director can take to prevent errors, or to correct them once the worst has already taken place. During the following discussion of the various aspects of television directing, suggestions are made in each case where such errors are likely to occur.

The director must be creative. It is important for a television director to have a creative spark, even though many types of television directing do not involve creativity in the usual sense. Almost any kind of show is a creative challenge, however. No two shows are ever alike, and their construction always involves some kind of original thinking. Such thinking is basic to good showmanship. It is sometimes known as "flair," and is easily recognizable in a director with talent. This quality is not quite genius, however, and few directors in theatre or film have merited that description. It is questionable whether a true genius could survive under the pressures and tensions, the restrictions of time, budget, and technology that exist in television. One might also wonder whether a genius would be likely to possess two other qualities which have been identified as necessary in television production: (1) a mastery of the tools of the medium that enables the successful director to make his ideas practicable; and (2) the personal charm and way with people that help him elicit cooperation from his staff and crew and thus get things done. In the opinion of the authors, the most successful television directors are highly talented, extremely sensitive and creative people, but also solid personalities, rather than geniuses.

The director must be able to work with people. Good personal relations are important in almost every kind of work, but they are absolutely indispensable in television, which calls for such a high degree of cooperation from everyone involved. Television is no place for the individual who expects associates and assistants to do their jobs just because they are paid to do so. Very often a television director must ask an associate to do more than just the prescribed job. In fact, he may have to ask for the seemingly impossible. The director must have the ability to inspire everyone with a personal interest in the production, as no one can be expected to do the impossible for money. It is standard procedure in many stations, by the way, to list technical directors, scenic designers, lighting engineers, and other key personnel in the closing titles, or "credits." A point is even made of using the same size lettering as that used for the names of directors, producers, and authors. This sharing of credits is a great help, of course, but it still will not substitute for personal charm and leadership.

Part of this charm is the secret of asking advice. If you are directing a show, the effect you want and how you want to achieve it may be perfectly clear to you, but it is still very wise policy to go to the man who will have to create that effect for you, to ask him for his suggestions on the matter. You may know his job as well as he does, or think you do, but he is still the man who must perform the operation. In this way you not only get cooperation so that the things you try to do become at least possible, but you also get a greater number of creative brains to work on the problem. As a result, you often find better ways of doing things and better ideas by which the show can benefit. Moreover, this makes everyone whose advice you ask a partner in the creative effort, and that much more eager to have everything work out perfectly.

The worst kind of director, and often the poorest in television, is the one who knows it all and feels his job as director requires him to tell everybody else what to do. If he does happen to know it all, he is still resented; and if he is faking, he can conceal the fact only from the sponsors and guests in the control room, if any—never from the crew with whom he is working.

The director must be self-confident. With all the skill and charm he can muster, the television director still falls short of full success if he lacks self-confidence. Often a high degree of self-confidence will make up for weaknesses in other areas. People tend to evaluate an individual by the value he places on himself, and if they sense this value to be high, they will be happier and more secure working under him. Even when a rehearsal is going badly, and the director is secretly worried about the show, he must still seem confident that all will go well by air time, if he is to avoid throwing the whole staff into a panic.

TERMS, CUES, AND DIRECTIONS

While terminology may vary from station to station, and while the cues or directions given by the director to the members of his crew permit considerable expression of individuality, many of the phrases used over the intercom system have become almost standardized. The ones that are listed here seem to be most commonly in use at the present time. As the young director joins the staff of any given station, however, he will do well to listen carefully to the particular pattern used at that particular station, and to modify his terminology and directions accordingly. It never helps to say, "Now at Station WOOF, we used to do it *this* way. . . ."

The following cues are shown in quotation marks to remind the reader that they are part of the *spoken* vocabulary of television production.

Cues Related to Shots or Camera Movement

1. "Tilt up"   The camera looks up, or down.
 "Tilt down"
2. "Pan left"   The camera looks from side to side.
 "Pan right"

These terms are usually used to slightly reposition the subject in the shot. It is not enough to center the subject. For example, the shot of the person in profile should leave more blank space between his nose and the edge of the screen than between the back of his head and the other edge of the screen. This could be adjusted, if necessary, by asking the cameraman to pan right or pan left. (See Figure 26.)

3.	"Frame up"	This term includes all the above and is used when the desired result is obvious, such as centering a title.
4.	"Focus up"	Get the camera into focus.
5.	"More (or less) head space"	More (or less) space wanted above the actor (tilt up or tilt down).
6.	"Single shot"	A shot of one person.
7.	"Two-shot"	A shot of two people.
8.	"Group shot"	A shot of a group.
9.	"Wide shot," "Cover shot," or "Long shot"	A shot that will cover the whole scene of action.
10.	"Medium shot"	Usually a shot of a person from the waist up.
11.	"Close-up"	A head-and-shoulders shot.
12.	"Tighten up"	Zoom or dolly closer to the subject. Allow less space around the sides of the subject.
13.	"Loosen up"	Reverse of the above.
14.	"Dolly in" "Push in"	Move the dolly (or pedestal) toward the set or toward the subject.
15.	"Dolly back" "Pull back"	Move the dolly (or pedestal) away from the set; pull it back and away from the subject.
16.	"Truck right" "Truck left"	Move the camera's mount to the right or left, keeping the camera itself focused ahead on the subject.

17.	"Pedestal up" "Pedestal down"	Applies to a counterweighted or hydraulic pedestal mount, used to raise or lower the camera.
18.	"Zoom in"	The cameraman uses the zoom lens to make the subject larger in the frame, panning or tilting, if necessary, to keep the subject properly framed.
	"Zoom out"	Opposite of the above.
19.	"Let actor in"	Camera holds steady as actor enters the frame.
	"Let actor out"	Camera holds steady as actor leaves the picture—does not attempt to follow him.
20.	"Take actor across set (or up stairs, etc.)"	Camera follows actor, panning, tilting, or zooming as necessary, without further cue.
	"Cross with him"	Similar instruction, leaving details of operation up to the cameraman.
21.	"Stand by for the rise" "Watch the rise"	Warning to cameraman of action to come. Also warns boom man to be ready to lift boom, to raise the microphone.
22.	"Flip in" "Flip out"	Does not refer to zoom lenses, of course, but to turret cameras. Cue to cameraman to turn lens turret to a tighter lens (flip in) or a wider lens (flip out). These terms are usually used orally, not written on a script.
23.	"One hold"	Camera One does not change the shot.

Switching Cues

The following terms are shown as they might be indicated by the director on his script, and all represent cues primarily delivered to the T.D. or switcher. The television director customarily "readies" each shot and each command to the audio engineer. For example, the series of commands to take the shot on Camera One are, "Ready One—Take

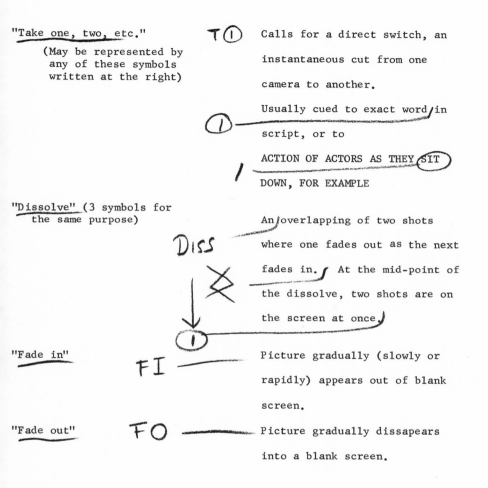

"Take one, two, etc." Calls for a direct switch, an instantaneous cut from one camera to another.

(May be represented by any of these symbols written at the right)

Usually cued to exact word/in script, or to

ACTION OF ACTORS AS THEY SIT DOWN, FOR EXAMPLE

"Dissolve" (3 symbols for the same purpose) An overlapping of two shots where one fades out as the next fades in. At the mid-point of the dissolve, two shots are on the screen at once.

"Fade in" Picture gradually (slowly or rapidly) appears out of blank screen.

"Fade out" Picture gradually dissapears into a blank screen.

Script 1.

One." The ready prepares the switcher. In some stations, the term "Stand by" is used. In giving ready commands, the beginning director should be especially aware of the potential confusion which may occur between "to" and "two." The switcher might confuse "Ready to take One" for "Ready Two." Again, an awareness of the standard readies and cues in a particular station is an important consideration, especially for the beginning director.

Audio Cues

The following terms are shown as they might be indicated by the director on his script, and all represent cues primarily delivered to the audio engineer.

1.	"Open mike," or "Open boom"	Turn microphone on.
2.	"Ready tape"	Warning for audio man.
3.	"Hit tape"	Come in strong—full volume at the opening of the music.
4.	"Sneak in the music (or sound)"	Let the start of the music (or sound) be imperceptible, then increase it gradually.
5.	"Cut the music (or sound)"	End the music (or sound) abruptly.
6.	"Fade out music (or sound)"	End the music (or sound) gradually.
	"Sneak out music (or sound)"	Fade the music (or sound) out imperceptibly, usually under dialogue or narration.
7.	"Music down" "Music down and under" "Music to background"	Hold the music behind speech or other sound, but do not take out entirely.
8.	"Music up"	Raise volume of music.
9.	"Cross-fade"	Fade one audio source out as another is faded in, so that they overlap for a moment.
10.	"Segue"	Let one song follow immediately after the preceding one without pause.
11.	"Give me a level"	A request to a performer to speak a few words in the tone of voice he will be using, so the proper volume level can be set.

It is a good plan, when writing cues into a script, to put them down in exactly the same words in which they will be spoken. Thus, a cue at the opening of a show should not read, "Warn music," which is a note from the director to himself, but "Ready music," which is the expression he will use. This saves a split second of mental translation, and split seconds are frequently golden.

Film Cues

1. "Ready film, dead pot"
   "Ready A (or other specific projector), dead pot"

   Be ready to start the film with the sound off.

2. "Roll film, dead pot"
   "Hit the film, dead pot"

   Start the projector running with the sound off.

3. "Dissolve to film, track up"
   "Fade in film, track up"
   "Take film, track up"
   or
   "Dissolve to A (or other specific channel), track up"
   "Fade in A, track up"
   "Take A, track up"

   Put the film channel on the program line with the film sound on.

Videotape Inserts

The cues "Dead pot" and "Track up" are also used for videotape inserts.

1. "Ready to roll VTR"
   (specific VTR number may be given)

2. "Roll VTR"

   Start VTR machine running.

3. "Dissolve VTR"
   "Fade in VTR"
   "Take VTR"

   Put the VTR on the program line.

The film and VTR cues are similar, but some videotape recorders require more roll time to come up to speed and lock the image in than film projectors do. Therefore the timing of the "rolls" and "takes" may differ from VTR to film.

Another problem in using videotape inserts is what to call them. A decision should be reached on how to distinguish between audio tape and videotape. One solution is to refer to videotape as "VTR" and audio tape as "tape." No matter what the individual studio decides, the policy should be adhered to consistently.

Special-Effects Cues

1. "Super One over Two"

   Superimpose the image of Camera One over the image of Camera Two.

2. "Wipe One into (or over) Two"

Using the special-effects generator, wipe the image of Camera One into (or over) the image of Camera Two.

3. "Key One over Two"
"Matte One over Two"
(also spelled "matt" or "mat")

The image of Camera One is keyed (electronically inserted) into the image of Camera Two. Because the wipe and the key are set up on the special-effects generator, the commands "Take effects," "Take special," and "Dissolve to effects" are sometimes used.

Cues Given at the Opening of a Show

The following series of cues is a typical opening for a live program, as the crew may hear them from the director.

Before Air Time

1. "Two minutes to air"
"One minute to air"

Delivered over loudspeaker to all in studio and control room.

2. "Opening shots"

Each cameraman is expected to line up on his first shot.

3. "Stand by—quiet in the studio"

Given over earphones at thirty seconds before air time. Usually repeated loudly by the floor manager.

4. "Ready tape"
5. "Ready fade in One"

Given quietly to the audio engineer and the T.D.

At Air Time

6. "Hit tape"
7. "Fade in One"

(Generally the opening title.)

8. "Open announce mike"

Cue to the audio person to open the announcer's mike.

9. "Music down"
10. "Cue announcer"

In some studios, the audio operator is expected to anticipate the announcement cue and have the mike open in time.

11. "Ready cue host"
12. "Ready dissolve Two"
13. "Music out"
14. "Cue host and ⎫   To floor manager to cue host.
15. Dissolve Two" ⎬ given together   (Live shot of host.)
16. "One—break to a close-up"   To cameraman.
17. "Ready One"
18. "Take One"   (Close-up of host.)

It will be noted that the customary opening of a program finds us dissolving from a slide or a title card to a shot of the host or M.C. In this situation we cue the performer first and *then* dissolve to him, to avoid seeing him reacting to his cue. If we were *fading in* a scene, however, it would be better to say, "Fade in One and cue Joe." The switcher then can control the timing of the fade, beginning it, holding it back until he sees Joe begin to react, then completing the fade-in. If Joe had been cued first, the fade would have had to come up immediately to avoid having his first line spoken from a blank screen. Whether the switching or the cue to the talent comes first, it is imperative that they both be given in the same breath. A delay of either can be a production crudity.

Shorthand Symbols for Common Cues and Directions

The previous list of cues is the complete "ready and cue" for each action desired. This method of cuing is desirable for the beginning director. Once television directing is no longer a frantic and emotionally shattering experience, a new and shorter method of cuing may be used. It is still a good idea to give complete readies, but "professional shorthand" may be used for cuing.

Readies	*Commands to "do it"*
Ready tape	Tape
Ready fade in ①	①
or	
Ready mike	Mike
Ready cue host	Cue
Ready fade in ①	①

The first thing a newcomer to a television station does, under ideal conditions, is to observe a few rehearsals or air shows, borrow a few marked scripts, and ask a few tactful questions about what terms are used and how scripts are marked. The T.D. is a good person to ask, if there is one; if not, ask a fellow director.

Studio or remote cameras are always designated by numbers—1, 2,

3—while film chains at some stations may be designated by letters—A, B, C—or Alpha, Beta—or higher numbers such as 10, 11, 12—to distinguish them more readily from the camera channels. A station with two studios may number its camera chains ① and ② in Studio A, while Cameras ③ and ④ will be found in Studio B. The film chains may also be called ⑤ and ⑥ or possibly ⑧ and ⑨, just to leave room for possible expansion.

To summarize then:

Shorthand symbols for Camera One might be ① or #1 or C1.

Shorthand symbols for a given film chain might be Film A or Film Ch. A or Alpha or may be represented by a number as ⑤ or ⑨, as the case may be. The same variety of systems would apply to a number of VTR inputs.

Shot Numbers and Camera Cue Sheets

For use in ambitious dramatic or musical productions, many directors number each shot in sequence. The shots assigned to each camera are then listed on narrow strips of paper which are taped at the back of the camera before camera rehearsals begin. When the cameraman has time between shots, he can snatch a glance at his shot list, or camera cue sheet (the two terms refer to the same thing), and get his next shot ready, often before the director can give him the "ready" orally. If a shot has to be changed in the course of rehearsal, the director merely says, "Change Shot 17 from a medium shot to a close-up," or even "Scratch [eliminate] Shot 17—we'll do without it." An added shot, conceived in rehearsal after the shots were numbered, can be described, for example, as 17a.

One other value of the shot-number system lies in its convenience in letting everyone know where he is in the script. For a director to say, "All right, let's try it again at the top of page four," is helpful to the floor manager and anyone else who is following the script. But for the cameraman, it is much more meaningful to hear, "Shot Number 23." Perhaps Camera One has shot 23; the person on Camera Two then knows that his next shot will be 24, for example. In a two-camera production, the shot numbers tend to alternate, except when slides or film clips come in between shots. Use of a film chain should properly be called a shot every time we dissolve or cut to the film chain. In a three-camera production, lasting sixty or ninety minutes, the shot numbers sometimes can run into the hundreds.

The following script illustrates several things. First, proper script form gives the director almost the whole left half (or right half in some

THE LOST CHILD by Alfred Bester

F.I.③ - Titles

✗ ② - L.S,- Pan
room to back door

to CU
sim trunks

T① MS, Paula

T③ CU swim trunks

T① MS Paula

WE OPEN ON THE LIVINGROOM OF THE GRAHAM HOME,
AN UPPER MIDDLE CLASS APARTMENT IN EAST SIDE
NEW YORK. THE IMPORTANT PLAYING FURNITURE IS
A SMALL KIDNEY DESK WITH A TELEPHONE ON IT,
AND A COUCH. A PILE OF LUGGAGE STANDS BESIDE
THE DESK. THERE IS A SMALL EMPTY BAG OPEN ON
TOP OF THE DESK. IT IS FOUR O'CLOCK IN THE
AFTERNOON; THE RADIO IS PLAYING.

PAULA GRAHAM ENTERS FROM THE REAR OF THE
APARTMENT. SHE IS IN A TRAVELING SUIT AND
CARRIES AN ARMFUL OF SUMMER CLOTHES FOR A
FIVE-YEAR-OLD CHILD. SHE PLACES THE CLOTHES
ON THE DESK, THEN NEATLY PACKS THEM INTO THE
OPEN BAG, SMILING AT THE TINY SWIM TRUNKS
MARKED "Hello" IN FRONT AND "Goodby" IN BACK.
SHE ALSO EXPERIMENTS WITH A TINY PAIR OF
WATER*WINGS.

AFTER THE BAG IS PACKED AND CLOSED, PAULA
PLACES IT ON TOP OF THE PILE OF LUGGAGE, SITS
DOWN AT THE DESK, AND DIALS A NUMBER ON THE
PHONE.

PAULA

Hello? This is Mrs. Graham at 215. Graham,

G-R-A-H-A . . . That's right, Graham. Apartment

2-C. I want to cancel our newspaper delivery for

one month. Until . . . (CONSULTING DESK CALENDAR)

. . . September 12th. (PAUSE) Well, yes. It's

a little more than a month. Yes. We're going away.

Oh. . . just a minute, Mr. Graham wants to know if

you can forward his magazines to him? Yes? Good.

The forwarding address is Mount Pleasant, Maine. . .

Mount as in mountain. . . Pleasant as in nice, good,

delightful. . . And Maine as in "So goes the nation."

That's right. Thank you. What? Thank you very much.

I'm sure we'll have a wonderful time.

T② MLS - follow
Paula to door

PAULA HANGS UP THE PHONE, LOOKS AT HER WATCH A LITTLE
NERVOUSLY. THEN CROSSES AND EXITS INTO THE REAR OF THE
APARTMENT. SHE RETURNS WITH A MILK BOTTLE, SITS AT TH
DESK, SCRIBBLES A NOTE, AND FOLDS IT INTO THE BOTTLE.
THEN SHE EXITS THROUGH THE ARCHWAY WITH THE BOTTLE AND
THE NOTE.

Script 2.

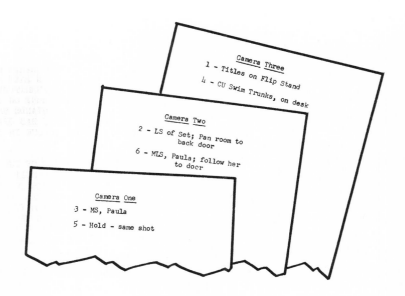

Figure 18.   Camera cue sheets as they would look for the beginning of
The Lost Child. Shot numbers would, of course, be entered by the director
on his script.

studios) of the page for cue markings. Using the far-left section for
readies and the area very close to the typed script for commands allows
the director to visually separate the two. To distinguish camera breaks
(directions to cameramen to move to their next shots) from directions
to cameras that are on the air, it is a good idea to box them in.

Here are the first half-dozen shots of a drama by Alfred Bester, as
seen in the director's copy of the script, then as typed on the shot lists,
or camera cue sheets, of the three cameramen.

Extent of the Director's Responsibilities for Cuing

Some studios have overdone the procedure of director's cues to the
point where he is made responsible for nearly every move that is made.
This is far from desirable. The director should be spared the responsibility of throwing any more cues than are absolutely necessary. Whenever a crew member can take a cue automatically from a previous element in the show, he should do so. The director should give a cue only
when he alone is capable of deciding the exact second at which the cue
should be given. "Take" cues are almost always of this nature, although
there are particular takes which must be made exactly on an action, can

be rehearsed thoroughly, and are usually more accurately done if performed without cue by the T.D. or switcher. A cue to *begin* action is usually given by the director, because he is also giving the fade-in cue, and the two must coincide. A cue to read commentary that goes with a film news story, however, is much better taken by the announcer directly from his own monitor when he sees the film appear. Routine operations, such as opening a given microphone, or panning with the action across the set, should be handled by the people involved without cues from the director, provided there has been time for rehearsal.

The exception to the discussion above is the student director. It is important that the beginning director familiarize himself with all aspects of the production and be able to handle all the responsibilities for directing the first few exercises. In this way, the director is aware of the timing needed for all cues and the new terms in each exercise are reinforced through personal use.

SUMMARY

By way of combining much that has been said in this chapter in easily digestible form, the authors have prepared and used with their students two lists of reminders. The first, "The Ten Commandments of Television," has been distributed to students, who have included, over the years, one rabbi, six Catholic priests, and nearly one hundred Protestant ministers. They have assured the authors that they find neither irreverence nor blasphemy in the document. The second item, "Television Mnemonics," is sheer doggerel, but we insist that it has both rhyme and reason, if admittedly no poetic value. Here they are, then, and may they help the reader, or at least amuse him.

The Ten Commandments of Television

1. Thou shalt show the viewer what he wants to see when he wants to see it.
2. Thou shalt not show a person speaking about an object that is out of the camera's frame at that moment.
3. Thou shalt have the right person on the screen at the right time; the speaker when he speaketh, the reactor when he reacteth.
4. Thou shalt not cross thy cables, but thou *shalt* cross thy cameras, shooting across each other's angle, when thy subjects are of equal importance.
5. Thou shalt not reverse thy screen direction by showing the same

person moving or looking left to right in one shot and right to left in the next.

6. Thou shalt not leave thy cameraman guessing as to what his next shot may be, but shalt ready each camera as soon as it is off the air.

7. Thou shalt not forget that the television screen is a small screen; and the close-up is the all-important shot.

8. Thou shalt not neglect an establishing shot, showing thy viewer the relations between this, that, and the other.

9. Thou shalt not cut from camera to camera for no good reason, or without motivation, or just to lend variety to thy shots.

10. Thou shalt not stay too long in black, lest thy viewer kick his set reproachfully, thinking it hath conked out again.

Television Mnemonics

(Things to remember in a jam—or just before you get into one.)

1. *First cue the talent, then fade in the shot;*
   T.D.'s react quickly, some actors do not.

In many situations, the talent takes his cue from the tally lights on the camera, in which case only one cue is necessary. When, however, in a dramatic scene, the actor cannot be looking at the camera, it is obvious that the switcher will react more quickly to the director's instruction, since here we have only one link in the chain of command, whereas an actor who gets his cue through a floor manager is at the end of a chain of *two* links. *Hence,* the ready is "Ready cue talent and ready dissolve One," not the reverse. The command may be "Mike-cue-dissolve One," but the complete ready sets everyone up for the shorter commands. Note, however, that the whole set of cues is given at once, in one sentence; there are no pauses between cues.

2. *When cutting scripts, please cut them all*
   Or else disaster will befall!

By the Law of Inverse Probabilities,* which states that anything that can possibly go wrong *will,* the one copy of the script which does not have the cuts marked on page 17 will fall into the hands of the lighting engineer, just because there are three crucial light cues on that page. It never fails.

3. *When troubles hover,*
   Go to cover.

You can "sit on a cover shot" until the performers find their places in the script, or you find yours, or things generally fall into place again.

---

* Also known as Murphy's Law or Gumperson's Law.

4. *When in doubt,*
   Fade it out.

A drastic step, to be taken only in extreme emergencies, but sometimes your only way out on a one-camera show. When caught with all your cameras down, fade out quickly, break a camera to the next person or object, and fade up as soon as possible. It works particularly well at the end of a program when somehow the closing title card is on the wrong side of the studio. But beware of the result of taking this admonition too literally, for reasons just below.

5. *Alas, alack—you went to black . . .*
   And stayed there!

Remember the Tenth Commandment: the American television audience is extremely allergic to a blank screen. Or, to put it in rhyme,

Viewers seldom stay serene
Before a blank and empty screen.

6. *The one transition you don't rehearse*
   Is bound to make you curse—or worse!

Hence, if you don't have time to rehearse the whole program, be sure to rehearse the opening, the closing, and any transitions from set to set or segment to segment. Also, in back-to-back programming out of the same studio, it is wise for both the director of the preceding program and the director of the one that follows it to rehearse all transitions between shows.

7. *When your seconds are too few,*
   Keep no secrets from your crew.

A director's crew is his most important asset, especially when there is some difficulty in the control room during taping. If the director tells his crew briefly what the problem is, they will be prepared for quick action when the director has decided what to do. Above all, never make a sudden drastic change while on the air without informing everyone on the intercom circuit of the change.

Good luck!

5 / Pictorial Composition

The composition of the picture is not the concern of the cameraman alone. It is of great importance in the work of many others who contribute to the production. The director, of course, is more involved than anyone else, since he is responsible for the appearance of the show. If the production is sufficiently complex to require a staging director as well as a television director, and perhaps a choreographer as well, these additional people will consider the composition of the final broadcast picture one of the principal aims of their creative work. Good staging of action or dance for television must be specially designed to make good shots. The scenic designer, too, will make sure that the set allows the director to frame interesting backgrounds for his shots.

Since many people who have nothing to do with the camera contribute to the composition of the pictures, it is evident that composition is as much a function of subject as it is of camera. Control over composition can be exercised in two ways: (1) through the handling of the camera—proper choice of field of view, camera angle, lens, and other factors discussed in detail in preceding chapters; and (2) through the arrangement of the various elements of the subject or scene. In most types of production, the television director is responsible for both the staging and the use of cameras, and he will exercise more control than anyone else over the composition of the picture.

Whether developed as a native talent or by diligent application, pictorial sense makes it possible for the cameraman, with or without the director's assistance, to pick a good composition automatically. If the composition is poor he must know it immediately, and know what to do to improve it. Usually this feel for composition comes only from long experience with pictures. Sometimes a cameraman will not become proficient until he has spent many months on the job. Working with good directors will give him valuable training. The director will commonly alter a cameraman's framing, ask for a wider or a tighter shot, suggest a different lens, or ask for slight panning adjustments for better balance. The cameraman will take the director's final word on questions of composition, and when he is working with a skilled director who has a finely developed sense of composition, he will learn rapidly.

One might well ask, however: Why is good composition so important to the television picture? Surely the average viewer is not an art critic; surely fast-paced action, the suspense of a plot, the personality of an actor, or the fine voice of a singer will be more important than the framing, or inner structure, of any number of shots. True, quite true. The point still remains, however, that a combination of good content and good composition will be still more effective than good content alone. Really bad composition, moreover, can seriously interfere with the viewer's enjoyment, or even his comprehension, of what is on the screen. Good composition provides more than sheer aesthetic value; it makes a contribution to what is being communicated by the screen to the viewer.

PURPOSES OF GOOD COMPOSITION

One way to put it is to think of the director as having four responsibilities to his subject, or four reasons for trying to compose his pictures well. These four may be stated as:

1. To show the subject clearly; to make it readily recognized or comprehended. This function is simple *communication* or *curiosity satisfaction*.

a   b   c

Figure 19.   Three purposes a shot can fulfill: (*a*) showing the subject clearly; (*b*) making a good composition; (*c*) achieving dramatic effect.

Nothing can infuriate a viewer more than the frustrating experience of not seeing clearly what he believes is happening. The viewer wants to know what is going on, and to see it easily. He is entitled to see the man who is speaking *when he starts to speak*, not seconds later, when the director has finally succeeded in getting a "suitable" shot.

An overabundance of spectacular effects that leave the viewer in doubt does not achieve any worthwhile purpose. A tricky angle, an elaborate superimposition, an extreme close-up, or a long shot will add to the dramatic effect only if the subject is clearly visible in the first place. Just as a line of doubtful meaning may elicit a comment of "Wha'd 'e say?" from the audience, a shot in which the subject or the action is unclear will bring out the much more serious "Wha hoppen?" reaction, which in turn leads rapidly to "So what."

2.   To show the subject pleasingly; to provide a subtle enjoyment, of which the viewer may not be conscious. This function is *aesthetic satisfaction*. In essence, the rest of this chapter is primarily concerned with this reason for good composition.

3.   To achieve, when it is appropriate, a dramatic or emotional effect; to create a mood or an atmosphere, as in the staging of drama, music, dance. Here composition supplies *emotional satisfaction*. The manner in which the camera is used may add a dramatic quality. Such factors as composition, movement, camera angle, and the like, subtly contribute to the viewer's emotional response. A shot may be placid or dynamic; it may give a character importance or insignificance. A big close-up provides dramatic emphasis; an extreme long shot may dwarf a performer against his background. The important thing is to make sure that the dramatic effect of the shot is in keeping with the dramatic effect of the scene as expressed by writer, performer, and director.

4.   To provide a variety of visual images, thus avoiding monotony and increasing the viewer's *interest satisfaction*. This is, however, much the weakest of all possible reasons for changing from one shot to another. The beginning director often falls into the trap of assuming that because *he* knows his shots are organized into some aesthetic pattern, the viewer too will be aware of this. When content is varied and interesting, the director, with his mind on technique, often tires of using a given shot long before the spectator, concerned only with the content, tires of seeing it.

It should be noted also that not every shot performs all four functions. A given shot may perform only two—to show the subject clearly and pleasantly for instance, and still be completely acceptable in a situation which carries no emotional overtone.

THE ILLUSION OF DEPTH

One aspect of pictorial composition which goes back to the cave drawings of Cro-Magnon man involves the problem of creating the illusion of depth, or of three dimensions, on what is essentially a flat, two-dimensional surface. A number of approaches to the problem of depth have been developed over the centuries by draftsmen, painters, still photographers, and film makers. We have already discussed the contribution of camera movement to the perception of scene depth or three-dimensionality of an object. Two other approaches to this problem are discussed here.

Foreground Objects

For several centuries, scenic designers for the theatre have utilized the device of placing objects in the foreground, or downstage area, to increase the depth of their stages. The most common application is the *wood wing*, a unit of scenery coming in from the edge of the stage and painted to represent a tree or some other object. Sometimes the branches soar up and over the proscenium, and are continued across the top of the stage in a *foliage border*.

Television has no proscenium; the camera's frame provides a constantly changing picture frame through which we see the action. It is possible to have an object just at the edge of the frame, however, as in Figure 20b. It is also possible to have some object, such as a pillar, a

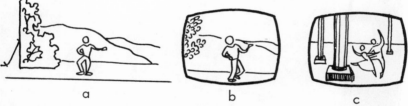

a   b   c

Figure 20. Foreground objects can help composition: (*a*) theatre wood wing; (*b*) foliage at edge of frame; (*c*) pillars at different distances emphasize depth of set.

tree, a stump, or a rock in the foreground of an exterior shot; a column, a brazier, or a massive candlestick can serve the same purpose in an interior scene.

Appropriate Lens Focal Length

The shorter the focal length of the lens that is used (and the wider the angle of view), the closer the camera must be to show the same subject field, and hence the more exaggerated is the depth dimension This is illustrated in Plate 10.

Start by studying the top left photo. This was taken at a relatively short focal length of 35mm (zoomed wide) from a distance of eight feet. The other pictures in the top row were taken from the same camera position but with different focal lengths. Thus three stages in a zoom effect are shown: from left to right, the effect of zooming in is illustrated; from right to left, the effect of zooming out.

SHORT ← FOCAL LENGTH → LONG

DISTANCE FROM MIDDLE C	35-mm	50-mm	135-mm	
8 FEET				8 FEET
4 FEET				4 FEET
3 FEET				3 FEET
	35-mm	50-mm	135-mm	

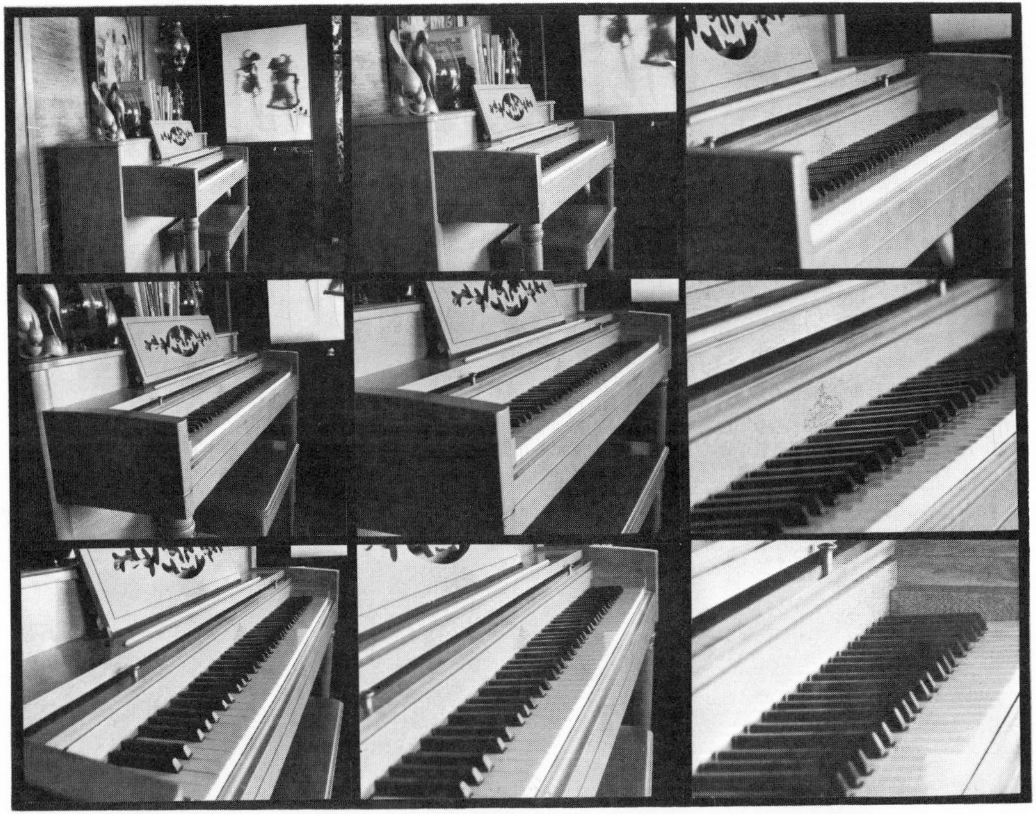

Starting again at the top left photo, and going down the first column, each photo was taken at the same focal length, but at shorter and shorter distances from the subject. In other words, a dolly-in effect is illustrated as you go down the column, a dolly-out as you go up. The same is true for the other rows and columns: all pictures in a column are taken with the same focal length; all pictures across a row are taken from the same camera position.

It is often said that a short focal length (wide angle) distorts perspective by exaggerating depth, while a long focal length compresses depth. This effect is clearly seen by comparing the three pictures that form a diagonal from lower left to upper right. They are comparable because they all show approximately the same field: the full piano keyboard. Note that the keyboard appears longest in the wide-angle picture at the lower left, and shortest in the long-focal-length shot at upper right. This is the difference in perspective that is often ascribed to the difference in focal length.

However, the difference in perspective is really a function of camera-to-subject distance rather than focal length of lens, as a little study of these photos will reveal. Compare the keyboard in the three photos in the top row (relate the near end of the piano to the music rack above). You will note that the perspective is the same, even though the magnification of the subject varies.

The difference between a zoom-in and a dolly-in can now be clearly observed, by comparing the lack of change from left to right across the top row (zooming) with the gradual lengthening of apparent depth and the opening out of the keyboard as the camera dollies in (down the column).

TECHNIQUES OF COMPOSITION

While there are many factors that contribute to a pleasing composition, there are a few which are so commonly used, and so readily achieved, that the beginning director is wise to include them in his shot planning from the very beginning.

Diagonal Arrangement

One classic rule states that "horizontal lines are static; diagonal lines are dynamic." If diagonal lines seem to move into or out of the picture, then the effect is even more active, but even the single device of arranging our subjects so that they do *not* form a straight line across the screen will generally improve the composition. Note the feeling you get

Figure 21.   Passive and active composition.

from the pictures on the left side in Figure 21, then compare them with the sensation you get from the right side. Which figures are more dynamic and which more passive? Note that in the two sketches at the right, the camera has been "canted" so that horizontal and vertical elements in the subject are no longer parallel to the horizontal and vertical sides of the frame. Here we encounter the third dimension of fixed camera movement: rotation of the camera around the camera-subject axis. Just as a ship may yaw, pitch, and roll, or a plane may turn, nose up or down, and bank, so a camera may pan, tilt, and cant.

Camera heads are not provided with means for adjusting the camera in this third dimension. Horizontal subject planes are always horizontal on the screen, verticals are always vertical. The composition effects shown in Figure 21 are special, not standard, and hence require special facilities, devices, or camera set-up to achieve. These will be discussed under special effects in Chapter 12.

Framing

Each aspect of camera handling makes a contribution to the pictorial composition, and several of these aspects have been discussed in some detail in Chapter 2. The framing of the shot, however, will be taken up here, as it is the adjustment through which the cameraman most frequently controls his composition.

The camera is practically always framing up a shot. When the adjustment necessary for the right composition is obvious, the director will simply ask the cameraman to "frame up." This would apply in the case of a simple title card or a close-up of a single person, where good composition consists only in centering the subject in the frame. The beginning director, however, may abuse this term "frame up." When the composition is very poor and serious changes must be made, instead of saying, "Pan left and tilt up just a little," he may say, "Frame it up, Two," leaving the novice cameraman at a loss to know what the director has in mind.

The framing is considered "tight" when the subject is crowding the sides of the frame, and "loose" when there is considerable space around the subject. A loose composition is always safer than a tight one, since the camera is ready for broader action without having to dolly back or zoom, but the tight composition is usually the most pleasing. In general, there should be enough space around the subject, and head room above it, so that it does not look crowded. On the other hand, the important parts of the picture should not be so small that they are lost to the eye.

Figure 22.   Tight and loose framing.

When the performers are spread too widely apart (as in the case of many stage dance routines) the camera may not be able to hold them both in the shot without using such a wide angle of view that both are entirely too small. In this case, either the camera must be placed at the side of the set, to shoot the dancers at an angle, or the performers must be instructed to separate in the direction of the camera.

Let us take stock for a moment. We have mentioned the two most obvious problems in framing: making the shot too loose and making it too tight.

Figure 23.   Camera angle helps composition when performers are spread too far apart.

Framing too loosely gives us waste space around the subject. Extraneous background elements may compete with the main subject for attention. Since any rule may be broken for a good reason, it may be wise to point out that a loose shot of one or more dancers is often necessary in order to include sudden broad movement. Choreography may be defined as the design of movement in space; sometimes extra space must be provided so that this design may become apparent.

Framing too tightly, even without the possibility of sudden rapid movement, often gives the viewer a crowded, cramped feeling; worse, tight framing may "amputate," or crop, elements of the subject that the viewer subconsciously desires to see. Again, the rule may be broken successfully for a good reason. In the drawings in Figure 24, a measure of amputation occurs. (Of course, any shot but a full-figure involves cropping to some extent, but "amputation" is used here in the very special sense of cropping the subject or subjects in such a way as to create unpleasant composition.) Why do you suppose that drawings A and B are "amputations" whereas drawing C, in the opinion of most

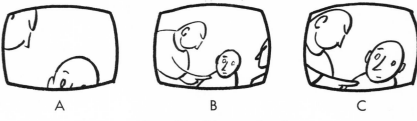

Figure 24. "Amputations."

directors, might be considered tight but would not be called an amputation?

The subject of amputation once more brings up the question: How tight should a tight close-up be? As pointed out in Chapter 2, there is some disagreement among the best directors as to the definition and limitations of a close-up. In general, one would not crop the forehead of a subject but would allow a margin of head space, as in Figure 25a. Yet for an intensely dramatic moment, or to make much of a character's reaction to a sudden stimulus, a director would be completely justified in framing the character as in Figure 25b. A director might also use such a close shot for an introspective moment, or for a scene revealing motivations which lie deep within a character. The tight close-up allows us to "look into" the character.

A large part of framing is concerned with what is called balance. This, again, is something which can only be done by feel. To give a simple

Figure 25.   How tight should a close-up be?

example: A person looking at the camera must usually be centered to seem in proper balance. However, if there is an object in the background to the right, or held in a man's outstretched hand, a better balance would center the man-and-object group, placing the man somewhat to the left of center.

Sometimes things outside the picture will affect the way it is balanced. For example: A profile shot of a person looking at something is usually framed with less space behind his head than in front to create proper balance. If, however, we are aware of something menacing him from behind, a better balance would show more space behind his head than in front. In each case, the unseen subjects beyond the frame of the picture have made the space on their side of the picture more important and have affected the composition.

Composition of a single head completely or somewhat in profile (with proper "look space") is perhaps most important in the interview, a very common format in television today. In an interview, it is most important, when shooting either the host or the guest separately, to

Figure 26.   Two examples of good composition. Balance may be affected by unseen subjects outside the camera's field of view.

allow ample look space so that we realize that one person is looking at the other even when the other is out of frame.

We must be careful not to assume, however, that a profile shot is the only exception to centering. Note that we said that a person looking at

the camera must *usually* be centered to seem in proper balance. This referred to centering him between the left and right edges of the frame;
centering his head midway between the top and bottom of the frame
would give us too much head space in most situations. In general, except for a single person looking at the camera, it might be well to avoid
having the center of interest exactly on the vertical axis of the frame;
it is almost always wise to avoid having it on the horizontal axis. In
Figure 27 the pillar exactly on the vertical axis is obviously bad composition; a castle archway in drawing B is acceptable if its base is below the horizontal axis. Drawings C and D are too mechanically sym-
metrical to be pleasing in composition.

Figure 28 demonstrates three compositions in which the major fault
is lack of balance. The last framing shows a pleasing balance of the
various elements of the picture within the camera frame.

It is important to note that not only in achieving good balance but
also in other phases of framing, of composition, and of all camera operation, there are many ways to skin the same cat. Two cameramen may
frame up the same shot in two different ways, equally pleasing. Then
again, a better cameraman, without knowing why, will consistently
frame up better pictures than his co-workers.

There is little that mechanical aids can do to assist in this creative
process. Some cameramen mark their viewfinders so that they will have
a center mark to refer to when panning with action. (The cameraman
generally "leads" a moving subject, keeping it always just behind the
center mark, in order to show the area into which it is moving.)

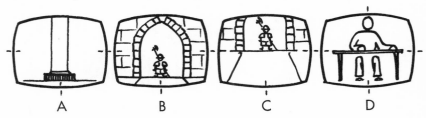

Figure 27. Dead-center symmetry is not generally the best composition.

Figure 28. Four possible framings on the same subject. One of these has
better balance than the others.

Difference in Size

If two or more people are included in the shot, they are quite often placed or the cameras are placed so that there is a *difference in size* between the two individuals. This means some persons must be closer to the camera than others. This difference in size can be utilized, if desired, to enhance a dramatic relationship, since larger relative size carries special emphasis and can convey a feeling of dominance.

Figure 29.   Staging the action so there is a difference in size between people can improve composition.

Difference in Height

Similarly, if two or more people are included in the shot, place them, or place the camera, so there is a *difference in height* between them. A higher position on the screen may also carry a feeling of dominance, no matter what the relative size may be. This can be achieved by arrangement of the performers at varying heights or by placing them at varying distances and either raising or lowering the camera somewhat from its normal eye-level position.

Figure 30.   Staging the action so there is a difference in height between people can improve composition.

Figure 31.   Variation in height can often be obtained by staging the action so that performers are at different distances from the camera and by using the camera either higher or lower than eye level.

CONTROL OVER SUBJECT

Backgrounds

Good scene design can make pictorial composition easy. There are some sets in which you just cannot help but get good shots, at least from the standpoint of design. A good designer considers the shots that the director wants to use, and he designs his set so that even when small portions of it appear, those portions will be pleasing in themselves and it will not be necessary to see the set as a whole.

The designer also considers the subject that is to appear in the foreground of the shot, the costumes, and the lighting involved. Horrible examples of the lack of this foresight crop up now and then when a dancer in a leopard skin, for example, is completely camouflaged and lost against a jungle drop. Backgrounds for dancers should be much simpler than sets for actors, since the dancer is seen predominantly in long shots and every movement of the body must be clearly visible.

The advent of color television has created new opportunities for scene designers and costumers. Now, color combinations are as important to color television as composition is in black and white. Though black and white may express mood through adjustments in shading and lighting, color television requires a far more complex balancing of color combinations in conjunction with lighting to produce a desired visual and emotional effect. Even the soap operas have utilized muted blues, greens, and browns for their sets, choosing strong costume colors to express the harmony or the discord that the situation requires.

Groupings

Any analysis of beauty in design and pictorial composition discloses the fact that *simplicity* is the keynote. It can almost be said that the simpler a line (or a form or a grouping), the stronger the composition will be. The grouping of actors in a shot serves to simplify the picture. By grouping people together instead of leaving them separated, we simplify the picture from a design made of many figures all the same size to a simple mass. Almost any shape or mass formed by a group of actors is better than a disorganized number of separate people. Possibly the grouping may consist only of moving a couple closer so that they make one form. (See Figure 32.)

If there are three figures, they may be arranged in one group or in two. Possibly all that may be necessary is to move one of the actors closer to another, or if one is in the background, move him so that his

Figure 32.   In the first picture, the figures are not grouped. In the others, grouping has improved the composition.

figure will be overlapped by that of another in the foreground and together they will make one shape.

Michelangelo is supposed to have said that a statue should be so designed that it could be rolled down a hill and nothing would break off. He was after simplicity of mass. The simplest possible forms are, of course, the cube, sphere, pyramid, or, in two-dimensional terms, the square, circle, and triangle. The T shape, cross, and X shape are also fairly simple forms. Of all these, the triangle is the most valuable for pictorial composition. Group people into a triangle, frame it properly, and a good composition will generally result.

Triangular Grouping

The triangle has been the basis of good strong composition almost from the beginning of graphic art. It is particularly valuable in a rectangular picture, because the spaces left around the sides of the triangle are themselves triangular in shape, thus repeating the same form throughout the picture, but in different sizes, all subordinate to the main triangular form.

Another very fortunate aspect of this form is that it lends itself beautifully to placing the center of interest in a dominant and compelling position, and we shall concern ourselves with the problem of dominance in just a few pages. The top point of the triangle is a very powerful spot in the design. There is, in a square or in a circle, no comparable point which can dominate the whole, unless one may choose to rotate the square into a diamond shape. The inverted triangle, on the other hand, has no dominant peak, and every point along the base or in the center of the form competes equally for attention. (See Figure 33.)

Naturally, the triangle as a device in composition must, like anything else, be given the right relative importance. It would be running the thing right into the ground, for example, to insist on forcing actors into

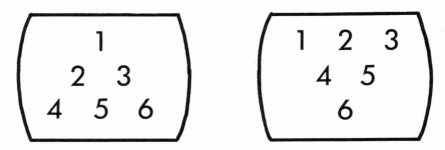

Figure 33.   Which number dominates in each of these groupings?

triangular groupings at the sacrifice of natural action. To make the triangular grouping simpler to obtain, and seemingly more natural, sets with different floor levels, various platforms or steps, are very helpful. Seating people on the arms of chairs, on hassocks, or on stools that are lower than regular chairs, or having some people sit while others stand, will also help toward this end.

Lighting as an Element in Composition

Lighting can be a controllable element in pictorial composition in certain studios, where there is the equipment, the time, the manpower, and the know-how to use it. This is particularly true in low-key scenes in which each source of light illuminates new objects and adds new elements to the composition.

By lighting a scene properly, it is possible to simplify the composition in many cases. Distracting elements in the background can be reduced in tone by cutting down the light on them so that they will no longer compete with the subject for primary interest. The right amount of what is called "separation" between subject and background can often be achieved by lighting. Backlighting will do this, by rimming the subject with a brilliant edge. Excessive backlighting, however, is an unnatural movie effect which does not help to convey television's peculiar feeling of actuality. A contrast in overall tone is often better for this purpose. The subject is either more brightly lighted than the background, or the background is lighter than the subject. This second possibility is of value in dance productions, where the form and outline of the figure are most important. When details of expression on the face of an actor must be seen, however, this tonal relationship cannot be so easily used. Contrasting colors, of course, provide "instant separation," but there must also be a difference in tone.

Sometimes a gradation in light across a background will itself add an element to the composition. A blank area in the background, a wall or floor perhaps, may be lighted in such a way (with spots) that it has a subtle variation of tone within it, or even moves from a high to a very low intensity, and yet remains the same simple plane. What we are talking about here is lighting a background with spots. If pieces of furniture, wall decorations, and the like are individually lighted, the result will be a "play" of light and shade across the background, rather than the flat effect of overall even illumination. A dark portion of a wall, for instance, on one side of the picture can be used to balance a waist shot of a single subject in which the person is off center, whereas if flat background lighting were used, the person might have to be centered. Again, gradations of color can sometimes serve the same purpose.

Motion-picture cameramen frequently light their background with small spots just for this purpose, so that the simple wall planes become rich in subtle variations of tone. This is not necessarily the unreal, stylistic device that backlighting has usually been. The unreal thing is to be seen when interiors are bathed in the merciless flat illumination of many television studios. In reality, interior illumination comes from a few sources, and often these are low sources, so that the upper portions and far corners of walls are naturally darker in tone.

Achieving Dominance

While pictorial composition is not the only means of making one of a group of subjects dominant (contrasting color is one obvious method), it is certainly one of the most useful. We think of dominance as important chiefly in dramatic productions, but it is almost equally vital in music, dance, and educational or informational programs. Accordingly, this is perhaps as good a place as any for a brief consideration of some of the more frequently seen methods of achieving the dominance of a selected element in a scene or shot.

We have seen how placing a performer at the apex of a triangle will give him a dominating position. The concentration of light on one actor will also pick him out from the others. Dominance may be achieved, moreover, by the use of converging lines of force. In Plate 11, for example, even though one actor stands at the top of a pyramid, his eyes and those of the woman direct attention to the man on the left. The converging lines of force, in this case, are invisible lines running from each of the actors to the spot at which they are looking, which then becomes the center of interest in the picture.

Another effective technique for achieving dominance is the use of differentiation of movement. If all the soldiers are in step but one, our eyes

Plate 11.   Which person is emphasized in this grouping? (Courtesy of the School of Radio Technique Studios)

will be drawn to that one. If the others in the file present arms while the one executes shoulder arms, we shall look at him immediately. The ultimate in differentiation of movement occurs when only one person is moving while the others are motionless, or vice versa. Some years ago a motion picture had a detective pursue a suspect into a stadium where tennis matches were taking place. Shooting from the opposite side, the camera showed a fairly large group, but the suspect stood out vividly. Why? He was staring straight in front of him, while the other spectators were turning their heads from side to side as they followed the progress of a tennis match.

Dominance of one subject over others may be achieved with a strong concentration of light. This same compelling effect can be achieved also by lighting all portions of the set with a dim, shadowless light, and striking the subject itself with a contrasting spot which gives it strong highlights and shadows. This is not peculiar to television, or to film. The theatre, for many years, has used not only lighting, but costume and make-up too, to make one character stand out. In color television, especially, these elements of contrast can be most effective.

Finally, two suggestions for improving composition in general can also contribute to the control of dominance. Difference in height usually puts the taller person at an advantage, but in a room full of basketball players, a short football quarterback would be down but definitely not out of our awareness. Difference in size, created by placing one person closer to the lens, can accomplish the same result. This device is used so often in television that the shot shown in Plate 12 has come to be called by some directors "Two Faces East." Unlike the tradition of the theatre, where the character who is upstage dominates those who are downstage, the person who is nearest us is so much larger that he is definitely dominant, *so long as he faces the camera, and therefore the audience.* Because television cameras are usually operated below eye level, a nearer person is also imaged higher in the shot, and hence receives even more emphasis.

Plate 12. Combination long shot and close-up, photographed from television screen. (Courtesy of NBC)

COLOR AND EMPHASIS

The advent of color television has created new opportunities, and problems, for scene designers, costumers, and lighting directors. Color theories usually ascribe three dimensions to color, one of which is tone (or value). Tone plays the greatest role as far as composition is concerned. The other dimensions are hue (blue, green, red, etc.) and chroma (brightness or intensity). Television engineers call the first of these three "luminance" and lump the other two together as "chrominance." The black-and-white camera is sensitive only to the tonal dimension, with which it is able to reproduce, quite satisfactorily, most of the visible world. The color camera, which can see and reproduce hue and chroma as well, provides some additional opportunities for creating emphasis.

An area of bright color, differing in hue from its surroundings, will generally attract first attention, and may easily supersede position at the apex of a triangle or at the convergence of lines of force. It is not likely, however, that it would exceed differential movement, and the eye is always drawn to moving objects in a static field, whatever their position or color.

In this connection it is interesting to note that none of the research studies have found any advantage in realistic color over black-and-white pictures in achieving cognitive learning. When color is used solely for emphasis, however, such as printing key words or important parts of diagrams in contrasting color, there is evidence that learners remember these elements more easily and retain them longer.

UNUSUAL COMPOSITION

Occasionally, the temptation will arise to do something very unusual and sensational in the way of composition. Rarely may this desire be indulged safely. Composition, like all other elements of production, must be the slave and not the master. It takes a strong motivation to call for a striking and unusual composition and prevent it from attracting attention to itself.

Figure 34.   "Framed shots," familiar examples of unusual compositions.

One of the best examples of the unusual in composition is the familiar *framed* shot. The camera looks into the room through the fireplace, or between the spindles of the balustrade. Sometimes one actor is framed by the arms or legs of another.

In the dramatic show, this special kind of composition demands a special motivation. It must be led into in some way. It is part of a series, dependent on the shot which came before and the one that comes after. A shot through the balustrade, for instance, cannot suddenly appear, in the middle of an ordinary sequence, without calling attention to the viewpoint from which the shot is taken and the camera taking it. The shot under the actor's arm is much easier to use in this respect, since it constitutes only a rearrangement of already existing elements. But to bring the stair rail into sudden prominence calls attention to it and probably to the camera as well. If the shot were of the subjective type, of course, the situation would be entirely different. Showing someone peering through the railing before cutting to the framed shot would turn all camera-consciousness into consciousness of the eavesdropper instead.

Sometimes a camera movement, which is itself motivated, may lead into the unusual composition. The shot might begin through the window, but with the camera too far in to show the window frame. An actor moving toward the window will then motivate a pull-back or zoom-out which will bring the window frame into view around the edges of the shot.

The opening shot in a sequence can often be quite unusual since it does not have to be particularly motivated, or led up to. Again, the shot up through the fireplace—the fire's-eye view—can sometimes be motivated when the actors are staring into the fire. We often see, and accept, the mirror's-eye view of the girl at her dressing table, or the oven's-eye view of the cook removing the turkey.

Another type of unusual composition is the *canted* or *cockeyed* shot where vertical and horizontal lines appear as diagonals on the screen. Diagonals are lines of action, of moving, kinetic objects, which impart a feeling of unrest. An unrealistic quality can also be suggested by this schizoid view of things. If the situation calls for it the canted camera may be used, but only when the motivation is very strong.

In the musical or variety show, these logical motivations are not as necessary. Anything that contributes, even superficially, to the visual interest of the production is desirable. Of course, the camera must not distract from the spirit of the performance; it would not be desirable, for instance, to use canted shots of a lovely singer, or of serious dancers, so that their actions seem to belie the law of gravity; but in the case of jazz musicians, trampoline acts, comedy dances, and the like, the canted shot can be very effective when properly used.

POOR COMPOSITION

In training people to recognize good composition when they see it, the consideration of poor composition is an excellent start. It is not hard to recognize poor composition, but it takes a great deal of knowledge and ability to know what makes it poor and what must be done to correct it. One of the prime examples of poor composition is the *odd juxtaposition*.

Unfortunate effects result from odd juxtapositions: near objects seem to connect with far objects when the camera is wrongly placed, and the classic example of the man with the halo around his head illustrates what may sometimes be seen. The juxtaposition of door and table in Figure 35 makes it seem as if the door and table are fastened together. Just a small change in camera placement is all that is needed.

One should not assume, however, that all unfortunate juxtapositions originate from objects in the background. One of the authors, watching a student director who had persuaded one of his sociology instructors to take part in a panel discussion presented as a class exercise, was startled to observe that his colleague had acquired a strange-looking beard. A closer look at the monitor revealed that the professor was seated just behind a cone-shaped table mike in just such a relationship that the microphone seemed to be growing from his chin, as in Figure 35. Of course, this was not as unfortunate as the case of the poor actor, playing the role of a betrayed husband, who seemed literally to sprout horns—until the viewer realized that the actor was placed in just the wrong way before a wall bracket or candelabrum.

Figure 35.   Odd juxtapositions. A slight change in lateral camera angle would improve each of these pictures.

SUMMARY

Every time a picture is composed, it is something new under the sun; there has never been anything exactly like it before. This is why rules of composition cannot apply except in the very loosest way. We may borrow a page from the designer's book, from the painter's, from the photographer's, but mostly we must use our own taste and judgment in determining just what devices are valuable for our particular purposes.

Yet rules do have a value; composing on sheer feeling may lead us to framing some pretty poor pictures if we have no standards of taste on which to base our feelings. In almost all art it is generally considered a good practice to master the rules before setting about breaking them.

Most rules of taste, unlike laws of optics or electronics, can be broken, and often to good effect, but only when the breaker knows why the rule came to be in the first place, why he now proposes to break it, and what purposes will be served thereby. Someone has said that *"training* tells us the rules; *education* helps us understand the reasons behind the rules; *experience* teaches us when and why to break them."

Only the experience of working with *pictures* can really develop the "feel for good composition" which the television worker must have. It is the hope of the authors that the study of this chapter, superficial as it is, will stimulate further thinking on creative composition, especially by those who operate the cameras. Television is, first and foremost, a photographic medium, and creative mastery of the camera's picture is essential to successful producing and directing.

6 / Production Elements and Techniques

So far we have considered two kinds of tools used by the television director: the cameras and lenses that make his pictures possible, and the cues and directions that make them take place. We turn now to a discussion of some of the various elements that the director combines as he creates those pictures. In this chapter we will be dealing with three of the production elements the director is likely to be concerned with. Because these elements are involved directly with the technical presentation of the television program, they will be discussed in some detail. These elements are: sound, lighting, and graphics. Other production elements will be discussed in later chapters.

THE AUDIO ELEMENTS

In many television stations, audio engineers are in charge of microphone placement and audio-board operation. While these engineers have the primary responsibility for achieving good audio pick-up and balance, the television director cannot and should not abdicate *his* responsibility.

With opportunities for training in radio production in the old tradition now available chiefly at educational stations, and with courses in radio production disappearing from the curricula of many universities, *the television director must take it upon himself to master the art of audio.* This chapter can describe only briefly the various audio elements. In fact, we will do little more than introduce these elements to the beginning director and producer; fuller acquaintance with them and eventual mastery can come only with actual use and intensive practice.

Audio production has always been erratic and problematical in television. There are three basic elements with which the director and producer need to be familiar: audio quality, volume, and balance.

Audio Quality

The term "audio quality" usually means the apparent "liveness" or "deadness" of the space where the sound originates. What we are talking about here is the brief period during which the sound reverberates. Except in a room where all surfaces are totally sound-absorbent, a sound will echo and re-echo as it reflects from surface to surface; these echoes finally reach a microphone via paths of differing length, at different times. We say echo, but only in a very large, poorly designed auditorium might a clearly defined echo be heard. Reverberation time, different for different rooms, even for different areas of the same room, is perceived and described simply as audio quality.

One problem is associated with the quality of one sound source versus a second sound source. All sound originating from the same general area, such as a studio, will have relatively the same reverberation period. When, however, extraneous sound (such as a laugh track) is inserted in a program, care should be taken that the sound of the recorded laughter is of the same quality as that of the scene being televised. It can seem phony to the viewers, for example, to watch a comedy series in which the sound quality is very "live" or very bright (with a relatively long reverberation period) and to have the laughter of the "studio audience" which is supposedly watching the program as it is being presented, seem very muffled because it was recorded in an area with a short reverberation period. Whenever possible, then, sound sources that are to be inserted into a program should match the quality of that program's sound. This is particularly important when a videotape segment, recorded outside the studio, is inserted into a live studio production. The real production point here is that if the two sounds do not blend, do not seem part of the same program, the inserted sound will seem false—just as it is.

Even in a production in which the audio is originating from the same studio, sound-quality problems can arise. Studios, because of set pieces and stage construction, often have live areas and "dead" areas. The greatest problem seems to arise in programs in which the sound is too live. Dramatic programs that are produced with bare sets (for example, the realistic representation of a police station) can, especially when boom mikes are used, have a sound quality that is too live. The shouting and angry actor seems almost to be in an echo chamber. The sound quality, then, can make the volume seem too loud for comfortable listening. In this situation, the director or producer will need to deaden the sound by the addition of set dressings or curtains to absorb some of the sound reverberations. Most television studios are constructed with sound-deadened walls and ceilings to prevent their actual large size being noticeable because of a long reverberation of the sound.

Volume

Volume is, of course, loudness or amount of sound. The television director should be aware that the volume of sound he hears in the control room is not necessarily what a viewer will hear at home. Sound in the control room is received through the audio monitor, which is the director's means of hearing what is going out on the air. (The level of sound on the control-room audio monitor is not necessarily the same as the sound being transmitted.) Again, the sound from the control-room monitor is for the convenience of the director; he can ask the audio engineer for louder or softer sound in the control room without affecting the sound being transmitted or recorded.

The volume of sound transmitted (or recorded) is controlled by the audio engineer through the audio board. Each sound input into the audio board is controlled by a separate "pot" (potentiometer) and the composite result is registered on the VU* meter. The VU meter registers

Plate 13.   Simple audio mixer with four pots to control microphone inputs, master pot, and VU meter. (Courtesy of Shure Brothers Incorporated)

modulation in percentage both in volume units and in percentage of optimum volume level. The VU meter should read close to 100 percent for the loudest sounds. These designations are not absolute; variations are discussed below.

Balance

Balance is the volume-level relationship between two or more sounds in a program. The director and the audio engineer need to work closely

* Volume Units

together to make sure that the various sound sources that are heard simultaneously are balanced—so that one does not overpower the other. Probably one of the most difficult sound techniques requiring careful monitoring for good balance is the voice with music in the background (for example, an unseen announcer introducing a show with music and titles).

While the single VU meter on an audio console gives a good indication when the sound is too weak to be heard on home receivers, or so loud that it will cause them to distort, it is of no help in adjusting balance. The VU meter registers *all* the sounds that pass through the audio console and it is frequently impossible to determine just which component may be causing the highest peaks. Thus balance must be a subjective matter; the director and the audio engineer must simply *listen carefully* to adjust the balance properly between the two sound elements.

In the master control room of the local station, sound from programs, films, network and local commercials, station I.D.'s, and promotional announcements is controlled. Care should be taken by the audio engineer and/or the director on duty that the sound levels balance between one program source and the one that follows.

Awareness of all these elements of sound is necessary to insure not only that the viewer can hear what is occurring in a program, but also that the sound elements will correspond to the desired visual images. Audio control is not simple in any medium which utilizes sound; it is most difficult in television and film productions such as dramas, where microphones must not be seen. In actuality productions, the performer can stand directly in front of a microphone or hold it in his hand.

Microphones

The voice of a performer, a news-program anchorman, and a singer and the sound of an orchestra all have one basic factor in common whether they are seen or not: the sound they make as they talk, sing, or play must be picked up and translated into electrical signals by a microphone. A microphone, then, is the second element in the production of sound for television, the originator of the sound being the first. We will discuss two basic ways in which microphones are distinguished: (1) method of transduction (discussed below) and (2) pick-up field. Depending on the desired effect, the limitations of the studio and equipment, and the type of sound source, the director or producer can choose the type of microphone that will best suit his purposes. There is no all-purpose microphone.

Method of Transduction

First and foremost, a microphone is a transducer—a means of changing the physical energy of the sound waves coming from the performer to electrical energy which can be boosted in power in the control board and then transmitted or recorded along with the picture. Originally, microphones designed for radio were adapted for television, but three types of mikes are currently used in television production: (1) dynamic microphones, (2) ribbon or velocity microphones, and (3) condenser microphones.

Fields of Pick-up

Even more important to the director are the fields of pick-up. The basic patterns are non-directional (also called omni- or all-directional), uni-directional, and bi-directional (used only infrequently or not at all in television studios today). (See Figure 36.) A non-directional microphone picks up from all sides, a uni-directional microphone from only one, sometimes very narrow direction, and the bi-directional microphone picks up from two sides. Simple dynamic microphones are non-directional, and the classic ribbon microphone of radio studios is bi-directional.

There are two other directional patterns that are often used in broadcasting: (1) cardioid and (2) poly-directional. A cardioid pattern is uni-directional and broad—heart-shaped, hence the name cardioid. The poly-directional microphone is one on which there is a screw-driver selector to choose between several fields of pick-up depending on the needs of the production. A discussion program in which only one microphone is used will usually require an omni-directional microphone. Boom-operated microphones are generally uni-directional or cardioid. Examples of specific directional patterns and their uses in specific production formats are discussed below.

Microphone Mounts and Placement

In the following discussion, we will be talking about microphones in relationship to the way they are placed in the television studio. We have divided microphones for this discussion into two types: (1) stationary and (2) mobile.

Stationary Microphones

Stationary microphones are generally used when the sound source is immobile. In actuality programs, it is usually acceptable for the stationary microphone to be seen in the shot. For example, in the case of newscasters and singers it is often not only permissible but expected that their microphones be seen. The basic types of stationary microphones are: (1) stand, (2) desk, and (3) hanging microphones.

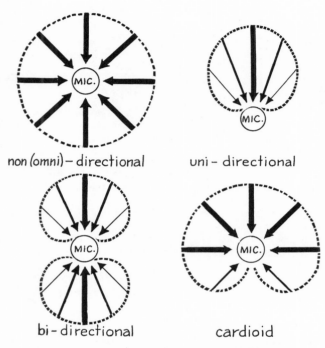

non (omni) – directional   uni – directional

bi – directional   cardioid

Figure 36. Microphone pick-up fields.

Stand microphones are most often used in television for announcers, narrators, and actors who are going to be off camera. An M.C. on a variety show or a singer can sometimes get away with using a stand microphone, but this is becoming less common. The stand is usually vertically adjustible. Announce microphones generally will be high-quality, uni-directional mikes (to control unwanted studio or audience noise) unless two performers are going to use the microphone at the same time, in which case a bi-directional mike is sometimes used. Care should be taken that the stand microphone is placed where it will not interfere with the cameras' getting a clear shot of the talent.

Desk microphones, as the name implies, are placed on desks, tables, or lecterns when the talent is to remain stationary. Used for panel discussions, newscasts, and interview programs, the best directional pattern

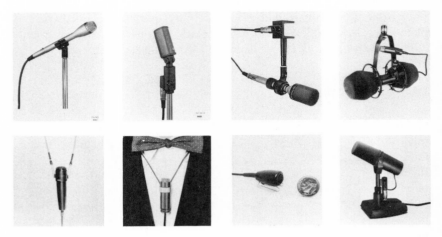

Plate 14.   Varieties of microphones. Microphones on stands: Shure SM61, *extreme top left,* represents a type of microphone that can be easily lifted from its stand and used in the hand of a singer, close to the mouth. *Top middle left:* Shure SM33, uni-directional.

Microphones mounted for boom use: *Top middle right:* Shure SM53, uni-directional. *Extreme top right:* AKG D-202.

Lavalier microphones: *Extreme bottom left:* AKG D-109. *Bottom middle left:* Shure 571. *Bottom middle right:* AKG C-510 Electret. All are omni-directional.

Desk microphone: *Extreme bottom right:* Shure SM7, uni-directional.

(Courtesy of Shure Brothers Incorporated and AKG)

will depend on the number of people to be covered and the nature of the program. Some floor or desk stands are designed so that the microphone can be easily removed from the stand and used in the hand if desired. This is not generally a noiseless operation and the audio operator must be very alert to turn down the microphone when someone begins to touch it directly.

When a single performer, such as a newscaster, is using a desk microphone, placement is especially important. The first consideration is that the microphone not be placed in such a position that it blocks the performer's face when he is on camera. Secondly, the format of the show will determine on which side of the performer the microphone should be positioned. If he is to look into camera at all times, it can make little difference. If, however, sometime during the show the performer is to turn to another camera or to a monitor, or someone else on the set, the microphone will pick him up better if it is placed on the side he will turn to. While most newscasters now use a small lavalier microphone (hung around the neck) or a tie-clip mike, many still use desk microphones.

When several people are in a panel discussion and desk microphones are to be used, it is important that all microphones be of the same type— otherwise the audio engineer will very quickly go out of his mind trying to adjust for various strengths, directional patterns, and qualities of sound. If each person cannot have a microphone, it is usually best to have a desk mike or a lavalier microphone for the moderator and a desk mike for every two panelists. If two panelists are on opposite sides of a table, unless the table is very narrow, a uni-directional desk mike close to each would be better than a bi-directional mike in the middle of the table.

Hanging microphones are often used in large sets where a boom microphone would take up too much space, microphone cords would be a problem, and cordless microphones either would not cover the action or would not be available. Performers must be aware that their positions under a hanging microphone are very critical; a slight change in the direction a performer faces may make him sound off-mike. A hanging microphone directly overhead will pick up sound from a cone-shaped area which may be visualized as an "audio pool," much like the beam from a spotlight. Performers, therefore, are restricted to the "audio pool," which means very limited movement. Sound quality can also suffer if a hanging microphone is placed too close to a piece of scenery;

Figure 37.   The hanging microphone and its audio pool.

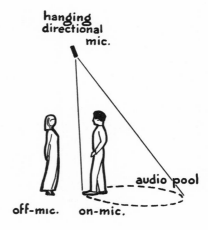

a nearby hard surface can act as a reverberation board for the sound. There are, of course, advantages to the use of hanging microphones in that they take up no space and do not cast unexpected shadows, but these advantages should be carefully weighed against the potential liabilities of sound-quality problems and limited performing area.

Mobile Microphones

Most of the microphones that are used in television are of the mobile variety—that is, they can be moved during the production. The most common types of mobile microphones are: boom, hand, and lavalier microphones.

Boom microphones are suspended from the end of a boom or stick. The boom allows quick movement to various desired areas within the studio: it can be panned, tilted; the microphone may be rotated to face any direction; and if it is the larger type, the boom may be extended or contracted. All this gives the microphone great flexibility. The entire boom assembly can also be dollied about the studio. The operation of the microphone alone requires one operator; if it is the larger type and will be dollied, two operators are required. The microphone boom allows a maximum of studio coverage with a single microphone.

The size of the boom-microphone assembly varies with the production needs and physical capability of the individual studio. The largest boom carries its operator and can cover two or three performing areas, but takes up considerable space. A medium boom (or giraffe) is operated while standing on the floor and must be dollied in and out, since the boom does not contract or extend. A smaller boom takes even less studio space, but must be repositioned more often to cover desired performance areas. A variation of the boom microphone which is sometimes used to cover a limited area, or when there are few microphones, is a fish-pole microphone, which is nothing more than a microphone mounted at the end of a hand-held aluminum or bamboo pole.

A boom microphone should be positioned above and in front of the sound source. The performer can be of considerable help to the boom operator if he is aware of the positioning of the microphone. A quick about-turn by a performer, followed immediately by speech, can easily outpace the boom operator's ability to move the microphone, and the performer will sound off-mike. In most situations, however, the performer will be concentrating on many production elements, so it is ultimately the responsibility of the boom operator to adjust the microphone to cover the performer. If the boom microphone is to cover several people in a scene or in an interview-discussion situation, it should be placed in a position to favor the weakest voice. Whatever the type of boom being utilized or the number of performers involved, the director should always be aware of the boom's positioning (both for sound quality and to keep the microphone itself out of the camera shot) and

Plate 15.   Microphone booms. *Top:* small, fixed boom. *Bottom:* large, movable boom. The operator may pan, tilt, extend or contract this boom, or rotate the microphone. If it is to be dollied in or out during a program, a second operator is required. (Top photo courtesy of Berkey Colortran, Division of Berkey Photo; bottom photo courtesy of Mole-Richardson Co.)

should avoid getting the shadow from the boom into the picture. In film shooting, when the crew can be sure that the camera will not suddenly have to pan left or right, the microphone is sometimes more advantageously placed just to the side of the shot, or just beneath, rather than above. This is particularly true when performers are looking and talking downwards. The overhead placement is rarely satisfactory for this situation.

The *hand microphone* is usually carried by a performer and is naturally seen on camera. All hand microphones are non-directional and most can be held as close to the sound source as is deemed desirable. This is important especially for variety programs, where singers of popular songs, in order to create a strong feeling of empathy in a love song or emotional involvement in a rock song, often prefer to perform with the microphone as close to their mouths as possible. When a hand microphone is used, there should be enough microphone cable allowed for the performer to work comfortably.

Lavalier microphones or lapel microphones are worn around the neck or clipped on the tie and may be either concealed or out in the open. People sometimes use them as hand microphones, but they are not made for close use. The pick-up pattern for lavalier microphones is non-directional. A variation of the lavalier is the FM microphone. This is a cordless microphone with a self-contained transmitter that sends signals to a receiver set which, in turn, feeds audio control. The only problems with lavalier microphones are that their quality is below that of larger microphones, there must be a microphone for each performer, and they tend to be less sturdy than other types of microphones. Nonetheless, their convenience makes them very popular in many stations today.

Recorded Sound

Most background music and sound effects for television are recorded. Some stations use record discs played on turntables, often located in the control room, but most stations have eliminated turntables and are utilizing audio tape recorders—either reel-to-reel or cartridge. There are obvious reasons for this change: audio tape will never jump a groove, repeating the same musical phrase over and over again, and audio tape can be marked with timing leader for easy identification for specific passages by the audio engineer. While audio leader is not without its problems and potential production dangers, the benefits and added flexibility of tape have persuaded most producers to prefer it to record discs.

Live Sound Effects

Manual sound effects are rarely produced in the studio any longer. There are a few exceptions—sounds which can be produced more efficiently or more artistically live. For example, the simplest way to get the sound of water being poured from a pitcher into a glass is to pour some water from a pitcher into a glass fairly close to a microphone. Footsteps and knocks on a door, or the scratching of a pen on a sheet of notepaper, are other obvious examples. If, however, we need the sound of a waterfall, or horses' hooves, or a locomotive, it would be inconvenient, to say the least, to bring the source of such a sound into the studio. Literally hundreds of sounds have been recorded on discs, tapes, and cartridges, and catalogues of several companies provide a ready source of sound effects for almost every conceivable situation. On rare occasions, the production staff may create special sounds for a specific effect, recording these well in advance and bringing them into the program as needed.

Filters

A filter, or more accurately a "variable-frequency filter," is an electronic device in the control room that permits the audio engineer to subtract or filter out high or low frequencies in many combinations. Taking out the lowest sounds and most of the high sounds gives us the familiar sound of a voice heard over a telephone; taking out other frequencies can create the effect of an intercom system. By varying the range of the frequencies being removed, we can get the inner voice identified with conscience or with the stream of consciousness, or get the mechanical voice of a robot.

Echo

Originally, the effect of reverberation was added to studio voices or sounds by the use of an echo chamber, a long narrow passage or a twisting labyrinth with concrete, tile, or plaster walls. The sound originating in the studio entered this chamber through a loudspeaker and the resulting sound waves bounced their way between the reflecting walls to be picked up by a microphone and then fed back into the audio console. Modern studios have electronic methods of inducing this added reverberation, but the effect is roughly the same: that of hearing the sound augmented by the resonance or reverberation of a large enclosed space.

So far, in this chapter, we have been discussing the element of audio, which is common both to radio and to television. We turn now to the visual elements, those which obviously pertain only to television (and film). In turning to them, however, it may be helpful for us to point out that the catalogue that follows is intended to provide only an introduction to these elements, not a handbook for their use. To describe them in detail would take far more space than we can allot for that purpose in this volume. The reader who wants more information about lighting or graphics will be referred to an appropriate source. In this chapter, he will merely meet these elements; for a closer knowledge, he must read further or study them in an appropriate course; for mastery, he will need both training and actual experience.

LIGHTING

The late Gilbert Seldes, when he was television program manager at CBS in New York, once said, "Lighting has two functions in television: One is to make it possible. The other is to make it interesting." Obviously, without sufficient light, the television cameras will not be activated, and there will be no pictures transmitted. Less obviously, a flat, even flow of light will activate the cameras adequately, and give the engineers little trouble. But flat lighting is rarely interesting. Thus, production people go to great lengths to achieve attractive and dramatic lighting, conscious always that the effect of that light on the video system must be kept in mind.

Amount of Light

The light level needed for basic transmission is called "base light" in many stations. This base light is an overall level that results from all the lights used in the studio in a particular area or scene. It is sometimes used to mean a base of a certain level to which other lights are added (in the sense of make-up base, for example). This concept leads to poor lighting practice, however—the setting of flood or overall lights first— and results in flat lighting.

The absolute exact amount of light is not as critical in television as it is in photography, where lighting and exposure (lens opening) must be very accurately matched. For example, the average vidicon camera picks up an identifiable picture with less than the 10-foot-candle illumination that is considered comfortable reading light. The picture may be grainy or the subject may "smear" as it moves, but the lack of light will not make the picture dark as it would in the case of a snapshot. As the light level is increased and the video adjustments are made to compensate, the picture becomes increasingly better until a maximum point is reached beyond which added light does not further improve the picture. In monochrome cameras, the optimum level for the image-orthicon and plumbicon cameras is between 80 and 100 foot-candles.* This is, of course, the level at which engineers would prefer to operate. However, a compromise is generally necessary. High light

* Ordinary classroom illumination varies between 20 and 70 foot-candles.

levels mean high heat levels, and in a small studio this can be a great disadvantage. High lighting levels also require more lighting units; and, with the light coming from many sources, the result tends to be, again, flat lighting. In actual practice, vidicons are even used in light of 50 foot-candles, producing acceptable pictures of less-than-maximum quality.

When using color cameras, the amount of base light needed is considerably greater. In a typical color-television camera, the light that enters the camera is divided into the primary colors of light—red, green, and blue—each of which goes to a different tube. Thus, any one tube gets only part of the total light and, therefore, more light intensity is needed for the scene. Most color cameras (usually utilizing vidicon or plumbicon tubes) require anywhere from 250 to 500 foot-candles.

When the total environment is illuminated by light of the same color, the eye easily adapts to white light of a wide range of colors, seeing either reddish white or bluish white as simply white. Not so the television camera, however. Therefore special light sources are needed for color television.

Generally, the light level that various television cameras require is as follows:

Plumbicon monochrome camera	80–100 foot-candles
Image-orthicon monochrome camera	80–100 foot-candles
Vidicon monochrome camera	200–250 foot-candles
Color cameras	250–500 foot-candles

Quality of Light

Another consideration is quality. This does not mean quality in the sense of bad or good, high or low. The range is between hard and soft. A hard light casts sharp shadows, brings out details of textures, and can be unflattering. Soft light casts soft-edge shadows, gives a generally more pleasing effect, and tends to flatter the subject. The difference in quality of light is partially determined by the intensity of the light and partially by the type of instrument used. There are two basic types of lighting: *diffused lighting*, which generally is produced by floodlights, and *directional lighting*, which is most easily produced by spotlights. (Floodlights *can* produce directional lighting, if they are close enough, and spotlights can be diffused.)

Specific Purposes of Each Lighting Instrument

Key light (the apparent principal source of directional illumination falling on a subject area)* is the first light to be set. Before it is placed and lighted the studio should have work lights only. It is best if there is only one instrument providing key light for a given area. The type of instrument found most useful in providing key light is the Fresnel spotlight. The key light creates lighted and shadowed sides to the subject, bringing out its sculptural three-dimensional quality. Obviously, then, flat light, which casts no shadows, is the opposite of modeling light.

Back light (illuminating from behind the subject) is another modeling light. It is particularly useful in preventing the subject from being lost against a background; when back light is applied, a lighted rim or edge sets the subject clearly apart from the background. Spotlights are

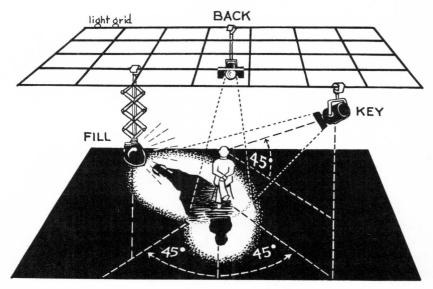

Figure 38.   The three basic lights—key, back, and fill—that should be set on each subject or playing area. Larger instruments can, of course, cover larger areas.

used almost exclusively for this purpose. It is a rare effect to see in nature. Because it is mainly an artifact of the motion-picture medium, many modern film makers avoid it as unrealistic.

Fill light (supplementary illumination to reduce shadow or contrast

* Lighting definitions in this section are from "Lighting Lingo," prepared by the TV Studio Lighting Committee for the Society of Motion Picture and Television Engineers.

range) is needed in all cases. Sometimes light reflected from the floor or other parts of the set and coming from instruments intended for other purposes will serve this function. A "scoop" light is usually used to provide the diffused quality necessary. It is always placed on the opposite side of the subject from the key light—so it can partially illuminate the shadow sides of the subject.

Set light or *background light* (separate illumination of background or set other than that provided for principal subject or areas), when needed, can be provided by almost any kind of instrument. If it is to be perfectly even, as in the case of a sky cyclorama, scoops or rectangular reflectors are probably best. Usually, the subject is placed close enough to the background to eliminate the need for additional set light.

Supplementary lighting. Included in this category are those lights that are used only for special purposes or effects. *Kicker light* (for additional illumination or highlighting of a subject and for extra lighting when necessary) is a spotlight placed in back or to the side of the performer, usually at a low angle. The *eye-catch light* is a small spot mounted on the camera where it will reflect from the performer's eye and give it sparkle. *Side light* (additional light to illuminate the subject from the side) is a spotlight placed opposite the key light to provide additional illumination.

It is important to remember that these supplementary lights are not always used. The basic lights used in television are: key, back, and fill.

Direction of Light

We are accustomed to light, both indoors and out, that comes from above. However, very rarely does light, even from the sun, come directly down. When it does, it gives the effect of very dark eye sockets and unpleasant, heavy nose and chin shadows. Thus, the main light for a subject (the key light) should be placed in such a manner that it reaches the subject from a front angle (generally 45 degrees up from the horizontal and within a range of 45 degrees left or right of the camera-subject axis). Back light reaches the subject from behind, not above, from as low an angle as possible without causing flare in the cameras, illuminating the edges of the hair and shoulders.

Lighting Balance

The relative intensity of key, back, and fill light is an important factor in achieving good lighting. Generally, fill light should be about half the intensity of the key light, and back light should be about the same as the key light. If the background is well lighted, this should produce the usual high-key scene (high-key lighting: a type of lighting which, applied to a scene, results in a picture having gradations falling primarily between gray and white in monochrome; dark grays and blacks are present, but in a very limited area). If the fill light is less than one-fourth the intensity of the key, and the background is dark in relation to the subject, a type of lighting results that is known as low-key.

It is very difficult to balance lights if the studio is not equipped with dimmers for this purpose. Except that spotlights can be adjusted to a wider or narrower beam, resulting in less or more illumination at a given point, one can vary intensity only by moving instruments toward or away from the subject, or adding and subtracting units.

Shadows

A common mistake by beginners in television lighting is to try to eliminate cast shadows. No light should ever be used to "wash out" a shadow. Most shadows are desirable; only occasionally does a person's shadow distract by falling on a particularly obvious area (such as a blackboard area where a teacher is trying to write equations). Instead of adding lights to wash out shadows, move the key light, or the subject, so that the undesirable shadow will fall on the floor or some other less obvious part of the background. In short, "Don't add light to bad light."

Microphone-boom shadows are, of course, always to be avoided. They are usually caused by key lights; fill lights should be so soft that they do not cause mike shadows. As with most shadow problems, microphone shadows show up worst when performers are working within a few feet of the background. If the background is farther back, the microphone shadow will be cast on the floor, where it is unnoticeable. Another solution to this problem is to "barn-door" the top of the key-light beam, so that light does not strike the microphone at all and thus a shadow is not produced. A barn door is a metal flap that can be hinged out or in to confine a spotlight beam and change its coverage area without changing its intensity.

GRAPHIC MATERIALS

The term "graphics" includes all still visual materials, whether they are original artwork produced in a size large enough for use in the studio or reproduced as slides or film strips. There are advantages and disadvantages to both procedures.

Slides

If your graphics are part of a program, putting them on slides means that you will not have to tie up a camera to show them. If they happen to be station-identification or announcement slides, they may be transmitted even when the studio is not in use. If you need to dissolve between a series of graphics, for instance, most projection equipment will have this capability, whereas if done in the studio, two cameras would be tied up on two easels.

Thirty-five-millimeter color slides (2 by 2 inches) have become a standard source of graphic material for television. Rare indeed is the television station that does not have at least one such projector. These slides are inexpensive and quickly made; some stations keep a copying camera always ready and loaded on a copying stand. Polaroid cameras can turn out positive transparencies in a few minutes' time.

Some stations are also equipped to use the older 3½-by-4-inch "lantern slides," although this is usually in the studio for rear-projection purposes, rarely in the projection room.

Film strips, also known as "slide films" or "strip films," are fairly common audio-visual materials, distributed nationally for many educational and industrial applications. A film strip is actually a series of still pictures photographed on motion-picture film. The only way that film strips normally can be used in television is to project them on a studio screen.

Studio Graphics

Projection-room slides must always be screened full-frame, however, whereas graphics in the studio, whether original art, photographic blow-up, or projected slides, may be shown only in part, with camera movement such as panning, tilting, or zooming. Also one can point to details on studio graphics, an action which cannot be readily done on slides in a projector.

The advantages of studio graphics go further. When everything connected with a production takes place in one locale, and all participants can see what is going on, things often run smoother. Also the whole production, graphics and all, can be rehearsed outside, transferred to the studio, and produced before the cameras in minimum time, especially if the floor manager, or production assistant who operates the graphics, can attend the outside rehearsals.

When titles are handled in the studio, they can be integrated with the program throughout the rehearsal period, whereas projection-room facilities, at most production centers, are used for so many programs

Plate 16. Floor manager flips graphics during KMEX-TV Los Angeles news program. (Courtesy of Berkey Colortran, Division of Berkey Photo)

throughout the day that they can be assigned to any given program for only a brief time. Often the titles are not actually integrated with the rest of the program until the show is finally aired or recorded. This will do only when they are straight titles and do not have to be superimposed or keyed over live scenes or timed accurately with the action.

On the negative side, a stack of graphics in the studio is always vulnerable to being knocked off its easel and thoroughly shuffled just before air time, while a stack of slides, once safely into its projection magazine, is certain to stay in order. Finally, if your graphics include a large number of items from different sources, each of a different size, and they are to be flipped over continuously before a single camera, they will have to be copied and reprinted to standard size. Making them into slides instead may be far less costly.

Title Cards and Crawls

The title card, or TC, is such an ever-present element in television production that it is given special consideration here, with other forms of graphic art described in the following section.

In general, title cards are printed or hand-lettered on fairly stiff cardboard; when only one or two are needed for a given program, they may be handled very simply on the shelf of an easel similar to those used by artists. A complicated set of half a dozen or more cards is sometimes

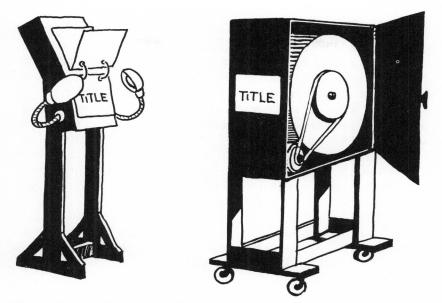

Figure 39.   The flip stand (or "hod") and the crawl machine (or "title drum").

mounted on a device known as a "flip stand." Holes are punched in the top of each card, thus permitting it to be mounted on the rings of the camera frame, giving the effect of a quick change of title, which has been called a flip.

For a smoother-flowing sequence of two or three titles, the director may prefer to use a pan card, a long stretch of cardboard upon which the successive "frames" of titling or other art work appear side by side. Although known as a pan card, this form of title is more often covered by a trucking movement. Panning across a flat expanse of cardboard will be effective if the card is not too long; otherwise the fact that the camera is no longer perpendicular to its field of view at the end of the

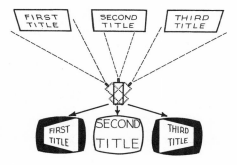

Figure 40.   "Keystone" effect is noticeable on the first and third title because the camera axis is not perpendicular to the plane of the title card.

pan will cause "keystoning"—the near side of the artwork appears larger, the far side smaller, to say nothing of the problems of holding focus. This effect is used extensively in advertising drawings dealing with television, since it suggests a dynamic representation of the television screen, but is not desirable in reproducing a title. Lettering that runs downhill or uphill is not easy to read. It occurs when the camera is not accurately at right angles to the title card or graphic. Of course, if the camera is trucking from left to right, the pan card could be as long as the studio wall, and the camera would still be head on to the artwork. A simpler solution is to slide the card past the camera, or curve the card so that all parts are equidistant from the camera lens.

A variation on the horizontal pan card is the vertical tilt card, in which the various frames of titling or other graphic material are arranged one below the other. The camera is usually focused on the top frame, then tilts down toward the bottom. Again, either the lettering must be kept small (although each frame must always be in the 3-to-4 aspect ratio*) to avoid a card more than four feet in length, or the camera must be capable of moving up and down in a plane parallel to that of the card. The counterweighted studio pedestal type of camera mount permits a smooth raising and lowering of the camera, but only through a range of about twenty inches. If the card is bent into a curve, however, so that the top and bottom ends are as close to the camera lens as the center, keystoning is no problem. For vertical title movement, however, most studios use a crawl device with variable-speed control.

The *crawl* is a long vertical title sheet, but instead of being mounted on a board or a wall, it is attached to a cylinder or drum. As the drum turns past a fixed camera, the lettering moves slowly ("crawls") up the screen; it can thus convey a great deal of printed information in a short length of time.

Many television studios today devote a small camera simply to the pick-up of graphics. When this camera is mounted overhead, shooting directly down in the manner of a copying camera in photography or an animation camera in film, graphics can be conveniently handled on a tabletop below it. The camera stays fixed, but elaborate effects of camera movement are possible by sliding the graphic material left and right, up and down, twisting it for the canted effect, while zooming in and out as desired with a manual control on the camera lens.

Other Graphics

In addition to providing program titles and credits, the graphics de-

* See below for a full explanation.

Plate 17.　Graphic device that embodies movement. The name of the climatic area is on one side of each reversible panel, a map on the other. The performer can flip it as he talks, or the camera can frame up in such a way that the floor manager can make the flip without his hand coming into the picture. (Courtesy of the University of Michigan)

partment of a station creates many other forms that convey visual information in drawn or painted form. Lettering is an important element to be sure, but graphics include not only printed words but also maps, charts, and diagrams. Often these graphics are given the appearance of animations, without the expensive techniques of motion-picture animation. Especially in informational and educational programming, such techniques can provide information consecutively and gradually, in contrast to the more simple forms which show all the information at once. Items may be revealed, added, removed, or changed readily and quickly before the camera on a well-conceived informational graphic. In the opinion of many television educators, the accumulative feature (as in the superimposition of additional information) is an important technique for integrating word and picture. Ingenious mechanical arrangements have been designed to be pushed, pulled, rotated, flipped, revealed or concealed, extended, contracted, or manipulated in any number of ways.

Sometimes graphics are incorporated into the setting. A map may run almost the full height of the back wall of a set, or a rear-projection screen may be set into a "window" in one wall. From behind the screen various graphics may be projected, either as simple slides or as complicated, animated creations in which dotted lines extend magically across maps, areas change their boundaries, and miniature ships or planes trace routes across seas or continents.

Figure 41.　One way to use slides in the studio. A projection box is constructed, with a mirror at the back, so the speaker may operate his own slides as he talks. He may, of course, use a remote-control, push-button slide changer.

The Design of Graphics

Whatever the form that a graphic may take, or the kind of projector which will transmit it, there are two factors that must never be forgotten: (1) the shape of the graphic must fit the shape of the television screen, and (2) the home receiver does not display all of the picture that the camera picks up.

The shape of the television screen is expressed by an "aspect ratio" of 3 to 4. This means that all television screens, whatever their size, are three-quarters as high as they are wide. For television graphics the implication is direct: Whatever actual size your television artwork may be, make sure that it is three units high and four units wide (three-quarters as high as it is wide). If you try to frame up anything with a different aspect, and show all of it, you will *inevitably* also have to show background areas somewhere beyond the graphic you want to display.

When you prepare artwork for television, besides making it fit the 3-to-4 aspect ratio, you must remember that border areas of your picture may never be seen by many of your viewers. This is due to faulty adjustment of home receivers, many of which are so cheaply made that better adjustment is impossible. Accordingly, the loss of border areas between camera and viewer must be accepted as one of the problems of television production.

To assure that border losses do not eliminate essential information from the receiver screen, the television graphic artist must keep his lettering within a central area which is called, accordingly, the "safe title area." In order to determine what this will be, he must first decide the actual area that he intends the camera to pick up and transmit. This is called the "scanned" or "picture" area. In the case of a studio title card, it is generally most of the card, out to within an inch of each edge. Naturally this will vary from one time to the next, since the camera will rarely set up exactly the same distance away from the title card. In the case of slides, however, the safe area is permanently set, an unvarying area will be picked up each time; the dimensions of this can be obtained from the station engineers. To determine the safe title area within a known scanned area, then, proceed as follows:

Divide the width and height of the picture area into tenths. Eliminate one-tenth along the top, the bottom, and each side. Call this the "supplementary area"; it will show on some receivers, but not on all. The inner area thus defined is the safe title area. Keep lettering and other essential material just within it; let backgrounds and nonessentials run out to the edge of the scanned area, or beyond.

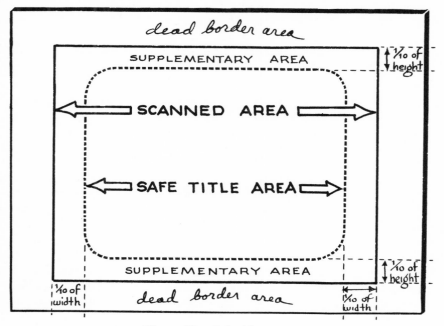

Figure 42.   Safe title area.

Graphics for television must be particularly easy to read. Complicated charts and graphs are too hard to see and understand in the short period of time allotted to them. The simpler the graphic, the better the chance that the audience will understand and retain the information.

As an aid in preparing graphic materials, use a cardboard mask whose outer dimensions fit the outer edges of the card to be used, and whose inner cut-out frames the correct safe title area. Once the standard size of cards is chosen and the scanned area of each determined, such a mask will save the mathematical problem of dividing a length into ten roughly equal parts, something many television students seem to find difficult.

Masks, Mattes, and Goboes

A mask or a matte is a device for blocking out part of the image coming into the camera, thus making areas of the picture black, a first step in creating split screens and other composite shots. This aspect of special effects is too detailed to be adequately explained here. A matte is generally attached to the camera (in a matte box a few inches in front of the lens, or built into the camera behind the lens). A mask that is not attached to the camera is generally called a "gobo." One might cut a hole in the shape of a shamrock out of a piece of cardboard and shoot through it to frame an Irish song on St. Patrick's Day, or make a heart-shaped gobo for St. Valentine's Day. An example of the use of a gobo is a window frame made of cardboard placed between the camera and the performer. As the performer begins a song, we see her through the window; then the camera zooms or dollies in to lose the window in the picture. A gobo, then, is used to suggest a place or a feeling, but is usually quickly lost in the picture. It need not be black, as a matte is, but may be decorated and lighted.

SUMMARY

The purpose of this chapter has been to provide the beginner with an idea of some of the many tools in the areas of audio, lighting, and graphics that are available to him. Again we must caution the new director to guard against the danger of becoming so enamored of techniques and effects that real content is neglected. The late Gilbert Seldes once cautioned his directors on the CBS–TV staff in the earliest days of American television: "Don't ruin the show for the sake of one shot." The true artist, craftsman, artisan is the master of his tools; he is not their servant.

7 / Directing "Residue"

Many television stations have adopted the term "residue" to describe all the odds and ends of short announcements (twenty-second, thirty-second, and the now infrequent one-minute commercials, station identification, and the like) which must be run between one program and the next. Although there is nothing creative about directing a series of short spots, especially if they are on film or videotape, it is nonetheless a television director's job and calls for the same skill and accuracy that is necessary in directing programs.

A growing number of television stations have automated the residue operation, programming all cues in advance. The director's job, under such circumstances, is to program the proper cues into the control tape (or computer, as the case may be) instead of calling them from a script at the time of broadcast. More will be said about automated operation at the conclusion of this chapter.

Stations have various methods of handling residue. A large network station will run all residue from a film control room, where a special residue director and technical staff are stationed at all times. Sometimes this director is known as the "broadcast supervisor" or the "coordinator." Some stations are not large enough to have a special film control room, but run their film and residue from the master control room, which then functions as a combination film and master control. The residue director or coordinator is then stationed in master control.

Small stations that have only one control room which must combine the functions of studio control, film control, and master control will, of course, have to run residue from the same control room as the studio programs. It is rare, however, that the same director will handle both. This has been attempted at some stations, by making each show director responsible for the residue that comes directly after or directly before his program.

A better method seems to be to make one director responsible for film and residue throughout a given broadcast period. This director may be termed the "film director" or the "duty director" and usually will be one of the regular production staff. The assignment will rotate from day to day, and the duty director may also have one or more programs to direct on the same day, provided they are not major productions that require his being away from the control room for long periods of preparation.

THE RESIDUE DIRECTOR'S SCRIPT

The residue director's "script" includes the entire broadcast schedule. He coordinates programs and spot commercials in much the same manner in which a program director coordinates the various scenes and shots of a show. Timing is fully as important. Just as the director is careful after a fade-out not to allow a black screen to linger more than a split second beyond its proper length, so the residue director must also keep his "show" rolling without dead spots. Dead air on radio has always been distasteful; on television it is even more serious, since much of the television audience sits within reach of the set and quickly reacts to a loss of program by switching to another channel.

The script that the residue director must follow is called the "log" or "technical routine sheet." Every traffic department puts this out in a slightly different form, but it usually contains the following information:

> Scheduled air time of each item
> Name of item (program, film, or commercial)
> Studio of origination (or number of film chain or videotape recorder)
> Source of sound (whether from film, live from studio, live from announce booth, etc.)
> Projector involved
> Announcer and director on duty.

Chart 1 is an excerpt from a fairly typical routine sheet taken from the operation of WBBM–TV in Chicago.

The chart represents about twelve or thirteen minutes of station operation starting at the station break just before six o'clock on a Tuesday evening and continuing through a news program with a break midway for two commercials until eleven minutes and forty seconds after six. The first two columns after the computer line reference list the "time on" of each segment and its duration; the widest column lists the programs and

LINE NUM	SCHEDULE TIME	DURATN MIN.SEC	LINE DESCRIPTION	MATERIAL REFERENCE	AGENCY MATERIAL#	TRANS SOURCE VIDEO/AUDIO	S I	PROGRAM SRC TP SUB
28200								
28300			STATION BREAK					
A 28301	5.58.58P	.30	SARA LEE INTL.DESSERTS (F)	K3002524	CFSL-0035- 30	K <-----	X	L N
A 28302	5.59.28P	.30	MIRACLE WHITE (F)	K3003204	BRSC-4023- 30	K <-----	X	L N
A 28400	5.59.58P	000.02	WBBM-TV ID #K1000064			K <-----		
28500								
28600			STUDIO CONTROL - NEWSROOM - STUDIO # 2 CONTROL RM					
28700								
A 28800	6.00.00P	000.10	CHANNEL TWO NEWS			VT/B SOT		L N
A 28900	6.00.10P	005.10	NEWS SEGMENTS			1N/2N		L N
29000			INTER- (1ST BREAK)					
A 29101	6.05.20P	.30	ARTHRITIS PAIN FORMULA	K3000648	AHAF-3032- 30	K <-----	X	
A 29102	6.05.50P	.30	MAYTAG (F) (SLIDE #25 & AVO ON CASSETTE)	K3000966	MYDW-0890- 30	K <-----	X	
29200								
A 29300	6.06.20P	005.20	NEWS SEGMENTS			VT/B&C		L N
29400								

Chart 1. Sample page from a typical station routine sheet.

commercial spots. Two thirty-second spots (29101 and 29102) are run during the program (for the exact time and place of these, the director, of course, follows his program script). While these first commercials originate on 16mm with sound-on-film, the introduction to the news program is on videotape.

It will be noted that the routine sheet can show which films are to be spliced together on the same reel. This is indicated by an arrow. For example, the first three films are all to be spliced together, with white leader (a sequence of blank frames) between. This is instruction primarily for the projectionist; to the director it means that these commercials will all be on the same film channel, and they can be run as one.

RESPONSIBILITIES OF THE RESIDUE DIRECTOR

It is up to the residue director to make many quick decisions during the course of a broadcasting period, as human and technical failures necessitate changes in the scheduled routine. His reports to the station manager after each day's broadcasting sometimes contain items such as this:

"Station slide on air but no announcement. Announcer had not notified residue director that he would take the station identification from studio instead of booth. There was no audio for one minute while the announcer was located."

This is human error. Technical errors occur also.

"Film was started but before it was rolling, film channel B blew out. Master control personnel tried desperately to patch it up, but unfortunately there were no spare fuses in master control. Coordinator requested that film channel C be used. The time lapse was about two minutes, during which time a station identification and a stand-by slide were put on the air." (This was because the film had to be rethreaded on a different projector.)

From this it should be evident that another very important function of the residue director is to be prepared with stand-by announcements and slides for every possible emergency. The announcer must have a book of these in the announce booth at all times, so that they can be called for by number, if a live announcer is used. Many stations have all announcements on "cart" (audio cartridge) which can also be selected by number when the need arises. Every slide in the projection room must also be numbered, so that emergency slides may be quickly located in the slide file and put on the air with a minimum of delay. In case of longer delays or loss of entire programs, the projection room will have a series of stand-by films of various lengths which can be entered into the program schedule on a moment's notice. In any case, it will be the responsibility of the residue director to choose the film or the stand-by slide and to carry the station through the emergency and back into the program smoothly.

Cuing Up Film and VTR

Bringing a film or VTR insert on the screen at the exact instant at which a newscaster or M.C. refers to it is important. Cuing film and VTR *accurately* is a technique that every director must learn. Most film projectors and VTR machines require a few seconds after they have been started to come up to speed, before the picture is suitable for transmission. The usual procedure with film is to attach numbered leader (society leader*) to the beginning of a roll. This leader makes it possible for the projectionist to set the film up in the projector in such a way that the first frame of picture will appear at a definite time after the projection has been started. The numbers on the leader run from 10 down to 3, after which a three-second section of black runs to the beginning of the film. After threading the film, the projectionist generally stops it when number 3 is in the gate and showing, and the director knows that it will take just about three seconds after he gives the cue to "roll film" before the picture is up and he can put the film on the air. In the event that several sections of film on the one reel are to be used at different points during a program, or before and after slide announcements, the technical director will run the film past its conclusion, watching on the preview monitor, and run off the beginning of the leader for the next section, stopping again when number 3 is again in the gate. Magnetic tape is also used to aid in cuing film. A magnetic strip is placed on the film at number 3 before the second film section. The film is allowed to run through after the director has switched away from it and it stops automatically when it reaches the magnetic strip. In using this procedure, the director is assured that the T.D. or the projectionist will not forget to stop the film in the cue position for the second film section. Videotape inserts, depending on the practice and equipment at individual stations, may require five or ten seconds before they can be put on the air.

In cuing the film segment, the director will mark his script and anticipate by three seconds the exact moment when he wants film on the air. This is usually about one line of script. When the film section approaches its end, unless the director is thoroughly familiar with the content of the film, he will need some type of cue mark to warn him

* So called for the Society of Motion Picture and Television Engineers, which developed the standard for this type of leader.

that the end is near. This may be done by stopwatch timing, but a more positive way is to punch a small hole in the upper corner of the frame, about ten seconds before the end of the film. A special punch is provided for the purpose. (One frame is usually not enough; it takes three or four punched frames to make sure the cue will be visible on the monitor.) Another cue punch is made on the film just one second before the end. To insure safety, a good plan is to add some kind of appropriate footage beyond the end of the film, or to extend the final shot a little longer, so that if there is any delay in getting the film off the screen and the next channel on, the viewer does not see a flickering of strange X's, numbers, and the like which usually appear on the end leader. Blank leader will serve if nothing else is available.

Some stations have developed an oral cuing system which dispenses with cue punch marks in the film itself. The projectionist who is running the film watches the reel carefully; just before it reaches the white leader (showing black and blank on the screen) he calls, "Film out," or "Running out," into the intercom. The director and other control-room personnel hear his call and react accordingly. People who have worked under this system develop an instinctive coordination based on their familiarity with the time lapse between the projectionist's warning and the actual end of the film, and rarely run past the last frame before dissolving or cutting back to the studio. The white leader also serves to separate one film segment on a reel from the next, making it easier for the projectionist to move on to the next unit.

There are some film projectors on the market that do not require time to come up to speed, but can be held stationary on a single frame of film, which then appears as a still on the screen. When the projector starts running, it causes this still picture to leap into action without any of the out-of-phase flicker and black bars which would show on the other types of projector. When these projectors are used, the procedure is to stop the film on the opening frame of picture and start it simultaneously with putting it on the air. (Some programs have made use of the effect of starting with a still.)

The Residue Director as Coordinator

Another duty of the residue director is to coordinate film and studio portions of remote programs. A baseball game, for example, will commonly be fed through the film control room so film commercials can be inserted between the innings. The film director will be in direct communication with the director at the remote point via audio cue line, or P.L. (for *private* telephone *line*), and will be told when to expect each commercial insert or station identification. The actual decision on when to insert the commercials must, of course, be made by the remote director at the ball game. An oral cue by the announcer at the game is usually the signal to come on with the film, although this signal may also be given by the director over the cue line.

AUTOMATED OPERATION

In a large station the complexity of the master control operation becomes so great that only a few irreplaceable experts can do the job. Over the last decade a constantly increasing number of stations have installed computer-controlled automated equipment. At first many stations used a large computer at some distant city on a time-shared basis (while a line to the computer was kept open at all times, the station was billed only for the few seconds in which the computer was actually working). With the development of the mini-computer, however, it became more common for a station to have its own local computer. In operation, the computer is programmed to respond to listed events on the run-down sheet just as a residue director should. It will pre-roll projectors so they are up to speed at the proper time, switch items on and off, meanwhile printing out a log of broadcast activities for the FCC report, for accounting, and for sales purposes. As smaller and even less expensive computers become available, the automation of technical operations will be possible for even the smallest stations.

The development of cassette VTR machines that can automatically play a large number of short videotapes in a predetermined sequence has been a great aid in the directing of residue. Most commercials, network promotional announcements, and the like are now distributed on short lengths of videotape. A station with four thirty-second commercials to run in succession would have to either: (1) thread up four VTR machines (since there would not be time to rethread), (2) splice all four commercials together on one reel, or (3) rerecord them onto another roll of tape. Both splicing and rerecording (electronic editing) are time-consuming. Most commercials are used several times in different combinations, so disassembly of spliced materials would also be required, something that is not difficult with film but hardly practicable with videotape, which is far more fragile and should not be handled any more than absolutely necessary. With the cassette VTR, the four short tapes are loaded in cassettes, placed in the machine, which then assembles them, dynamically, as the broadcast proceeds.

The cassettes that these machines use are about 3 by 6 inches in size and 2 inches deep to accommodate the 2-inch tape. They contain a take-up reel and a supply reel that can hold up to six minutes of tape at the

Plate 18. Ampex ACR-25 Automatic Video Cassette Recorder/Reproducer. This machine has a magazine that will hold up to twenty-four cassettes, each containing separate program segments (commercial spots, promotion announcements, etc.) of from ten seconds to six minutes in length. After loading, all handling (threading, cuing, etc.) is automatic. (Courtesy of Ampex Corporation)

15-inches-per-second running speed. Cues which determine where the machine will begin to play the tape, where it will end, and whether in each case a cut or a fade is to be used can be placed on the control track.

The cassettes are placed in a movable magazine (Plate 18), from which any cassette may be random-accessed in about ten seconds (several ten-second commercials may be run in sequence). When finished, the tape is automatically rewound, unthreaded, and returned to the magazine. Two such transports are provided, of course, so that continuous operation is possible. The operator may take out and replace cassettes at any time.

If it is not to be used again for some time, a videotape may be taken from its cassette (in the same condition it was when it arrived at the station, except that it has been played once) and stored until needed. This equipment is also usable for simple automated editing. As long as the segments to be assembled do not exceed six minutes in length, they can be automatically assembled according to the editor's cues, and recorded on another VTR machine.

From the automation of the videotape playback it is a short step to the full automation and computer control of all residue. It should be made clear, of course, that automation can never replace art (at least not *yet*), and the television *program* director is in no danger of technological unemployment. However, the directing of residue, as we have seen, is perfectly routine, practically void of any need for artistic judgment. In short, it will always require a director to create and record even the simplest thirty-second television commercial, but a machine can put it on the air at the proper time.

It should also be pointed out that in any automated station the traditional step-by-step directing of the operation while the broadcast is in progress is replaced by the step-by-step *programming* of the operation in advance. Of course, programming in advance is also a part of live direction of residue—the programmer is the traffic manager or possibly the program director of the station. All the major decisions are thus normally scripted in advance, and the residue director merely follows the run-down sheet as accurately as he can. Programming a computer is, in a sense, putting the script directly into the machine, with the surety that the machine will carry out the program at least as accurately as a residue director, and in many cases far more so.

The elimination of human error (and its attendant expenses for reimbursement of disgruntled advertisers) is, of course, a great advantage. All possibility of error is not eliminated, however; machines can fluff, flub, and boo-boo as well as humans, with the possible additional factor that when the machine makes an error, it will be a beauty. KNXT's computer went berserk one evening when it was just being "trained for the job," and in its neurotic frenzy put everything under its control on the air at once. Film projectors rolled, audio-tape cartridges for a dozen different kinds of announcements began a great babble of voices, and seven camera chains combined forces in one magnificent superimposition—or so goes the story. Not even the most excitable residue director ever managed to accomplish this supreme degree of chaos.

8 / Directing Unrehearsed Studio Programs

By far the most common type of live television directing is the "off-the-cuff" variety. Network shows as a rule do not fit into this category, because most of them are thoroughly scripted and rehearsed, with the exception of parts of NBC's *Today* show, game and panel shows, and talk shows. The great majority of the small station's non-network programs must be done without studio and facilities rehearsal. All the creative decisions of camera handling, cutting, and the other aspects of production must be made while the show is on the air.

The Host-Director Team

Unrehearsed programs may be presented in a manner that is so completely informal that the host of the show will himself do a good share of the directing. Performers are often heard speaking directly to the cameraman: "I want the audience to get a good look at this little thing I'm holding. See if you can get a good big close-up of it for me." Most of the afternoon local interview shows and the public television station "auctions" are produced in this manner.

The Director's Script for the Impromptu Show

If any script is used for the off-the-cuff show, it is only a format or routine, listing the non-commercial elements of the production. The commercial announcements that must be used are listed in some formats, along with the order of the various musical numbers in the program, and any other production details that may have been arranged in advance. If film or slides are to be included, the routine sheet may indicate the exact projector and channel on which they are to be used.

142

SEMI-SCRIPTS FOR EDUCATIONAL PROGRAMS

Some educational TV stations have developed forms, or typographical layouts, that assist the director in his task of following a studio instructor through an elaborate series of slides, graphics, and other visuals. These forms, or formats, are especially valuable when rehearsal time is limited or nonexistent, and when the instructor does not work from a fully written out script but from an outline of his ideas.

One example of such a semi-script is reproduced below.

```
                         SCIENCE:  QUEST & CONQUEST
                         PROGRAM 19
                         THE CHANGING CLIMATE
                         2ND DRAFT
```

GLACIER MOVES DOWN

    Teaser

TC: SCIENCE - WIRES

MUSIC: THEME

SUP: CLIMATE

ANNCR: The changing climate, the story of climate on our

earth. A story which began a million years ago.

FLIP TO SCIENCE

This is a part of science, a part of the story of Quest and

Conquest.

    BOOKS

University of Michigan Television is pleased to present the

noted author, teacher and biologist, Marston Bates.

Here now is Dr. Bates.....

    BATES

BATES: Miami - climate.............. Boston - weather

Today: consider climate....... average of weather for a
particular place........

Climate is the result of three things.......

WALK TO GLOBE

One........ Angle of earth ....

MOVE GLOBE AROUND SUN

Incidentally our word climate.........

SUP: INSERT CLIMATE

Greek Klima........ meaning incline

FLIP TO INSERT KLIMA

Secondly, atmosphere around globe.........

Thirdly, ... our climate is a result of topography

FILM.... MOUNTAINS AND SEA

Three things :
    (1) Inclination
    (2) Atmosphere
    (3) Contours

MOVE TO MAP....TROPIC, TEMPERATE...ARCTIC

Describe...........

Script 3. (Courtesy of Alfred H. Slote and the Television Center of the University of Michigan)

Note that the "lines" or spoken elements (shown in upper and lower case) are only fragmentary, indicating the topics the speaker will discuss, especially those key words or phrases that will function as cues for the introduction of title cards (TC), studio graphics, superimpositions, or studio action (all shown in caps). In this case the director preferred also to underline and overline these cues for added prominence. A margin for the director's cues is provided at the left, as well as space between lines for additional key words and cues to be written in if the director needs them, for example when the speaker makes changes.

The *Quest and Conquest* script is representative of a production that was allocated at least three hours of studio facilities for a half-hour program, a ratio of 6 to 1. Most ETV production, however, cannot afford such a generous ratio; a director often considers himself lucky to have ten or fifteen minutes prior to a program to check his key shots, arrange his graphics, and find out what major moves the speaker intends to make.

Following the script is another kind of run-down form into which the same program on changing climate has been entered. If there had been no opportunity for the teacher and director to work together, and if the teacher had filled in such a run-down, this would then provide the director with the basic information needed to put the program on tape. The teacher or "performer," who often acts as his own producer in ETV production, is encouraged to allocate unit times to each segment of his program early in his planning, adjusting these as needed during his outside rehearsals, so the director may use the cumulative timings to help him bring his program out on time. The typed entries on the form, plus the timings at the right, would be on the form when the director receives it; cues are shown at the left as a director might have written them.

Series _Science: Quest and Conquest_ Principal Talent _Bates_

Program _The Changing Climate_

Director _Marshall Frank_ Recording Date _Feb 6_

Producer _Alfred Slote_ Date of first broadcast _Mar 2_

DIRECTOR'S CUES	CONTENT UNIT	AREA	UNIT TIME	CUM. TIME
FI ①	GRAPHIC: MOVING GLACIER	Easel, left		
	Teaser	Voice over graphic	:15	:15
②	TC: SCIENCE WIRES	Easel, right		
sneak	MUSIC: THEME		:10	
SUP ④	SUPER: CLIMATE	Slide		:25
① on books	ANNCR:		:15	
FLIP ②	FLIP TO SCIENCE			
lose sup ①	BOOKS	Display table		:40
T ②	BATES:	Center area	3:30	
① to TC climate	Miami-Boston def. of climate...			
	Climate result of 3 things...			
② follow		Walks to globe		
SUP ① SUP: INSERT CLIMATE	1. Angle of earth word "Climate"	Moves globe		
FLIP TO INSERT KLIMA	Greek "Klima"			
lose SUP	2. Atmosphere			
roll film	3. Topography			4:10
⑤	FILM: MOUNTAINS AND SEA		1:15	5:25

Chart 2.

THE DIRECTOR AND THE FLOOR MANAGER

One of the first techniques the director must learn for any type of show is how to cue studio action so that it begins at the same time that the picture is first seen on the television screen. Nothing looks quite so amateurish as a show which begins with a shot of the performer waiting or peering out of the corner of his eye for the signal to begin. The performer should never be seen taking the cue.

The director will use the floor manager for many purposes during the ad-lib show as a link between the control room and the host. Time cues may be sent to the performer so as to wind up the show on the right second, and people may actually be moved around if they happen to place themselves in an inconvenient spot for camera coverage. This, however, is to be avoided, especially if the people are not seasoned television performers, as the floor manager's gestures may puzzle them and attract their eyes off screen. The performer must take his cue without showing any sign of having received one. The floor manager can help the performer by giving the cue in the performer's "line of sight" (standing as close as possible in the direction in which the performer is facing so he can attract the performer's attention).

Above all, the performer must not nod or directly acknowledge the floor manager's cue. The latter may continue to give the performer the cue long after it has been seen, but the performer must accept this procedure. The link between control room and newcaster or anchorman is made simple and direct on some shows by the use of headphones on the set, so the director can inform him as program segments are ready to be introduced.

In the informal type of show (which is probably much better television) the host will look at the floor manager, even ask him what he is trying to convey, and sometimes bring him into the shot. Very few floor managers realize that once the show has been placed on this basis —once the attention of the audience has been called to them—then it is no longer any secret that they exist. Any further secrecy, resort to hand signals, or care to keep out of camera range, is not only unnecessary, but the exact opposite of what the audience wants. And the director, too, is bound by the desires of the audience. The viewers must be given what they want to see. Once the performer has called attention to the floor manager or the cameramen, especially if the performer has called them by name, the director has no choice but to show them in the picture. Mike Douglas and Johnny Carson are among the performers who occasionally like to speak to members of the floor crew.

The floor manager will often help the performer by holding notes, and sometimes entire lines, written large on a white card, close by the side of the camera. In order to read, however, he must take his eyes away from the camera lens, and the fact that he is reading can be very obvious. The closer the floor manager can hold the card to the lens, the better, of course. The earlier TelePrompTer devices were hung just below or just above the lens turret, a slight improvement over a cue card held to left or right of the camera. The TelePrompTer device provided a script typed in gigantic capitals for easy legibility at a considerable distance. A roll of paper, some eighteen inches wide, was used; its edges were perforated so that it could be driven by sprockets. Several could be used at once at various places in the set and all roll in synchrony. More modern versions of the TelePrompTer reflect the text from the surface of a sheet of glass placed at an angle directly in front of the lens. Thus, the performer can look right *at* (though not always *into*) the lens and one must look very closely at his eye movement to know that he is reading.

In any event, using notes or an outline, whether on cue cards or on a prompting device, is more effective than reproduction of the whole script verbatim, since the performer needs only an occasional glimpse of an outline and by ad-libbing his lines generally turns in a better television performance. This is particularly true, in the opinion of the authors, in an educational or informational program. An experienced announcer reading commercial copy, however, or a skillful newscaster, can develop the knack of reading from a prompting device so skillfully as to mislead all but the most knowing viewers into believing that he is either speaking extempore or from memory.

CONTROL OF TIMING

Television is organized on a network basis; all shows must begin and end on time. Independent stations, not connected with a network, still adhere closely to time schedules because the public tunes in by turning the dial when a previous program on some other channel has concluded, or, more commonly, when some program in which they are not interested begins. When a program has been announced in the press as beginning at 9:00 P.M. and a viewer tunes in at that time, he will take a dim view of a station that has not concluded its own previous program or has already progressed two minutes into the new show.

Some educational stations, during the hours of broadcasts to the schools, allow approximately five minutes between one program and the next. They fill this interval with a series of slides, identifying the coming lesson and also reading "Three minutes to go," "Two minutes to go," and so on, or broadcast the image of a clock giving a countdown to the start of the next telecast. Under this system, accurate control of time becomes less important.

Most commercial stations, however, follow multiples of a quarter hour; some now use multiples of ten minutes, with a minute and thirty seconds between programs for local station identification, local spot announcements, and whatever switching is necessary all along the line to change the network feeds.

Television in other countries often seems quite unusual to Americans, especially in regard to the casual attitude most foreign broadcasters have toward timing. Where there is only one television channel in communities, there is no problem of coordination with a time pattern. If a delay occurs, there is likewise no great worry about losing the audience to a competing channel. Foreign stations will often let programs run their natural length; and if they run under, the station will often leave a slide and music on for as much as ten minutes, if necessary, until the scheduled time of the next program, or until the next program is ready to begin.

Certain programs in this country are carried by some stations only in part. When new stations join a program in the middle, it is just as necessary to make the middle break on the exact second as it is to end the program accurately. If a program runs for longer than an hour (such as a remote pick-up of a ball game), station identification can be more flexibly timed. Even when this is a network show, however, no attempt will be made to put the station breaks exactly on the hour, since no stations will be joining or leaving the net, and a break at any set time might interrupt an important play. The break is usually made as close to the hour as possible, however.

The length of the show is estimated as closely as possible in advance by tallying the times of all the various segments and commercial spots. Once this general timing has been arrived at, it is adjusted to meet the required air time and made final. The length of each segment is marked beside that section on the program outline, and the clock time at which each segment is to begin and end is marked beside that. The schedule for the final minutes of a typical program outline, reproduced below, illustrates a successful method of preparing such a timing sheet. The director will provide as many people as necessary with copies of this list, including floor manager, host, and control-room assistants.

Element	Running time	Time in	Time out
Intro. to special guest	:15	8:22:55	8:23:10
Interview with guest	2:30	8:23:10	8:25:40
Intro. of music	:15	8:25:40	8:25:55
Musical number	2:10	8:25:55	8:28:05
M.C.'s good night	:40	8:28:05	8:28:45
Closing titles	:40	8:28:45	8:29:25

Cushions help timing. The *cushion* for controlling the length of a show is standard procedure. A cushion is any portion of the program that can be contracted or expanded during the air show so the program can be made to end on time. Naturally the cushion must be the last thing on the show, since it is only then that the director can know whether he is a little short or a little long.

The closing titles usually make a pretty good cushion for a show, especially if they are fairly long. When titles are on a drum or a crawl in the projection room, they can be run either rapidly or slowly up the screen, and the announcer can gauge his own speed of reading by the clock in the announce booth. When closing credits are run with background music, their length is even more flexible.

The musical theme that begins and ends a program is the most common cushion in television. This signature usually comes in just before the closing titles and may continue after them, provided there is something to look at. This may be a closing graphic, a set with performers, or even an empty set.

IMPROMPTU CAMERA HANDLING

The handling of cameras on the unrehearsed show calls for fast thinking, accurate guessing of what the performers are going to do, and a very intimate knowledge of cameras and the cameraman's problems. It is very difficult for a director who has not previously worked with a particular camera crew to handle his cameras well on an unrehearsed show. This type of production is usually attempted only by staff directors who have complete familiarity with the studio facilities and the cameramen. It is important to note that, in the teamwork between camera crew and director, it is just as often the cameraman who contributes the creative effort and gets the good shot at the right time.

If any routine or pattern for camera work can be laid down to follow on the ad-lib show, it probably would consist of only one axiom: Be prepared. When anything is likely to happen, a camera must be ready to pick up anything. If we are holding the performer in medium shot and he is seated, certain types of action may follow. He may rise and walk around; he may speak to someone else; he may call attention to a small object in his hand, or to someone or something outside the picture we have on the screen.

The director will usually keep one camera with a fairly wide angle of view, so that if the performer should suddenly rise or begin to move around on the set, this cover shot would include his full figure and could be quickly switched onto the line. Of course, a director can play it too conservatively and never dare use this camera for any other purpose. This makes for very dull camera work. If the director knows how long it takes to get on the cover shot, he can use that camera for other purposes, standing ready to give the order to line up the cover shot whenever he thinks the action is about to widen out. During the time when he does not need the cover shot, he may use both his cameras for close-ups (one of the host and the other of the guest, in the case of the interview show).

A good director will never let two cameras show him the same or nearly the same picture. If one camera is showing a two-shot, the other camera will be used for close-ups. The director knows that it will serve no useful purpose to cut from a two-shot to another two-shot of the same people. The exception to this rule is the reverse angle, already described in Chapter 2. Let us repeat that reverse-angle shots are equal in composition but opposite in emphasis, and this is what justifies cutting from a shot of two people to a *quite different* shot of the same two people.

The following figures illustrate four different, increasingly complex formats that are commonly used in unrehearsed programs. A simple interview program with guest and M.C. on a small sofa behind a coffee table is shown first. As the associated run-down of the first few shots illustrates, Camera One begins on an easel graphic and then goes to a close-up of the guest. Camera Two dollies back from a close-up of the M.C. to include the guest as he is introduced.

The second example is a typical camera set-up for a panel show involving an M.C. and three participants, and covered by two cameras. If panel members respond in order, it will be safe to use Camera One in close-ups. If you do not know who is to speak and when, use a two-shot so the respondent may be quickly covered.

This routine is a simple starter. An improvement would be an establishment, somewhere near the beginning, showing the spatial relationships of M.C. and panel members. (It will also please the produc-

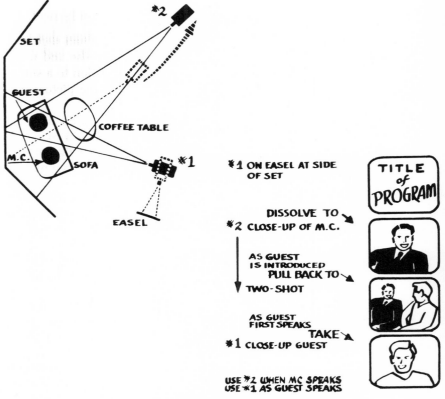

SET

GUEST

COFFEE TABLE

M.C.

SOFA

EASEL

*2

*1

**1 ON EASEL AT SIDE OF SET

DISSOLVE TO
**2 CLOSE-UP OF M.C.

AS GUEST
IS INTRODUCED
PULL BACK TO
TWO-SHOT

AS GUEST
FIRST SPEAKS
TAKE
**1 CLOSE-UP GUEST

USE **2 WHEN MC SPEAKS
USE **1 AS GUEST SPEAKS

TITLE
of
PROGRAM

Figure 43.   Typical camera set-up for an interview show.

tion manager of the station by showing his beautiful free-form table.)

An establishing shot could be arranged by placing Camera One (and its title easel) farther from the group so it can cover all four people. Then the introduction of the panel can be done by close-ups on Camera Two. If the introductions proceed from right to left, Camera Two can then pan on to the M.C. and you are back on the above pattern in shot 4.

The third example is a panel show with four participants (or contestants if it is a quiz format), the M.C. separated from the others behind his own small table. Three cameras can simplify it for the director, but can complicate it for the viewer if they are not used properly. Again, a few opening shots are diagrammed and sketched. Note that when more cameras are used, they tend to be placed in static positions and left there, providing little challenge or training to camera personnel or directors.

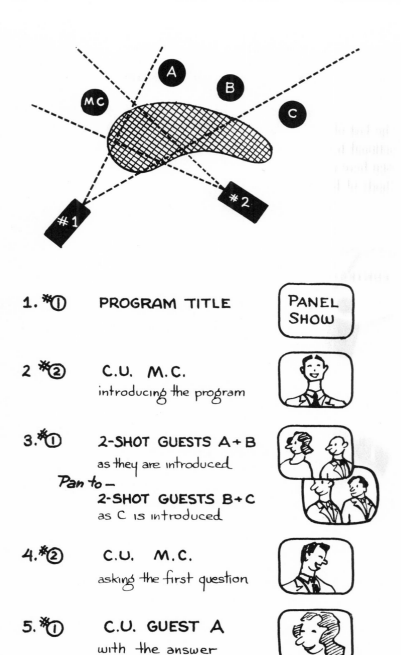

1. *①   **PROGRAM TITLE**

2. *②   **C.U. M.C.**
introducing the program

3. *①   **2-SHOT GUESTS A + B**
as they are introduced
Pan to —
       2-SHOT GUESTS B + C
as C is introduced

4. *②   **C.U. M.C.**
asking the first question

5. *①   **C.U. GUEST A**
with the answer

Figure 44.   Typical camera set-up for a panel show (two cameras).

The last of these examples is a science demonstration typical of instructional television, again utilizing only two cameras. The example chosen here is somewhat more complex than the preceding and shows methods of handling movement from one set to another. A studio of

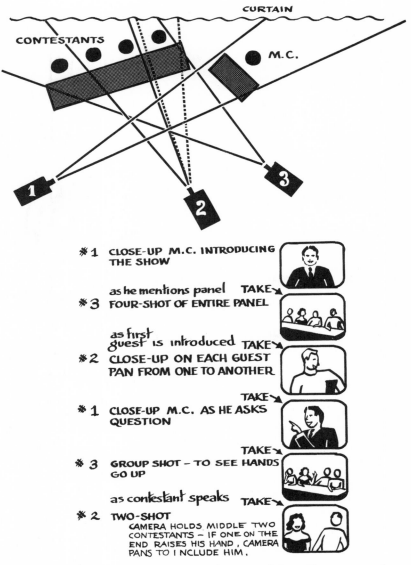

Figure 45.   Typical camera set-up for a panel show (three cameras).

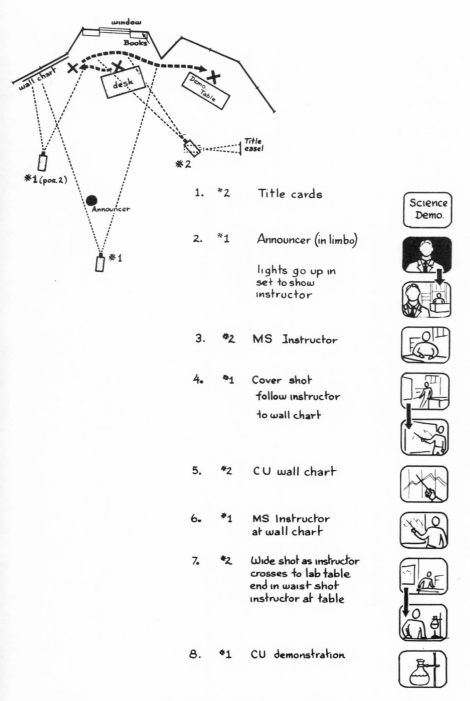

1. #2   Title cards

2. #1   Announcer (in limbo)

          lights go up in
          set to show
          instructor

3. #2   MS Instructor

4. #1   Cover shot
          follow instructor
          to wall chart

5. #2   CU wall chart

6. #1   MS Instructor
          at wall chart

7. #2   Wide shot as instructor
          crosses to lab table
          end in waist shot
          instructor at table

8. #1   CU demonstration

Figure 46.   A science demonstration for two vidicon cameras.

more than average size (for a training situation) would be necessary in order to do the opening in depth as it has been shown. Also, the studio must be equipped with dimmers for the light effect. Naturally, both of these are expendable.

Note that three locations are used and in each of these, for the duration of the scene involved, one camera plays the role of cover camera, while the other takes the close-ups. Note also that these roles change in the last scene, and the camera which was devoted to close-ups before is now the cover camera.

SUMMARY

In the unrehearsed program, the director's responsibilities and problems in relation to cuing, control of timing, and movement of cameras will vary with the format of the production, the performers' freedom of action, and the policy and facilities of the station. In general, however, the directing of unrehearsed studio programs requires a combination of quick reactions, ability to foresee what will happen, and complete command of available facilities. A great deal of preparation must be made while the program is on the air. On the other hand, many unrehearsed programs use the same format day after day, and established camera patterns and combinations of cues become almost automatic.

9 / Directing Remote Programs

The remote program is a show which originates outside the studio itself. Often it is an event which would take place whether television cameras were present or not. There are intermission periods in most such events, however, during which nothing really happens, and this time must be programmed for the television audience by the station staff. These natural intermissions provide the network or station with time for commercials, station I.D., and other thirty- or sixty-second announcements and promos. If you have ever been to a stadium where a game is televised, you may have noticed that the game seems to move more slowly than a non-televised game. More time than an actual "time-out" is needed for television purposes and the national sports organization involved agrees to this in a contract with the network or station. Sometimes more than the sporting event itself must be produced. When there are unexpected delays—because of rain or accidents on the field, for example—the burden of maintaining audience interest is usually placed on the commentators, who are prepared with background information, color, and history of the teams and of the sport in general, so they can ramble on at great length, if necessary.

The cameras are placed where they can get the best shots of the field, players, and stadium spectators without interfering too much with the view of the stadium spectators. Some cameras are stationary, usually provided with zoom lenses for a wide choice of shots, while other cameras, mounted on large-wheeled dollies, often motorized, roll along the sidelines capturing the action on the playing field or in the stands. Still other cameras are hand-held and wireless, operated by cameramen moving at will within the stadium.

Directing the sports-event broadcast is a matter of cutting between cameras, keeping a camera ready wherever action will develop, and controlling replay and slow-motion coverage. This is particularly difficult in the coverage of football. Directing the televising of a football game is one of the most difficult assignments in television, and perhaps the most challenging. Elia Kazan, in an address to students at Wesleyan University, remarked: "The best-directed shows on TV today are the professional football games. Why? Study them. You are shown not only the game from far and middle distance and close-up, you are shown the bench, the way the two coaches sweat it out, the rejected sub . . . and a stop-action shot showing just why the penalty was thrown."* Televising football calls for an individual who not only knows cameras and equipment cold, but one who is thoroughly familiar with the game as well. It has been said that the cameramen and director for a televised football game are as much a part of the game as the players on the field. Shots that are too wide can make the players look like ants. Close-ups taken at the wrong time (especially when they are a split second too late) can easily cause the viewer to lose sight of the play and ruin his enjoyment.

Aids to the Remote Director

The director of a major sports event is rarely without help. Besides his sportscasters and technical help, he is often part of a producer-director team. A network pick-up often has a producer who operates in quite a different fashion from the producer of a studio program. Financial responsibilities and details are left to a unit manager, while the producer sits at the director's side in the remote truck, a portable control room, and takes over many of the director's duties while still exercising total overall responsibility. In one network, the pattern calls for the producer to predetermine the basic pattern of camera coverage, in pre-game conference with the director. The producer determines when commercials are to be inserted, which promotional announcements are to be cut in, when the scores of other games are to be announced or superimposed, and similar items of non-action material. He also sets up the camera pattern for the national anthem, the toss of the coin, the kick-off pattern, the half-time break, and other segments of the program. The producer often controls communications from the mobile unit to the play-by-play announcer and the color man and may even call for isolation camera or instant-playback or at least make the decisions as to when such items are to be called for. The director will be busy enough following the play and calling for shots on half a dozen cameras, or more!

In the crowded quarters of the average remote truck, there is barely room for the T.D., the director, and the producer to sit side by side before the bank of monitors. The A.D. (assistant director) sits behind the producer or the director, keeps an open telephone line to the control

* Elia Kazan, "All You Need to Know, Kids," *Action*, Jan.–Feb. 1974, p. 9.

studio from which the film or videotaped commercials originate, maintains a private line to the "sideline man," who signals the officials for an extra time-out or warns them during a normal time-out when the commercial has ended and play on the field may be resumed. The A.D. is also in touch with the announce booth, where another assistant may hand extra copy, such as late scores, to the sportscasters. The A.D. is also in communication with a graphics or visuals area, where statistics, scores, and other graphic information are constantly being changed and readied for the graphics camera, which will superimpose these letters and numbers over a shot of the field. Decisions as to which information is to be superimposed at any given moment are given to the A.D. by the producer, with the director calling for the supers.

Handling Interviews

The broadcasting of sporting events is made more difficult than other types of programming by the time-outs, half time, player injuries, and other periods of non-play which can be a challenge to the commentator and the director. Through the years, the interview has been used to help fill the time when there is no action on the playing field.

Often the program begins with the commentator and his associate or "color man" talking informally about the game. This can be superimposed over the empty stadium to maintain the feeling of being at the game. Throughout the game, the networks often have a man on the field to interview the players when they are on the bench. This practice is limited to the extent that the program must not interrupt play or interfere with the coaching staff. Half time may find the two commentators reviewing the play of the first half, until other action begins on the field —marching bands in collegiate football, for example.

One of the most exciting types of interviews is the locker-room interview after the game. This activity is usually reserved for playoffs or championship games and gives an added emotional impact to the broadcast. All these interviews are highly informal. The director should strive to give the audience the feeling of the moment, even if the shot is not "properly" composed. He should just show the people—the "feeling" will result. The interview of a player should give the viewers information that will interest them and keep them involved.

Control of Timing of a Remote

The timing of a remote is usually no particular concern of the director's, since he has no control over the length of the event. It is usually allowed to run to its completion, and the station schedule is left sufficiently flexible so that it can be adjusted to fit a variation from the expected length. A special phone line is always kept open between the director at the remote point and a coordinator at the station, who is usually in master control or in the film studio. The director forwards any information he may receive as to the time when the event is expected to end.

The private phone line is also used to warn the coordinator when film commercials are to be inserted into the program from the film studio back at the station. Usually the commentator has been instructed to use a cue phrase, often the score of the game, which will signal the film director to fade out the remote feed and fade in the commercial. The decision as to when the commercials are to be inserted is, of course, up to the remote director or producer, who then watches the commercials on the off-the-air monitor and begins the show again as soon as each commercial break ends.

Surveying the Site

The first survey of the field or other site of the remote is usually conducted by a two-man team consisting of the director assigned to the remote pick-up and a member of the engineering staff. At this time they fill out a detailed form which calls for information such as the location of mobile-unit trucks, each camera and microphone, special camera mounts that may be required, and the construction of platforms, dolly tracks, and the like. After this has all been approved, multiple copies of the report and plan are distributed to all personnel responsible for the event. Pages 162–65 are selected from the NBC survey report for a major sports event, the Super Bowl IX game, held in New Orleans in January 1975. While not the complete survey, the map and the first few pages of location information reproduced here can give the reader an insight into the problems that are faced in planning and producing a major remote broadcast.

Instant Replay

One of the important contributions that television has made to the enjoyment of sporting events is the instant replay. The capability of repeating a play in the short period before the next play begins doubles the viewer's opportunity to understand what is happening. Added to this is a new time dimension, slow motion, which has been called the "temporal close-up." With the Ampex HS-100, thirty seconds of action is recorded on four sides of two rotating video discs sixteen inches in diameter. The recorder is run continuously; as soon as the discs are filled they are progressively erased and filled with new material. Thus the last thirty seconds of play is always ready to be recalled.

Plate 19.   Video disc recorder for instant replay. Ampex HS-100 Color Slow
Motion Sports Recorder/Reproducer.   (Courtesy of Ampex Corporation)

Fast forward and fast reverse motion ($4\frac{1}{2}$ times normal) allows the
operator to locate any desired point within four seconds. He may then
run the recording at normal, $\frac{1}{2}$, $\frac{1}{5}$, or variable speed, using the vertical
row of selector buttons shown under the operator's hand in Plate 19. In
variable-speed mode, the operator uses the handle at the left to gradually slow the action down or stop it. He may also advance or reverse
the action frame by frame, or reverse at any speed under the variable
control.

A large clock dial with a white timing pointer keeps the operator in-
formed. A red pointer that normally rotates with the white pointer is
stopped by punching the "cue" button, usually at the beginning of a
play, while the white pointer continues to run. After the play the recording may be quickly reversed (or fast-forwarded, whichever is quicker)
until the white pointer matches the red.

TULANE - SUPER BOWL STADIUM 1975
NEW ORLEANS, LA.

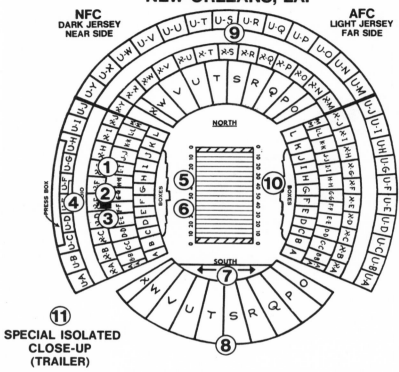

NFC
DARK JERSEY
NEAR SIDE

AFC
LIGHT JERSEY
FAR SIDE

⑪
SPECIAL ISOLATED
CLOSE-UP
(TRAILER)

① LEFT 25 YD. LINE
② 50 YD. LINE TV ANNOUNCE BOOTH
③ RIGHT 25 YD. LINE
④ 50 YD. LINE PHOTO DECK
⑤ MOVING CHAPMAN CRANES

⑥ MOVING CHAPMAN CRANES
⑦ MOVING CRAB DOLLY LOW
⑧ RIGHT END ZONE
⑨ LEFT END ZONE
⑩ PCP HAND HELD CAMERA

Chart 3.   (Portions of NBC sports survey reprinted by permission of the National Broadcasting Company, Inc.)

SUPER BOWL IX SURVEY REPORT

PROGRAM: SUPER BOWL IX   DATE: JANUARY 12, 1975

LOCATION: TULANE STADIUM   AIR: 2:00 CST
                                                  (3:00) EST

MOBILE UNITS

Parked adjacent to fence at the Northwest side of Stadium near the Claiborne Street Entrance.

CAMERA LOCATIONS

POS. #1 ... Left 25 yard line ... West side, behind vomitory
            in upper deck, Section UG. Platform to be constructed
            over Rows #13 & #14 at height of Row #13. Platform
            to be made as vibration proof as possible.
            Seats Eliminated: Row #13, Seats 11 through 17.
                               Row #14, Seats 11 through 19.

POS. #2 ... 50 yard line ... West side -- Radio Booth, partitioned
            South end of Booth.

POS. #3 ... Right 25 yard line ... West side, behind vomitory in
            upper deck, Section UD.
            Construction duplication of that at Position #1.
            Seats Eliminated: Row #13, Seats 11, 14 through 19.
                               Row #14, Seats 11 through 19.

POS. #4 ... 50 yard line ... West side, Photo Deck new designation
            -- Booth #2. South side of Booth on existing mount
            adjacent to NBC Radio Announcers.

POS. #5 ... Near (West) sideline ground level ... Moving vehicle
            ... Chapman Nike Crane. To move from end zone line
            to end zone line. Plywood track to be installed.

POS. #6 ... 2nd Nike Crane -- to work adjacent to Position #5.

POS. #7 ... South end zone on grass behind restraining wall.
            Camera mounted on an Elmac Dolly with lens height
            just above wall. A track to be constructed to move
            dolly from corner to corner.

POS. #8 ... South end zone on existing platform, beneath Scoreboard.

CAMERA LOCATIONS (CONTINUED)

POS. #9 ... North end zone on existing platform, centered between
            goal posts.

POS. #10 ... PCP 90 Hand-Held Camera. RF, with microwave dish
             to be mounted on existing platform on top of
             Northwest stands. Triax cable to be run to
             entrance of both Locker Rooms.

POS. #11 ... "Studio Camera" in trailer parked adjacent to Mobile
             Unit.

CAMERA LOCATIONS (POST GAME)

    A) AFC CLUBHOUSE

    B) NFC CLUBHOUSE

    C) INTERVIEW ROOM

    D) (PCP) INTERVIEW ROOM

    E) EXTERIOR

ANNOUNCE LOCATIONS

NBC-TV -- Radio Booth at 50 yard line, West side. Exterior of
          Booth to be painted with NBC Logo included. Interior
          to be panelled with construction to include removal
          of post between windows, table and monitor rack
          installation.

NBC RADIO -- 50 yard line ... West side, photo deck. New
             designation -- Booth #2. Announcers on North
             (left) side of camera Position #4.
             -- One (1) off-the-air monitor with audio on-headset
             TV audio feed.

CBC -- West side photo deck. North (left) of NBC Radio on
       other side of existing panelled partition. (Partitioned
       part of new designation -- Booth #2).
       One (1) monitor with return video.

SPECIAL MONITORS (CONTINUED)

CAMERA ROOM: One (1) Special Monitor and
                      One (1) Air-Monitor

END ZONE CAMERA #7
LOCATION: One (1) B & W Monitor.

VIDEFONT ROOM: One (1) Color Monitor.

INSIDE EACH CLUBHOUSE -- (WWL TRUCK AUDIO)

Two (2) Hand Mikes
Two (2) IFB-Telex
One (1) Monitor -- Network return
Camera and Interview platforms in each room.

NOTE: Simulcast from Clubhouse on TV and Radio.

FIELD -- NEAR SIDE

Two (2) Hand Mikes
Two (2) IFB-Telex
One (1) Monitor -- Network return

ADDITIONAL MIKES

Crowd Noise Mikes
Parabola Mike for band pick-up -- manned pre-game & Halftime
Two (2) RF Directional Mikes -- Far & Near side manned
Tie into PA system -- to and from

NOTE: Plus special halftime audio requirements

LIGHTING

Announce Booth -- Talent on Camera & Chroma Key
Field -- Near side -- Talent & interview positions
Both Clubhouses and Interview Room
From field to Clubhouse Area
Stadium lights turned on at TV request.

10 / Directing the Fully Scripted Program

While there are many types of television programs that are fully scripted, we are limiting our discussion in this chapter to what is probably the most difficult and challenging: the television drama. Few television stations at the present time are able to produce fully scripted dramatic shows of any great complexity. Most complex productions are done only in the network-originating stations and in a few of the larger independent stations, but are beyond the scope of most of the smaller operations. Many dramatic productions are done by independent producers as weekly segments of continuing series which all involve the same basic characters. A pilot is first produced, usually on film, and if this is sold the networks show it as part of their regular programming. Many television programs are produced on videotape—the usual technique is to rehearse an entire segment or scene (not just one shot, as in film production), tape it, and retape it if necessary. These taped segments are then edited together much in the manner of film. Most of the techniques discussed in this chapter were developed in the early 1950's, when television drama was produced live; the basic concepts are still used in the production of videotape segments, live telecasts of soap operas, and programs produced before a studio audience which are shot (either with television or film cameras) as complete theatrical performances.

In small stations where there is limited studio time (and limited videotape), live techniques must be used. Retakes will require later editing, as well as additional studio time and videotape, and so are avoided. Even without this austerity, the larger part of live-television practice is still followed. The student director must learn to direct fully scripted programs by live-television techniques because he will surely be required to do so, probably early in his career. Our detailed description of a live-television drama broadcast, presented later in the chapter, once represented the essence of television direction and production. It is retained in the current edition because it describes a television era

166

whose influence has been broad and whose techniques will be integrated into many future media.

Live television should not be forgotten.

VARIOUS APPROACHES AND SYSTEMS

It is possible to direct a dramatic production without camera rehearsal if the cameras are never expected to move. It is the repositioning of cameras that takes the larger part of rehearsal time. If a dramatic production is thoroughly rehearsed outside the studio and the actors make all the changes themselves, walking up to the camera when close-ups are required, using only certain playing areas to which the cameras are directed, the show can be produced without the cameramen knowing anything about it before air time. This does result, however, in very uninteresting camera work. The best camera shots are usually those in which the actors are arranged in depth, some people being closer to the camera and thus larger in size on the screen, while others in the background are smaller. This kind of shooting cannot be done without rehearsal. The unrehearsed dramatic show must almost of necessity be done in flat shots without depth. Still, the fact that the shots are planned, if only in the mind of the director, means that better shooting can be done than if the show were to be picked up by the ad-lib method.

In the usual ad-lib technique the director will keep one camera on a cover shot, risking close-ups only rarely; and the result will be a series of medium and long shots, none of which is fully satisfying to the audience. The difficulty is probably this: When any type of production other than the dramatic show is done, it is accepted as television; but a dramatic show asks for comparison with the motion picture. The audience is used to seeing big close-ups, accurate cutting, smooth production all around, and subconsciously, perhaps, expects the same thing in the television dramatic show.

Most dramatic productions require a great deal of pre-production planning, rehearsal, and tight control. Teamwork during studio rehearsal is essential, and much depends on the method of directing that is used. Discussed below are three of the main types of systems presently used in television stations and production centers.

The Technical Director (T.D.) System

Under this system the director calls the shots, but for years was not allowed to give any instructions to the cameramen except as they were relayed through the T.D. The technical director was thus a kind of head

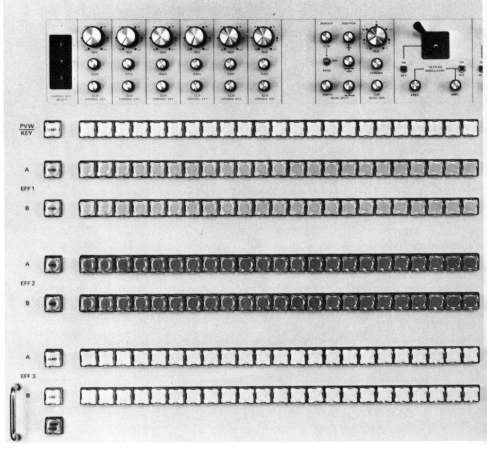

Plate 20. Example of an elaborate production switcher: Grass Valley Group 1600-7G. This control panel, 20 by 44 inches in size, contains almost 300 buttons, providing for 24 input sources in three mixer/effect systems. It can produce almost all conceivable switching and electronic effects. Simple switching, as described in the caption for Plate 8, may be done with the mixer/effects system at the bottom (EFF 3). This is a double re-entry switching system; the output of the Effects 1 system can be re-entered into the Effects 2 system, and the outputs of both of these can be re-entered into the Effects 3 system. Extra buttons are provided in the Effects 2 and 3 buses for this purpose (center bottom). Thus it would be possible to dissolve from one

cameraman, as well as a supervisor of all the other engineering facilities of the studio. This system was found useful in the production of fully rehearsed shows if and when the T.D. was a highly capable individual with an understanding of production values and showmanship. In smaller stations, and on shows where ad-lib cutting and spontaneous directing of cameramen was necessary, this system broke down because of the necessary time lag between the director's giving an order and the

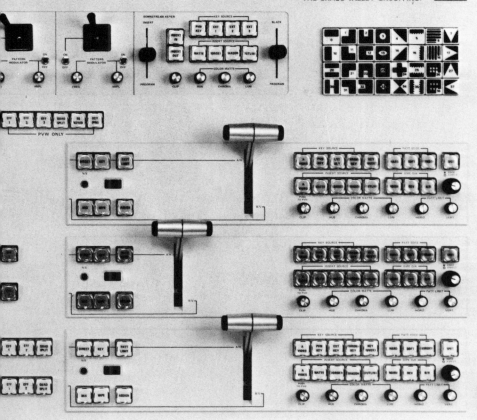

two-camera effect (set up on EFF 1) to another two-camera effect (set up on EFF 2), or to superimpose four cameras and still have the capability to dissolve from all this to some other single source.

Sixty-four different wipe effects can be made (32 patterns, each reversible), with sharp or soft edges, border or shadow lines, and there are joy-stick positioners to move effects about over the screen. The top selector bus feeds a preview monitor so that any source may be previewed; supers, wipes, as well as keying and matte effects may be set up and previewed just before they are actually done. (Courtesy of the Grass Valley Group, Inc.)

cameraman's receiving and acting upon it. Eventually, the technical-union contracts covering T.D.'s were liberalized to allow the director to work directly with the cameramen on "unrehearsed" shows.

The Switcher System

By far the most common system in use today is what is called, for lack of a better term, the "switcher system." In stations using this system a technical director is employed, but he has less production responsibility than under the T.D. system. The switcher's job is only to operate the switching system under the director's orders, although the switcher may also be in charge of the engineering facilities in the studio and he may indeed be called the technical director. The distinguishing characteristic of this system is that the director may communicate directly with the cameramen. Most studios which operated originally under the T.D. system described above have so liberalized their methods that directors now have nearly as much freedom as they do under the switcher system.

It is interesting to compare, in this connection, the American methods with those used in Europe and elsewhere. Under the European system, switching generally is done by a woman, on the theory that dexterity and speed of reaction are most necessary here, and most likely to be found in the female. The responsibility for technical quality is then vested in a technical director who has no part to play in the production, beyond supervision. The technical director may, as at the BBC, have an elaborate control desk and switching console with which he can keep a constant check on the quality of all the technical aspects of the production. His panel of switching buttons may be almost as complicated as that used by the program switcher, but it allows him merely to preview all cameras and effects, and has no function in the actual broadcast.

The Director-Switching System

A third system eliminates the switcher entirely and puts the switching buttons under the hand of the director. This has been called the "director-switching system" or "self-switching system" and is in use in small production centers and in many places for directing remote programs. It makes for accurate cutting, since there is no appreciable delay between the director's decision to cut and the actual punching of the button. Directors who have used this method over a considerable period of time say that operating the switching system is no great chore, that the punching of buttons and the working of dissolve levers become practically automatic, and can be done entirely by touch without looking at the control board.

As a matter of fact, these directors say that they prefer working the switching system themselves for this reason: When the director gives an order to take or to dissolve, he must then devote his entire attention to the technical director until this action is accomplished. He mentally punches the button himself, or pulls the handle, and watches the result on the master monitor. If the T.D. does not execute the order as quickly as desired, or in quite the right manner, a certain extra amount of energy goes into this mental operation in the attempt to make it go right. All this is saved if the director can do the job himself. This argument, of course, presupposes relatively simple switching and would not hold much water where particularly complex effects were involved. Some of the studio switching systems in the network studios contain hundreds of punch buttons, controlling not only the program line but two preview monitors and special-effects channels as well. Another important deterrent to use of the director-switching system is the local union rules which often limit the punching of buttons to engineering personnel, at least in most of the larger cities.

Directing Drama from the Studio Floor

In discussing the various methods of directing, a word should be said about a technique developed many years ago at CBS by Wyllis Cooper and now in very common use. Under this system, the director runs all his rehearsals from the studio floor instead of the control room. With only one monitor before him on which he can see the program line, he places himself in a strategic location, almost among the cameras, and works out his camera shots from there. Switching instructions are given to the T.D. in the control room; the audio engineer is also on headphones; and the assistant director is usually in the control room to keep his timing records and production notes on the script. It is only when the program goes into the first complete run-through that the director goes into the control room. This has the very real advantage of allowing the director to work very intimately with the cameramen as well as the actors; their every problem is immediately evident to him, and he always keeps a clear picture in his mind of where the cameras are positioned.

It is not uncommon for television studios to be so crowded with sets that the control-room window (if there is one) does not give a satisfactory view of the studio floor. Working only by the pictures on the monitors, the director finds himself making frequent trips in and out of the control room to solve the various staging and traffic problems. It is virtually impossible in any studio for the director to stay in the control room throughout the rehearsal period, and the easier it is for him to step out on the floor and back again, the better the studio is laid out. The Wyllis Cooper method simply carries this to its logical extreme and keeps him out on the floor during most of the camera rehearsal period— or even right through to the end of videotaping.

Lest the reader think that this is an archaic form of directing, no longer in use, it is important to note that directing on the floor had a marked increase in popularity in the 1970's. The usual pattern was for a "primary director" to work on the studio floor during the videotape recording, with a co-director calling the shots in the control room. As recently as the end of 1974, the Directors Guild of America described the situation as one in which "there is a Director member [of the Guild] directing the actors on the floor and another member in the booth." Because there had been several instances in which the director on the floor considered himself *the* director and did not wish to share director credit with the member in the booth, the National Board of the Guild ruled: "Only a Director who selects shots, times camera changes, and approves audio and visual elements of a show may receive solo directorial credit on an electronic show. These decisions are customarily made in the control room."*

BLOCKING OUT THE SCRIPT

After the director has prepared his various lists of facilities and production requirements, and conferred with people in each of the service departments, he must sit down with his script and laboriously visualize the show. Simply reading through a script is easy—and the director may do this to begin with just to get the idea of the story. Reading a script and *visualizing* it takes time. The director must ask himself on every line, "What are they seeing now?" and force himself to visualize the picture on a television screen. People who have not had television, film, or theatrical experience may find this particularly difficult. It is natural to visualize as we read; all of us, reading a novel, see the characters in our mind's eye, but not through the eye of a camera. A director with stage background will read the script with a visual picture of actors on a stage. Only experience in the use of cameras will train a director to see close-ups, two-shots, shots that pan, truck, dolly, or zoom, as he reads the script.

As soon as the director has a clear idea of the kind of production he wants to do, he will go to the set designer and together they will rough out a set. Later, the designer will have a floor plan ready which will show the positions of all sets and furniture accurately and to scale. The director takes this floor plan and uses it as a sort of base map on which to chart his camera placement. The director's most useful instrument at this time can be a device called a "shot plotter." Whether manufactured or homemade, the shot plotter is basically a protractor on which are

---

* *Action,* Nov.–Dec. 1974, p. 34.

marked the horizontal lens angles for the standard camera lenses; a shot plotter can also be used for a variable-focal-length lens. A shot plotter may be a simple triangle, cut from clear plastic, showing the field of view of only one lens or zoom position; or it may have several sets of lines imprinted on it, representing the angles of several lenses or zoom

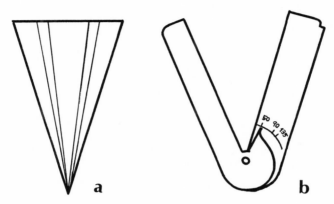

Figure 47. Typical shot plotters. In (*a*) the horizontal angles of view provided by three standard focal lengths have been inscribed on a piece of clear acetate. The outer boundary may be used to represent the widest angle of a given zoom lens; the inner lines, its narrowest angle. In (*b*), the "Bretzplotter," the two arms of the plotter open and close to form the various angles. The range of a zoom lens may be marked as a continuous line on the scale.

positions. Placing the shot plotter on the floor plan, the director can determine one of three variables involved in each shot: (1) the position of the camera, (2) the lens, and (3) the field of view of the shot. If two of these are known, the shot plotter will determine the third. Thus, if the director knows the field of view he wants and where he wants to place the camera, he can determine which lens to use. If he knows the lens and the field of view, he can determine where he must place the camera, and if he knows the lens and camera position, he can determine how much of the scene will be in the camera's field of view.

Perhaps the first step in this entire process is to determine which cameras are available for each scene. This entails a very rough blocking out of camera positions, scene by scene. If only two cameras are available, the problem of camera coverage will be more difficult for a drama, for example, but the problem of camera placement will be simpler, in a sense, because fewer alternatives will be possible.

If we use as an example a dramatic program with three cameras available, we can begin with the major premise that in general Cameras

One and Two will cover the sets to the director's left on the studio floor, while Two and Three will take those on his right. Two is thus the roving camera, able to join either One or Three. A major scene that requires all three cameras can have them, of course, no matter on which side of the studio it may be set.

In short, the director will determine the four things listed below in the paper stage of camera blocking. If the paper work has been done correctly, he should not have to alter many of these decisions later in rehearsal, and yet should not have imposed any unnecessary or arbitrary limitations on himself. He will determine:

1.   Which camera, or cameras, will be used in each scene (for the major portion of the scene);

2.   Which cameras must be released from a scene early so they can reposition and be ready for a following scene—which cameras, in other words, are available for the opening and closing of each scene;

3.   Which cameras will carry the key or pivotal shots within each scene;

4.   What other shots can be used.

What the director will not do at this stage is to work out his exact plan of cutting from shot to shot, or the exact lines on which he will use close-ups or medium shots, unless, of course, these are key shots on which the whole meaning of the scene depends.

Whatever action is planned during the paper stage of blocking must be related in a practical way to the number and positions of the available cameras. If more than one director is involved in the production, as when a staging or a dance director is working out the action, and the television director is merely handling the cameras, frequent conferences between the various directors are necessary at this early stage.

OUTSIDE REHEARSAL

Dry rehearsal outside the studio is the principal technique which makes the incredibly rapid process of television production possible. Most of the problems and the details of movement and camera shots are worked out during these rehearsals, so that when the time comes for rehearsal with cameras there will be as little of the trial-and-error operation as possible. There are several physical aids to accurate planning of camera shots which the director will make good use of at this stage.

First of all, he will transfer the floor plan of the studio onto the floor of the rehearsal hall. This should be done accurately with a tape measure, with the outline of walls, furniture, and set pieces marked on the floor with chalk. Many directors use masking tape instead of chalk, finding it does not scuff off and can be quickly removed if the room is

THE LINE OF DUTY *

(FADE IN ON A LONG SHOT OF A
VERY BARE SUGGESTED COURTROOM.
THERE ARE FOUR CHAIRS ... WOODEN,
STRAIGHTBACK, UNCOMFORTABLE. THREE
ARE OCCUPIED. TO ONE SIDE STANDS A
WOODEN PLATFORM, TWO STEPS LEADING
UP TO IT. ON IT, A LARGER CHAIR
WITH ARMRESTS. THE SCENE IS LIT
SHARPLY WITH PIN SPOTS. ON THE
FLOOR, BETWEEN THE CHAIRS AND THE
PLATFORM, WE SEE THE ELONGATED
SHADOW OF A BARRED WINDOW WHICH
WE CAN IMAGINE BEING ABOVE AND
BEHIND THE WITNESS CHAIR.)

(SITTING IN THE THREE CHAIRS ARE
THE SERGEANT, THE MAJOR, AND THE
PRIVATE. STANDING BY THE WITNESS
CHAIR, BESIDE THE PLATFORM, LOOKING
UP AT THE INVISIBLE BARRED WINDOW
STANDS THE COLONEL. ALL ARE IN
UNIFORMS, WHICH ARE DARK, SEVERE.
THE SHINY BELTS AND BOOTS GIVE THEM
A TOTALITARIAN APPEARANCE AND THIS
WILL SERVE AS OUR ONLY CLUE AS TO
THE MILITARY NATURE OF THE UNIFORMS.
NOW, VERY SLOWLY, THE CAMERA TRUCKS
FORWARD TOWARDS THE COLONEL. AS
THIS HAPPENS.........

........TITLE CARDS ARE SUPERIMPOSED
OVER THE PICTURE. THE LETTERING IS
BOLD, CRISP, OFFICIAL AND COLD.
WITH THE LAST TITLE CARD.....
                         LONG
.....THE COLONEL IS HELD IN A MEDIUM
SHOT, PROFILE. WE CAN SEE THE OTHER
BEYOND HIM. OVER THIS PICTURE, WE
NOW HEAR THE ANNOUNCER'S VOICE. HE
SPEAKS SLOWLY, CLEARLY ... VERY CLOSE
ON MIKE.....ALMOST WHISPERING, GIVING
THE IMPRESSION THAT IF HE WERE TO
SPEAK LOUDER, HE WOULD DISRUPT THE
GATHERING.)

ANNCR:

(OFF SHOT) It isn't necessary to

give the characters names. Neither

is it necessary to place the action

-1-

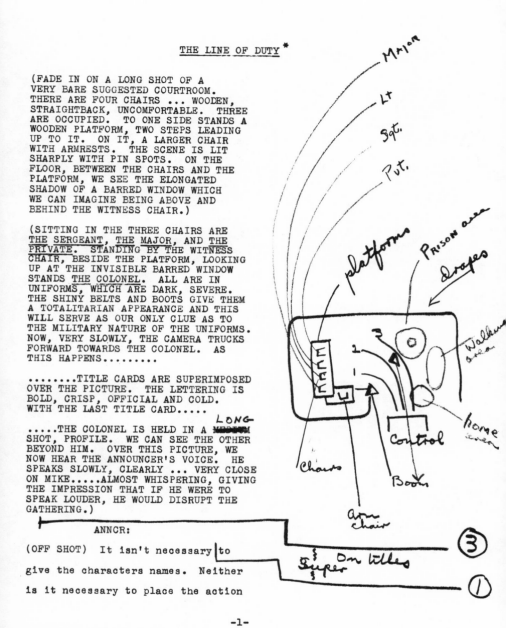

Script 4. Example of director's thumbnail sketches on the margins of a
script: Albert McCleery's script for *The Line of Duty*, by Guy de Vry.

Plate 21.   NBC rehearses the opera *Amahl and the Night Visitors* to piano accompaniment in an outside rehearsal hall. *Top:* The three kings stand at the door. *Bottom:* The mother is discovered stealing the gold. (Courtesy of NBC)

to be used for any other purpose. Rehearsal chairs will do to simulate furniture of all kinds: beds, sofas, walls, pillars, doorways, and so forth. It is always best to find something as close as possible to the final furniture that will be used on the air, however, since a great amount of the action centering on a chair or a sofa will depend on the actors' sitting on the arms or leaning on the back of the prop, and these positions cannot be planned at all when no better substitutes than straight chairs are available.

Having the outlines of the set and the positions of furniture, doorways, and key props accurately established, the director can then proceed to work out his action and movement, both of actors and of cameras, hoping that they will not have to be changed to any great extent when the actors finally are on the studio set. If the set outline that is laid out on the rehearsal-hall floor is made just a little tighter than the studio set itself, the actors will feel less crowded when they get into the studio.

As the actors rehearse, the director will be constantly on his feet playing the part first of one camera, then of another, as he views the action from each camera position. It is important for the director to know exactly where a camera will be positioned for any particular shot, and it is also important for him to know what various shots the camera can take from any particular position.

One factor which must not be lost sight of during dry rehearsal is the audio pick-up problem. If the director does not consider his microphones, he will have people talking in all parts of the set and find in studio rehearsal that a lot of his staging must be revised because he cannot hear the dialogue. Some television directors, deplorably, actually have forgotten about audio and simply dumped the entire problem in the audio man's lap at the beginning of the rehearsal.

STUDIO REHEARSAL

The following narrative describes a half-hour television drama as it was produced live in a typical network television studio before the days of videotape, but since the routine for taping and live broadcasting is basically the same, the terms "air time" and "taping" will be used interchangeably. Most of the techniques described are applicable to present-day media, and must be mastered by the aspiring director. While videotape production has borrowed much from the film medium, film has also been influenced by live television. Today's director must be sufficiently versatile to work in all these media.

On the day of the show the director usually will spend eleven or

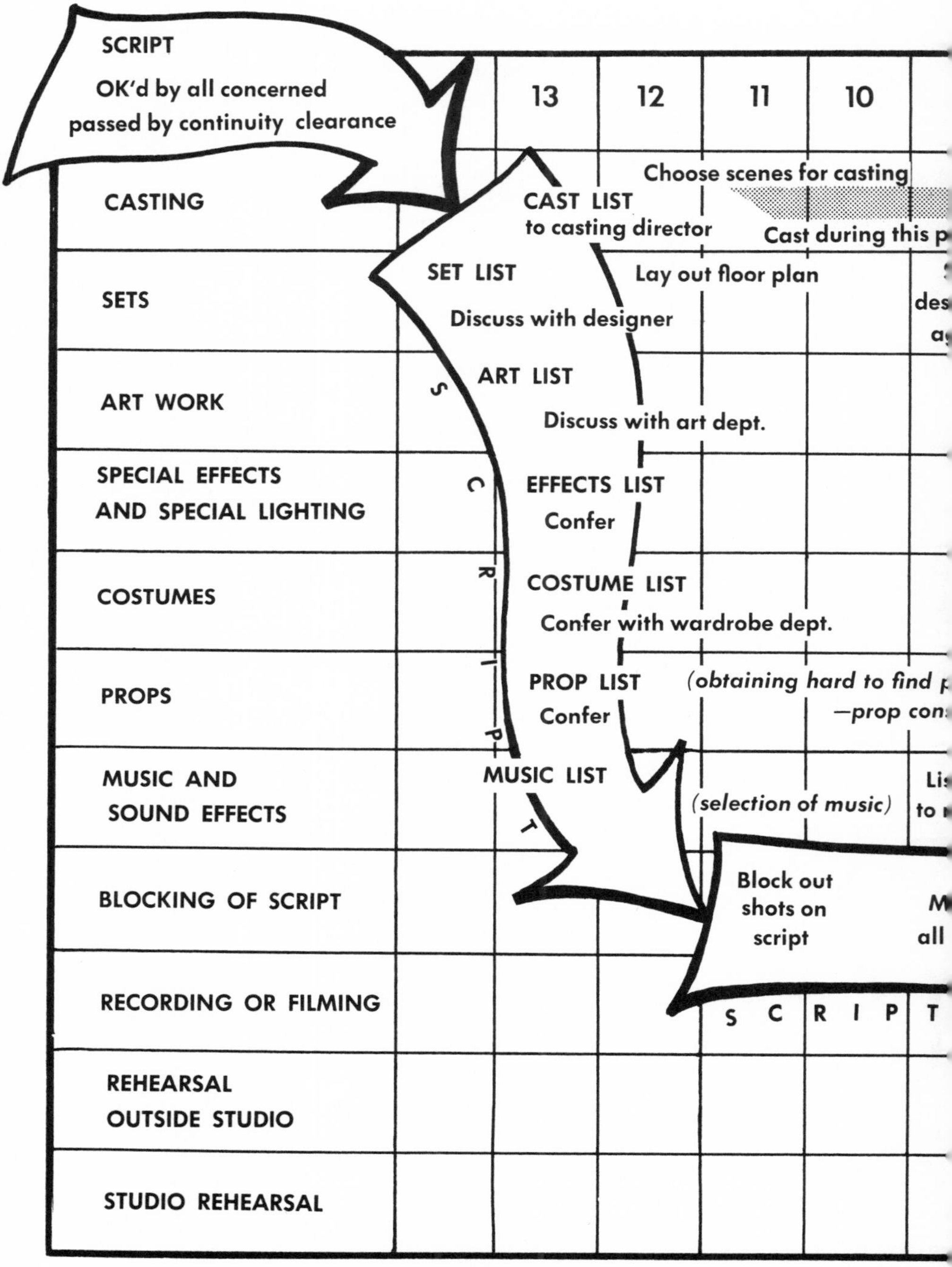

	13	12	11	10

SCRIPT
OK'd by all concerned
passed by continuity clearance

CASTING
Choose scenes for casting
CAST LIST
to casting director
Cast during this p

SETS
SET LIST
Lay out floor plan
Discuss with designer
des
ag

ART WORK
ART LIST
Discuss with art dept.

SPECIAL EFFECTS
AND SPECIAL LIGHTING
EFFECTS LIST
Confer

COSTUMES
COSTUME LIST
Confer with wardrobe dept.

PROPS
PROP LIST
Confer
(obtaining hard to find p
—prop con

MUSIC AND
SOUND EFFECTS
MUSIC LIST
(selection of music)
Lis
to

BLOCKING OF SCRIPT
Block out
shots on
script
M
all

RECORDING OR FILMING
S C R I P T

REHEARSAL
OUTSIDE STUDIO

STUDIO REHEARSAL

S C R I P T

Chart 4.

1 WEEK BEFORE	6	5	4	3	2	DAY BEFORE	DAY OF SHOW
ng complete							
exact floor lay out			Check on sets			Check	
		Give art dept. complete cast list for closing credits				Check	
						Check	
		Send actors for measurements		Send actors for final fittings		Check	
n props for rehearsals n permissible)						Check	
						Check	
		Keep changing script				Prepare scripts and cue sheets	
		RECORD OR FILM		PLAYBACK OR SCREEN			
READ OR WALK THRU	BLOCK ACTION		DRY REHEARSAL				CAMERA REHEARSAL

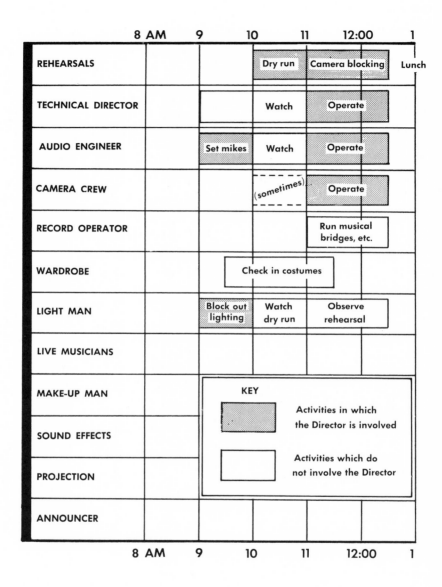

	8 AM	9	10	11	12:00	1
REHEARSALS				Dry run	Camera blocking	Lunch
TECHNICAL DIRECTOR				Watch	Operate	
AUDIO ENGINEER			Set mikes	Watch	Operate	
CAMERA CREW				(sometimes)	Operate	
RECORD OPERATOR					Run musical bridges, etc.	
WARDROBE				Check in costumes		
LIGHT MAN			Block out lighting	Watch dry run	Observe rehearsal	
LIVE MUSICIANS						
MAKE-UP MAN			KEY			
SOUND EFFECTS				Activities in which the Director is involved		
PROJECTION				Activities which do not involve the Director		
ANNOUNCER						
	8 AM	9	10	11	12:00	1

Chart 5.   Activity chart of VTR day: an analysis of hour-by-hour activities of all personnel involved in the show on the videotaping day. If the show were being taped before a live audience, the taping session might run on for

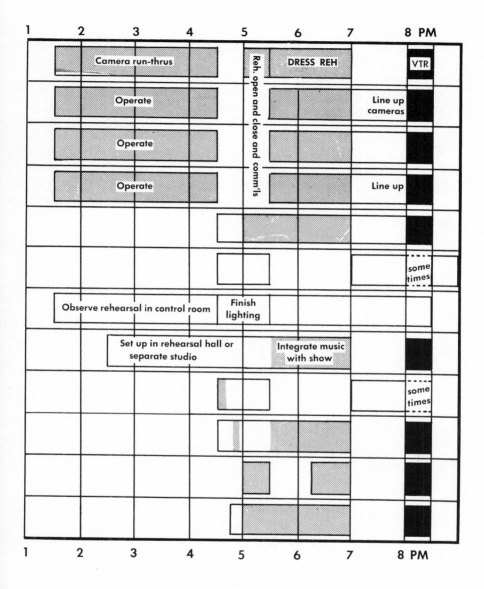

an hour, or be repeated for a second live audience at 10 P.M. If there were no audience, recording might go on until midnight, or be resumed for several hours on the following day.

twelve hours in the studio, sending out for coffee and sandwiches, and eating on the run. Ideally, camera rehearsals should be devoted to training the studio crew in the routine of camera shots that the director has firmly in mind. In practice, the director will usually find many things that he wishes to change once he sees the actual shots on the camera monitors. If he makes good use of his creative cameramen he may add or simplify according to their suggestions, or those of the technical director. There may be unusual or tricky shots that the director has planned and which can be finally decided upon only when the cameraman attempts to execute them. When very limited rehearsal time is available, however, the wise director will have already chosen his shots, and will simply direct each cameraman in the shots that are planned. This is better than trying out several ways of shooting the same action and choosing the best. When there is only a three-to-one rehearsal ratio, for example, there may not be enough time to work over anything twice, or even to run through the entire program in a dress rehearsal. In such cases, the director must come in with definite shots predetermined and hold to them. If he tries two or three possibilities for each shot, from which one is chosen, the cameraman and even the director may forget by the time the show is on the air or in the process of being taped which shot was decided upon. A quick job of memorization is required of everyone, and the simpler and more straightforward the rehearsal, the easier this task will be.

The director arrives in the studio early in the morning of the rehearsal day to inspect the set that has been erected. During the first hour, the director may familiarize himself with the set, checking on the various shots he has planned. The composition of the shots will often be different from what he has imagined, because the sets are now in place and these background elements will figure into the composition of every shot.

Ideally, the set should be dressed before rehearsals begin. By "dressing" is meant adding all the necessary bric-a-brac, pictures on the walls, curtains at the windows, and so forth. The scenic designer is usually present to discuss the set and make (or argue against) any changes the director may require and he will supervise the dressing of the set so the atmosphere is right. In very-low-budget shows this is something the director must do himself, sometimes in the last ten minutes before dress rehearsal or just before the show goes on the air.

The audio engineer will also be present and will want a script of the show and a general idea of where the dialogue will be coming from. He places his mike booms and other audio inputs where the director has suggested, unless he has better suggestions, and begins lacing microphone cables through the overhead pipe grid for whatever hanging microphones may be necessary.

The lighting engineer will be examining the set and finding out where the major playing areas are located so he can block out an arrangement of lights. He may have begun designing the lighting on the day before, working from a floor plan on which major playing areas have been indicated by the director. The lighting engineer will direct the stage electrician in the angling and placement of these basic lighting units. Any special lighting requirements are discussed with the director at this time.

The technical director, who works very closely with the director throughout the rehearsal day, is on the set during the first hour and taking part in all the above discussions, suggesting means of meeting the audio problems and the lighting requirements.

Meanwhile, the wardrobe man is busy receiving and checking in the costumes for the show, sending back for items that have been omitted, and verifying sizes and other details. If there is doubt about any item, he will take it to the studio and try it on the actor who must wear it, but usually he does not enter into the studio activities again until just before the dress rehearsal, when he supervises the dressing of the actors.

By mid-morning, the actors arrive to be shown their dressing rooms, take a first look at the set, and go through at least one complete run-through without stopping. This is for the benefit of the T.D., the floor manager, the audio man, the lighting man, and sometimes the cameramen, too, if they can be present. If there are moves for the stagehands to make during the production, it is valuable for them to be able to watch this dry run also. It puts a complete picture of the show in everyone's mind, which is very valuable at the beginning of the rehearsal. This is also the first opportunity that the actors will have had to use the actual furniture and hand props, and certain adjustments in staging may have to be made.

At about eleven o'clock, the entire technical staff is present, cameras have been adjusted technically (during the dry run), and the camera rehearsal is ready to begin. Some time may be lost before the camera cables are run to the most convenient outlets in the studio walls, and there are the inevitable technical delays when one or another piece of equipment fails to function properly and must be repaired or replaced by similar equipment from another studio. However, the fact that two hours have already been spent in the studio by the technical director and the audio man will eliminate most of these starting delays. If this preliminary time is not provided, the director often loses a full hour straightening out various technical problems before his rehearsal can actually begin.

Camera Blocking

Usually, an hour and a half of camera blocking is scheduled, with the entire crew in operation and the lighting man standing by in the control room to observe the lighting on the camera monitors. In many studios the electrician who operates the lights during the show will have his own monitor near the light-control board (or a remote-control unit for lighting may be in the control room). The lighting man will prefer to watch the rehearsals from the control room so he can be aware of each production problem as it comes up and discuss the lighting with the director and technical personnel whenever necessary.

In most situations, the first stage of camera rehearsal is called "camera blocking," and is usually understood to mean the working out of camera shots and coordination of camera and actor movement. "Camera run-throughs," which come later, constitute more complete rehearsals of the show with fewer interruptions. Each director, however, will have his own way of conducting a camera rehearsal, and it will be necessary here to describe several of the more common methods of procedure.

Methods of Studio Rehearsals

Some directors like to take the show as a whole and work it out as a unit, not going back over anything until the whole show is completed, and then run through the entire program immediately in a second rehearsal. Others take the show in tiny bits and pieces, perfecting each small part before going on to the next. Probably the majority of directors separate the show by scenes or acts, work through all the shots in each scene, and then go back and run the scene again to crystallize it all in everyone's mind. In summary, here are some of the most common methods:

A. Rehearse the show in its entirety.

Stage 1. Bulldoze your way through the entire production, stopping only at moments of complete confusion, paying no attention to shots that are missed, but simply telling the cameramen where they should have been and correcting errors later on in the next run-through.

Stage 2. Run a stop-start or stop-and-go (sometimes called the work-through or stagger-through) in which each shot is properly set.

Stage 3. Do a complete run-through, and a second run-through if time permits.

Stage 4. Do a dress rehearsal.

B. Rehearse the show in its entirety without the rough run-through at the beginning. Same as above without Stage 1.

C. Rehearse the show by sections, a scene at a time.
Stage 1. Run roughly through the scene to give everyone the general idea of the action.
Stage 2. Stop-start the scene, correcting each shot.
Stage 3. Run the scene over to crystallize it before going on to the next. (Repeat 1, 2, and 3 for each scene.)
Stage 4. Do one complete run-through of the entire show.
Stage 5. Do a dress rehearsal.

D. Rehearse the show by sections without the rough run-through at the beginning of each scene.

E. (Not recommended, but often done at smaller stations.) Stagger through the entire show, leaving ten minutes (hopefully) before taping or air time for last-minute corrections and instructions. *No run-throughs and no dress rehearsal.*

It would appear that the use of videotape makes methods C and D the most desirable, since each section, once rehearsed and perfected, could be recorded once and for all. Stages 4 and 5 of C would thus be eliminated, the fourth stage then being the taping of the scene instead.

The Work-Through

The most important stage of camera rehearsal, whichever method may be employed, is the stop-start work-through. It is during this period that the cameramen learn exactly where to place their cameras, the lens or zoom position for each shot, and the routine for cutting that the director will use. If there is no time for anything else, the work-through must be done. Many a production has gone on the air without a dress rehearsal, without a complete run-through of any kind, and come across to everyone's surprise as a successful show, simply because the camera shots had been properly worked out. It is of very little value to try for complete run-throughs if the cameramen are not clear on their shots. The work-through will take the major portion of the camera rehearsal time, and should not be curtailed, even if run-through or dress rehearsal might suffer.

The preferred procedure is to work through the show until late afternoon and try for one run-through before dinner. The dress-rehearsal period after dinner is long enough to allow for a second run-through as well as the dress rehearsal.

At the dinner break, when the studio crew goes out to eat, the lighting man can take over the set for any major changes of lights that he was not able to make during the afternoon rehearsals. Some of the cast may be scheduled to be made up at this time, usually eating sandwiches during the process. It is wise to begin make-up at this point, just in case the dress rehearsal runs late and there is not much leeway between rehearsal and air time. If there is a large cast, or complicated make-up to put on, it may easily be that the entire cast could not be taken care of by the make-up department during the period between seven and eight.

Before reporting at about 5:30 for dress rehearsals the actors are expected to get into costume. The wardrobe man will probably accompany the actors onto the set and make minor repairs and adjustments whenever he can find an odd moment during the rehearsal. The director's production assistant will have put down notes of things which had to be fixed but were not serious enough to stop the rehearsal, and the director (and the technical director, in many cases) will take up each of these things with the proper crew members, or members of the cast, before they get away.

The sound-effects man will have arrived just before the dinner break. The director will spend a few minutes with him, listening to the various possibilities in each case and making selections where necessary.

At 5:00 the director has scheduled the use of projection-room facilities and the assistant director will interrupt him in his various conferences in the studio and remind him that he had better rehearse his titles soon or he won't be able to rehearse them at all. Either he or the assistant will have delivered the necessary artwork (or film or slides as the case may be) to the projection room and settled with the projectionist which film channel will be used and just what cues are necessary to change from slide to slide. If prerecorded videotape inserts are to be used in the program, the director can watch them in the control room.

The director will check the framing of the titles, and their order, and will rehearse the opening and closing of the show. For this purpose, only a skeleton crew is necessary—the sound operator, the T.D., and the announcer. If the show uses film commercials, this may be the first time that the director sees these films, or he may not see them until they go on the air, run by a residue director from a film or master control studio. Since rarely is any attempt made to integrate film commercials into the action of the show, the director will need only know the timing and the general content, and the closing line or action at the end. This will cue him for the start of the studio action that follows. In programs prerecorded on videotape, the commercials may be edited in later.

At 5:30, if no one is delayed, the entire cast will be on the set in costume, carrying the last of their coffee and sandwiches with them, the live musicians who have been rehearsing in a separate studio will set up in the space provided (or stand by in their separate studio), and the director will make ready to integrate the entire show. The only things that might not be present are the titles and film from the projection room, since projection-room facilities cannot always be assigned for the entire dress-rehearsal period.

Last Run-Through and Dress Rehearsal

During the last run-through and the dress rehearsal, the director will try to keep going without interruption. If cameras or actors do things wrong, the director tells his production assistant to make notes about them. Only in the case of complete confusion does he stop the run-through. As soon as the run-through is over he takes his assistant with him and dashes out onto the floor to give everybody the corrections or changes he has noted down. The technical director will often assist him by taking the notes which apply to the cameramen and crew, gathering these people together and giving them their notes at the same time.

An accurate timing can be taken on the show only when the first continuous run-through is made; it is very difficult for the assistant director to achieve any accuracy in timing during the work-through period. If the show has been properly timed during out-of-studio rehearsal, the timings on these later run-throughs should not be too surprising, and should not entail any great changes in the script. However, a number of new factors are always introduced when the show is run on the set, with the cameras and the real props: the tempo of acting may change, or the actual time consumed in the movement of the actors may be different from what it was in the rehearsal hall.

Some directors rely heavily on their scripts, even up to the last dress rehearsal and air show. Others find that they have the show so well memorized by the time the camera work-through is completed that they no longer have to look at the script. Most directors will rely on the assistant director to follow the script during the show, however, and read off to him any cues which are not connected with the straight flow of the program. Advance warning to a cameraman to move his camera to a distant spot must be entered in the script a page or so ahead of the point where the camera is to be used in order to allow time for the move, and this necessity will probably be overlooked by the director unless he is reminded of it by someone who is carefully following the script.

Generally, a one-hour period is allowed between dress rehearsal and air time, for last-minute changes in every department. It also serves as a period of leeway in case the dress rehearsal is delayed. This time is badly needed by the make-up department and as much of it as possible should be used for this purpose. Sometimes, in productions where make-up and other last-minute preparations have not been necessary, the dress rehearsal has been allowed to run almost up to air time. This used to be common practice in radio production, but is not at all wise in television. As a matter of fact, the engineers in every station sooner or later put a limit on how close to air time the rehearsal can go, and automatically take the facilities away from the director for the last fifteen minutes before air, whether he likes it or not, simply because there is so much last-minute technical "lining up" to do. If more than fifteen minutes is allowed, the crew will be happier, and if there can be as much as an hour's leeway, a large part of this time will be spent in careful lining up and adjustment of cameras.

During this final hour the director will dash about from one person to another, checking on everything. Is the special-effects machine set up properly? Will this actor positively remember to come into the room *behind* the sofa instead of *in front?* Are the title cards in correct order? Does the floor manager have all the hand props ready and at the entrances where the actors can pick them up and carry them onto the set? The answers will always be yes to all these questions, yet there is the one time out of a hundred when the title cards are *not* in correct order, and the director is wise who checks on everyone, or who has his assistant check on everyone. This precaution may not be so necessary in a big commercial show where everyone feels the Great Importance of the undertaking and knows very well that an error will result in a change of personnel.

When air time comes, of course, everyone is on his toes. The test of good operating personnel—studio crew, actors, prop men, everyone—is that when the show goes on the air they can rise to a level of quicker thinking, faster reflexes, and more efficient operation. The excitement of going on the air does this for some; for others it undermines their efficiency by making them nervous and tense. A third group, usually those who have been in show business for many years, are completely unaffected by air time and go about their business in a routine and efficient way. Videotaping a whole program sometimes lowers the adrenaline level—unless the program is being recorded before a live audience.

The Control of Time

In spite of the most careful planning, the timing of a show, once it is in the studio, may come out quite different from what it was when the show was rehearsed outside. The show may be shorter if the tempo of the acting is speeded up under the tension of actually being on the air, or it may be longer if an actor has fluffed his lines and the cast has had to ad-lib for a while before getting back on the track. This time problem may not show up until the last few minutes of the show. Then something drastic such as padding by slowing down the credits must be done.

THE LIVE SHOW ON THE AIR

There can, of course, be no substitute for experience, but observation is the next-best thing. For the reader of this book who has never stood in a control room while a live television show was on the air, we have tried in the following pages to re-create what goes on during a typical broadcast of a live drama as it was done in the past. The taping of a situation-comedy performance in theatrical fashion (no stopping) before a live audience, or the live broadcast of a television soap opera, would be, in many ways, quite similar.

Before we begin, we feel it necessary to point out that our imaginary control-room events are set in a situation in which the director would be speaking directly to the cameramen, shifting cameras to their new positions from notes in his own script, and calling for changes of lenses or zooms himself.

Ready to come into the control room with us and watch a live production?

It is three minutes to air time, and the director has just relayed that information to the floor manager through the latter's headsets. The floor manager calls out, "Three minutes—stand by, please." Actors take their places, and quiet falls on the studio floor.

One minute later the director calls, "Two minutes," and once again the floor manager repeats the time. The technical director punches up the cue line on the preview monitor. The director with well-concealed anxiety glances at the blank screens in front of him, and then at the studio clock. "How about pictures?" he says. "All right," the T.D. says to the cameramen, "uncap cameras—opening shots."

Another minute has gone by and the one-minute signal has been passed down the line. The director calls for a preview of his opening title, which comes from the projection room. The T.D. calls down to the projectionist through his intercom, saying, "Stand by for Slide 27 on Chain 8." The director feels a sudden clutch of apprehension. "Is the announcer in the booth?" He stands up, cranes his neck, and peers through the control-room window. Two flats of the commercial set are between him and the announcer's booth. The floor manager appears around the corner of the set and gives the O.K. sign.

The slide comes up on the cue-line monitor as the second hand passes twenty seconds before air time. The director says, "Stand by on the music."

The inexorable second hand stands straight up, and on the cue-line monitor the network or station identification slide fades out. We're on the air!

The director calls out, in one breath, "Hit the music—fade-up opening slide!" And, as the first notes of the theme are heard, the T.D. smoothly moves his fading lever and the opening title of our program appears on the screen.

DIRECTOR: Music down and under—announcement!
The announcer reads his opening copy into his microphone, and, as it begins, the director is already saying, "Ready dissolve One." The T.D. punches another button on his switching panel and waits for the director's cue, as the announcer finishes.

DIRECTOR: Music up—dissolve One.
The T.D. moves his dissolve lever back. On our screen the main title blends into a live studio shot, the first shot of the show.

DIRECTOR: O.K., now, One. Pan right slowly and start dollying in.
The camera pans smoothly across the set.

DIRECTOR   (to floor manager): Cue actors!
The floor manager throws the cue to the actors, and, as the camera reaches them, they begin the opening business or lines of the show. Immediately the director's eye moves to the monitor screen of the camera which will take his next shot.

DIRECTOR: Just a little tighter, Three. (The camera zooms in a little closer.) Ready Three. . . . Take Three!
The T.D. punches the button that puts Camera Three's picture on the air and the show is well on its way.

So it goes, we hope, for the next twenty-eight or fifty-eight minutes, until we approach the last minute of our program. The director has once more proved that the best way to get over thin ice is to keep moving. Refusing to lament over fluffs, flubs, and bobbles, he has kept his mind and his eye on the shot coming up, forgetting whatever embarrassing aspect there may be to the shots that are past. At last the closing shot of the show is called.

DIRECTOR: Ready Three. . . . Take Three. Stand by on commercial film.

The T.D. alerts the projection room, and previews the first of the closing titles. The actor speaks the closing line and makes his final exit.

DIRECTOR: Roll film.
Bring in the music.
Fade out Three. Fade in film. We're on commercial.
How are we for time?

ASSISTANT DIRECTOR: Should have been into commercial film twenty seconds ago.

DIRECTOR (cheerfully): We'll just have to roll the titles fast! Projection! Give me a forty-second roll on titles instead of a minute! Ready to dissolve to titles.

The T.D. punches the appropriate button, and all watch the monitor on which the commercial film is now nearing its closing frames. The first cue mark flashes in the corner of the frame.

DIRECTOR: First cue. . . . Ready to dissolve. . . . Dissolve to titles.*

The T.D. moves the dissolving lever once again, and the closing credits float rapidly up the screen. Everybody takes a breath, and forty seconds later the last title is dissolved into the network or station identification slide by the engineers in master control.

T.D.: O.K., that's it.
DIRECTOR: Thanks a lot, everybody.

The show is over—but the director's work isn't. He will go out on the floor to thank his cast and crew, laugh at incidents which seemed agonizing just a few moments before, and generally reassure people that all went well—especially when it didn't. These polite amenities are constantly interrupted by stagehands pushing by with the scenery or props, as they make haste to clear the studio and start setting it up for the next show. What has taken hours to set up must be torn down in as few minutes as possible.

---

* In some large stations the assistant director takes over at the end of the show proper and puts the closing credits on the air.

In the midst of these somewhat confused farewells, an engineer calls to the director over the control-room intercom: "You're wanted on the phone!" The director heads for the nearest telephone with all the eagerness of a condemned man heading for the execution chamber. The caller may be only his wife, but it is even more likely to be the sponsor or the advertising agency that handles the account. It's the account executive of the agency, all right, who has noticed none of the horrible blunders, but is quite upset about the style of the lettering on the new title cards. The agency man adds, however, that he has been watching the show with the sponsor and his wife, and that both were very pleased.

The director heads for his overcoat, a cup of coffee, and home. Tomorrow may or may not bring a day off, but it is sure to bring another script on which the first week's work has already been done. And the whole cycle begins again.

11 / Film and Videotape

Film and videotape are media which, while they can both exist entirely separate from television broadcasting, provide a large proportion of the program material used by television stations. This may include motion-picture features made originally for theatrical release, features made originally for television (but which may also be later shown in theatres), and half-hour episodes of television series that are produced on film or videotape. In addition to this, film and videotape are common production elements in television programming; it is in this connection that we shall take the greatest interest in them. Finally, videotape, at least, is used constantly at all television production centers for recording and playing back programs—a storage-and-delay process, if you like—making it possible to produce and record a program at a time that is most convenient to studio and performers, and to transmit it at a time most convenient for its audience.

FILM PROJECTION EQUIPMENT

Every television studio, except the very simplest or most temporary, will have a "film chain." This may consist of no more than a standard 16mm film projector projecting into a small television camera. When more than one projector is required, the station will have what is called a "film island." This is a cluster of several projectors (usually at least two 16mm projectors and one or two slide projectors of the 35mm size) surrounding a television camera. The projectors are directed into a "multiplexer"—a series of mirrors, prisms, or lenses—which allows any of the images projected from the several sources to be channeled into the television camera. The number of film chains per studio ranges from only one to highly complex facilities such as the BBC's news room with its sixteen film chains.

Associated with the film projection room, but often occupying a space

193

of its own, a station usually will have several videotape machines. These are usually capable of both recording and playing back programs, as audio tape recorders are, although there are some machines that perform only one of these functions.

Plate 22.   Film pick-up camera and multiplexer. The addition of three projectors (film or slide) shooting into the three sides of the multiplexer at the right would form a film island. Camera is in unit at left, with local operating controls (used for set-up, preview, etc.). Monitor above functions as a "viewfinder" for the film pick-up camera. (Courtesy of International Video Corporation)

VIDEOTAPE PRODUCTION

In television studio production today, most programs are taped in segments that are later assembled by an editor. In producing a variety show, for example, the skits may be taped on one day and the song-and-dance numbers on another. A guest star may come in for an exclusive taping of his numbers. A variety show, then, may be done not only in two or three separate taping days, but even in different studios. Except that segments each consisting of many shots are recorded, and it is these chunks that are later assembled, videotape production is similar to film production. In film, of course, every shot is taken separately.

Another technique, characteristic of many small-budget stations and student productions, is almost like live television production. Using this method, the director, cast, and crew attempt to tape an entire production at once, going as far as they can until something goes wrong. They then back up the tape until they find a good edit point (a cut to another shot, a different set, or a fade to black). Having started taping again

Plate 23. Broadcast standard videotape recorder: Ampex AVR-1. Accommodates two-hour reels; playback is completely under automatic control; contains its own sync generator. (Courtesy of Ampex Corporation)

and gone safely past the point in the program where the mistake or technical problem had occurred, the production is continued until it is completed or another problem arises. The director's goal in this is to reduce post-production editing to an absolute minimum.

Videotaping could be, and was expected to be, as fast and efficient as live production, but it could never make it, except in cases of sheer economic necessity. Actors were far more likely to blow their lines than in live television, and directors felt free to retake as often as they liked. (Frequently a director, even in film, will make a long series of takes, and in the end use the first one.) Moreover, a director is not quite as keyed up and alert when he knows that if he makes a mistake he can always retake. It happened in radio when audio tape came in, and it happened again in television.

FILM STANDARDS

It was early in the history of film production that the 35-mm-width standard was adopted, although many others had been proposed. Later the 16mm size was agreed upon for amateur uses, followed by 8mm and much later by Super-8mm, which uses a film of the same width but with a much larger picture area. The 70mm width was specially developed for wide-screen theatre presentation. Network and complex production facilities use 35mm equipment for the most part, but smaller stations make great use of 16mm because it is easier to handle in comparison to 35mm and is considerably less expensive all around. Though Super-8mm film is used by some television stations, relatively few are equipped to project film in this format.

The 16mm film can be utilized in either of two formats: silent (with no sound printed or incorporated on the film) or SOF (Sound On Film). Many small stations use silent film for newcasts and other production requirements, and, as will be discussed in Chapter 12, silent film can be televised directly in negative (using polarity reversal), eliminating the cost of having a positive print made. Sound news film with a separate sound track is also often run this way.

The sound track on SOF film is either *optical* or *magnetic*. While many stations have equipment that can handle both, the most commonly used is still optical sound. Most non-theatrical sound films are distributed in this format.

VIDEOTAPE STANDARDS

Physically, videotape is very similar to audio tape. Magnetic tape is coated on one side with a film of iron-oxide particles. When an electronic signal comes from a camera or other video source and is fed into the videotape recorder, the electrical impulses magnetize the iron-oxide particles on the videotape—thus "imprinting" the picture on the tape just as audio tape is magnetized by the pattern of electrical energy that comes originally from a microphone.

As with film, videotape is available in various sizes or "formats": two-inch, one-inch, three-quarter-inch, half-inch, and quarter-inch. At present, two-inch videotape equipment is used by most stations because of its superior quality. Rapid development is being made, however, in an attempt to bring other formats up to broadcast standards.

Broadcast Standard Recorders

The original broadcast standard system uses two-inch videotape, recording video tracks across it from one edge to the other at a rate of about 50 to the inch. Sometimes called "quad head" (four recording heads), the VTR machine drives the tape at either 15 inches per second or 7½ i.p.s. when somewhat less quality is a reasonable sacrifice to make for half the tape cost. Most of the area of the tape is used for video-recording. A narrow audio track runs along one edge of the tape; a third track, a control track, runs along the other edge. This consists of the sync pulses that are used to synchronize the videotape recorder signal with the signals of the studio system's production, monitoring, and transmission facilities. The control track is also used for a "cue track" which is utilized in editing. The control track can also be simultaneously used as a second audio track. For example, the director's comments and commands over the intercom system could be recorded for teaching purposes. An interesting facet of this system is that the audio and video information may be recorded separately. Thus, in some studios, an engineer may "lay in" the audio track (such as mood music) first, before the video is recorded, or add it later.

The Helical Scanning Process

All portable, low-cost VTR recorders, whether they use one-inch, three-quarter-inch, half-inch, or quarter-inch tape, are based on the helical scanning design. In the helical scanning machine, either one or two heads spin horizontally inside a vertical cylinder around which the tape moves in a spiral or helix (hence helical). While the heads spin, the tape winds gradually downwards until its wrap is complete, then it is taken up on a rewind spool. Thus a recording or playback head inside the cylinder first contacts the tape at its bottom edge, then makes a long slanting track across the tape, and leaves the tape by its top edge. Meanwhile the tape moves slightly forward so a second track may be laid down just behind the first by the next passage of a head. Most helical scan machines record an entire frame (1/30 sec.) on each slanting track. Thus when the movement of the tape is slowed in playback, the playback head plays each track more than once, producing the slow-motion effect. When the forward motion of the tape is stopped, a

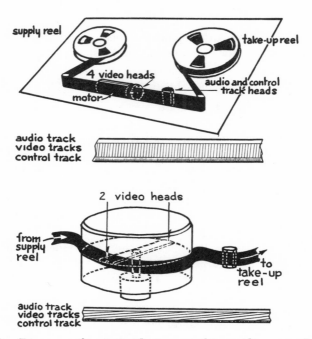

Figure 48.   Diagrams of typical videotape machines. *Above:* standard broadcast type: four heads, transverse track, 2-inch-wide tape. *Below:* one type of helical scan recorder: two heads, slant track, ½-inch tape.

single track is played back over and over, producing a still picture. As in the quad system, the audio track runs along one edge of the tape, the control track (with the sync-pulse information) along the other.

EDITING TECHNIQUES

Conventional film editing involves two main steps: (1) the breakdown and proper ordering of the rolls of film that come to the editor with the shots in the order in which they were exposed in the camera, and (2) the trimming of heads and tails from each shot and joining them together in a smooth and creative fashion. The editor usually divides the work print he is given for editing purposes into small rolls of individual shots or takes, labeling these and putting them in the correct order. When he begins to assemble the film he may have to choose between several takes for the best shot to use, and he must project them for himself on a small viewer, an essential part of his editing equipment. He may also hang a large number of takes and shots on a rack above a large clean barrel, so he can reach them quickly and make his decisions as rapidly as possible. At best, however, conventional film editing is a time-consuming process, often taking weeks to edit a half-hour film.

Videotape Editing

The editing of videotape allows the producer of a program, as in film, the freedom of shooting scenes in the most convenient sequence and assembling them later into the proper order. One method of tape editing is mechanical: the tape is actually cut physically (as in film editing) and taped together. Because physical cutting lessens the life of the tapes, and splices can wear or damage the videotape recorder heads, mechanical editing has been largely replaced by electronic editing.

Electronic editing is actually rerecording. While this can be done with any two videotape machines, one playing back while the other records, it is not possible to assemble two segments together without a few moments of picture break-up between them. For smooth cuts a VTR machine with "editing capability" or a separate device known as an "editor" or "editing control system" is required. The editor has the ability to recognize predetermined sync pulses on the control track at the edit point, and places the new material on the tape without picture roll.

Two helical-scan VTR machines are shown in Plate 24, set up for editing with an editing control system between them. The recorder on the left, on which the roll of original material is placed, is sometimes called the "master" and the other the "slave." When the editor is ready to make a tape-to-tape edit, the first of the two shots to be joined will have been recorded on the right-hand (No. 2) machine. Using the slow-motion and freeze-frame capabilities, the editor first selects the point at which he wants to end the shot and cut to the next picture. With the reel containing the second shot on the left-hand VTR, he then runs that tape back and forth until he selects an edit point where he wishes the second shot to begin. With the system in "Edit rehearse" mode, he can then rehearse the edit, without recording anything, to see if his judgment was correct. When he is satisfied, he puts the system into "Perform edit" mode and presses the "Roll" button. The edit is then made as desired, and the rerecording of the tape from the left-hand to the right-hand machine continues until manually stopped.

What actually happens is this: When the "Edit rehearse" or "Perform

Plate 24. Equipment set up for editing one-inch videotape. Master VTR, for original recorded material, on left; slave VTR, on which final edited tape is being assembled, on right. Between them is TRI EA-5 Editing Control System. (Courtesy of Television Research International Inc.)

edit" button is pushed, both machines run backwards a predetermined distance and stop. (The term "park" is often used for this action when it is done manually.) When the editor is ready, he pushes the "Roll" button and both machines start, come up to speed together, and the cut occurs at the exact moment the editor has selected, both picture and sound.

Camera-to-tape editing may also be done with a VTR that has editing capability, or with the addition of an editor. This is the technique that is used for electronic single-frame animation. The edit point is first selected on the videotape, and cued to automatically roll back to its parking spot. With the camera feeding the desired next shot, the editor may either rehearse his edit or perform it by pressing the "Roll" button.

The most important step in editing is the planning of what is desired on the final version. During the original taping, record two- or three-second pauses on the beginnings and endings of segments where you may want to edit. It is easy to shorten a recorded segment but it is impossible to lengthen it. When recording on location, it will save later editing time if you plan your production so that segments are recorded in the order in which they will be used. Sequences can always be changed in the final editing.

The recorded material should be previewed as much as time permits and possible edit points noted, using both visual and audio cues as reference points. There is one basic technical problem to keep in mind —any technical problem on the original tape is always amplified when the tape is edited. Drop-outs,* crinkled tape, etc., can, therefore, influence the selection of material to be included in the final edited tape.

POST-PRODUCTION

Post-production may be defined as putting the final touches on a nearly completed videotaped (or filmed) commercial or program, or as the total combining of bits and pieces of videotape into a full unit, ready for broadcast. The process may range from a relatively simple procedure such as the addition of opening titles and closing credits, to modifying a sound track by working in sound effects, music, or narration, up to combining dozens of short pieces of tape into a full reel—to say nothing of replacing a short scene, in which something went wrong, by inserting a similar equally long sequence recorded at another time.

Titling

When a program is produced in a station, the titles and credits are usually recorded along with the program. In other cases, titles may be recorded later and edited into the program (see the videotape editing section in this chapter).

Titles may be achieved graphically, using artwork for background with titles printed on the background material, or may be produced electronically by using a machine called a "character generator." When a character generator is used, the credits are generally "typed" in advance and recorded on a disc in the machine until needed. They may appear on a black screen or superimposed on a pictorial background.

An electronic roll is often used to move credits up the screen as if on a title drum. These credits may be keyed or matted in over any source— slide, studio card, a shot of the last part of the videotape, a "frozen

---

* Drop-outs are short white streaks that flash in the picture area, caused by impurities or irregularities in the magnetic coating.

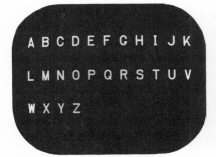

Plate 25.   Typical character generator. This system incorporates "floppy disc" storage; each 8-inch disc can store 1000 pages of alphanumeric display. Each page is addressed and can be retrieved in 0.5 second. A page contains 10 rows of 22 characters each. Will roll (bottom to top) or crawl (right to left) at various speeds, and flash individual words. *Lower left:* input keyboard; *lower right:* numeric key set, to address and retrieve stored titles, and disc memory in rack mount. (Courtesy of Datavision Video Products, 3M Company)

frame" of performers on the set, a shot of an empty set, or any other background.

Dubbing

After a program has been recorded and edited, the problem of distribution arises. Network prime-time programs are sent directly to affiliates through a relay system spanning the country. Other programs, such as evening newcasts, are sent several times for broadcast by affiliates in one of several time slots.

In a non-network situation, most distribution is done by mail. This requires the station or production center to copy, or "dub," each program many times for mass distribution. The procedure requires at least two videotape recorders, one for playback of the original program and one for recording the dub. An extension of this is practiced when multiple copies of a program are required. National Educational Television, Inc., in Ann Arbor, Michigan, and the State University of New York (SUNY) in Albany, New York, use a high-speed recorder (ten times normal speed) that runs a mirror-image master tape in contact with five other tapes in succession, thus making five copies. A more recent system which uses a high-speed dubbing device can transfer a one-hour video-tape to five slaves on the same machine in less than ten minutes.

Dubbing tapes of broadcast quality requires competent engineering staff to interconnect the videotape recorders, compatible equipment, and sufficient time for distribution. An original videotape can be dubbed hundreds of times, much like the film negative used to make release prints for theatres. Dubbing a half-inch videotape, perhaps of a program which a student director wishes to use as a sample of his work when seeking employment, is well within the reach of most students.

To sum up, videotape editing, post-production, and dubbing are techniques whose mechanics can readily be learned under the watchful eye of a sympathetic engineer. To quote Richard Marcus, former engineer and producer of the BBC: "The mechanical aspects of editing, both in film and in videotape, are relatively easily taught to intelligent people, provided the equipment is reliable enough to be operated by push buttons. The creative aspects, however, are something quite different." It is clear, then, that editing is far from being merely a physical or technical operation, and that the creative producer or director cannot relinquish control of editing, except in cases of the very simplest tasks of assembly.

12 / Special Production Elements and Techniques

We turn now to certain visual elements which can enhance or severely detract from the finished television production. We would point out that the catalogue that follows is intended, like the information in Chapter 6, to provide only an introduction to these elements, not a handbook for their use. To describe them in detail would take far more space than we can allot in this volume. Here, however, the reader can get a quick overall view of at least seven of these special tools of production.

VISUAL ELEMENTS IN THE STUDIO

In producing any but the simplest television production, consideration must be given to the production elements of make-up, costumes, settings and props.

Make-up

With the present size of the television screen, the close-up is the all-important shot, and the face of the performer (with the exception of the dancer) is a key instrument of dramatic communication. In a non-dramatic presentation, such as a newscast or an educational program, a chest shot or a waist shot is commonly used, but the face of the performer must be featured if the viewer is to feel in contact with him.

For detailed instructions on make-up, the reader is referred to the volume mentioned below,* but he is reminded that television make-up need not be elaborate. In nondramatic programs, just a touch of pancake may add greatly to the total effect, although many small stations do not

---

* For a book on make-up, the reader is referred to Vincent J. R. Kehoe, *The Technique of Television Make-up* (New York: Focal Press, 1969).

bother with make-up at all, except for actors and singers. There is no denying that "five-o'clock shadow" makes a difference in the appearance of any announcer or interviewer; so, too, does the shine on the glowing scalp of a distinguished authority. Here, then, are a few simple general suggestions that have been found helpful.

In most cases, use cake make-up, not grease paint. Cake make-up is easier to apply and to remove, and much cooler. Use the shades recommended for television by the manufacturer, such as Max Factor's Pancake N series, Nos. TV–1N (light pastel pink) to TV–11N (deep brown). The Pancake series for color television is CTV–1W through CTV–12W.

For men, remember that you are not trying to make them look handsome—you just want them to look clean and well groomed. Cover but do not entirely obliterate the beard, which makes itself present on camera long before five o'clock; a grease-base make-up called Beard Stick is commonly used for this. Often no other make-up is needed by a man, unless he has a high forehead or balding scalp that needs special attention. This tends to be oily and may show the reflections of a neat row of studio lights, so we use pancake right up to a substantial hairline, even though it makes thinning hair even thinner.

For women, ordinary street make-up is usually sufficient. It is best to suggest the use of a medium- or dark-red shade of lipstick for black-and-white television. Pink and orange lipstick are too light in tone—they register the same as flesh and look like no lipstick at all. Pink, however, is usually used in color television.

Whatever make-up you use, try to check it on camera ten minutes or so before air time, so that you can change it if it looks strange or artificial. No attempt has been made to describe character make-up for drama in this limited space, but two rules we might mention are:

1. Don't use so much make-up that it will *show* as make-up in close-ups. Just as stage make-up can look pretty horrible when you meet an actor backstage, it is not suitable for the closeness of the television camera.

2. Not only be sure to check make-up on camera well before air time, but if you do make any changes, be sure to check the change—the "improvement" may be worse than the original condition.

Costumes

As used here, the term "costumes" is intended to include the everyday clothing worn by guests on panel shows, as well as the specially designed and selected costumes provided for actors, singers, and dancers.

Almost all kinds of everyday clothing may be worn on television, with only a few notable exceptions. Black, in large amounts, such as dark suits or dresses when seen in close shots, can put a strain on the television system and thwart the video engineer's attempts to present a suitable picture. It is difficult to show the shape of black or very dark objects; wrinkles and shadow sides do not show up as a darker tone, because the entire object registers as black. This phenomenon is usually due to the presence of small areas of very light or bright white tones somewhere in the picture.

Even small areas of pure white in a scene containing, for the most part, tones in the middle range will cause too great a contrast and again strain the camera—and the video engineers. While it can and has been done, it requires everything in perfect working order, new tubes in the camera, particularly skilled men on the video controls, and these conditions cannot always be relied upon. The once familiar masculine uniform of navy-blue suit, white shirt, and black or dark-blue tie is still a good one to avoid. Most television performers keep a wardrobe of pastel-colored shirts, which look perfectly white on monochromatic television and, when worn with the correct colors, will also look good on color television.

A black halo effect, sometimes called "flare," often surrounds white areas when the image-orthicon camera tube attempts to cope with excessive contrast. The vidicon will exhibit a "sticking picture" under these conditions; the image tends to disappear slowly, causing smear if the object is moving, or a momentary ghost effect where the white object has just been. A black streak to the right of the white area may also occur.

While objects such as sequins occasionally appear on network programs, they require careful lighting. Flashing metallic surfaces, such as earrings or brooches or tie clasps, will sometimes reflect key light so strongly as to be ringed with a black halo. Long dangling earrings are distracting, especially when swinging in pendulum fashion, even when not composed of highly reflective surfaces.

When it comes to monochrome television, color or hue is not as important as *value*. Value (sometimes called "tone" or "shade") may be roughly defined as the degree of lightness or darkness in a given color, as a dark red or a light green. Similar values of different hues will look alike on black-and-white television, whereas different values of the same color will look entirely different. Thus a light-green tie on a light-brown shirt may register as the same tone of gray and disappear against the shirt. Ditto the light-blue bathing suit against the pink girl. When contrast is desired, we must make sure that there is sufficient variation in value, and not be misled by a difference in hue.

Whenever there is any doubt about the suitability of the costume a person intends to wear, it is a good rule to have him bring two outfits to the studio, so that one may be substituted for the other if difficulties develop. With experience, the producer or director soon learns which combinations of color, value, and material are safe and which ones to avoid as dangerous.

Settings

The term "settings" is used here, rather than "scenery," in order to suggest a wider scope—to include the entire studio background. The French term *décor* might serve better, since this brief discussion will include not only the scenery but also the properties, or "props," and set dressings.

In general, television studios tend to use five types of scenery: drapes, cycloramas, flats and other modular units, set pieces, and projected scenery. Drapes are usually suspended from tracks, or "travelers," along

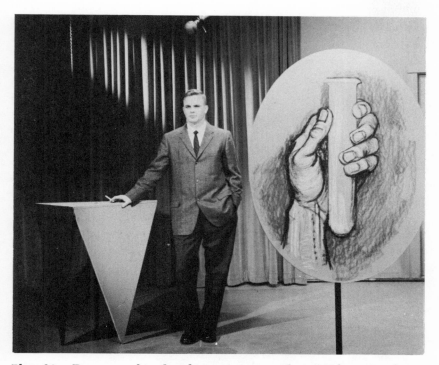

Plate 26.   Drapes combined with set pieces provide a simple setting for an educational program on chemical engineering. Note that the drapes can be moved aside to reveal a hard wall. (Courtesy of the University of Michigan)

which they travel to open and close, and may be shirred into interesting folds. They are useful in that they can provide a background for any number of programs with very little modification.

Cycloramas, or "cycs," are smooth expanses of cloth, usually suggesting an unending stretch of sky. They may be light or dark in original color, or may be made to look lighter or darker (in black-and-white television) by varying the lighting. In color production, colored lights change the hue of a neutral cyc to a marked degree. Like drapes, cycs may be used alone or may be combined with set pieces. Plate 27 shows a background cyc.

Flats are the familiar units of canvas or plywood on wooden frames, traditional in the theatre, and are often used in television to provide realistic settings. Flats are the most common example of scenery that is made in standard sizes, or modules, large units being just twice or three times the dimensions of smaller units so they may be combined in a variety of ways and will always fit. Four by eight feet is a common module; both four-by-four and two-by-eight units, for example, may be combined with these.

Set pieces are generally small units of scenery used against a background of some sort, usually a cyclorama. They can be stylized frames,

Plate 27. Set pieces and a cyclorama provide an imaginative setting for a series dealing with our legal heritage, *The Blessings of Liberty.* (Courtesy of the University of Michigan)

screens, columns, or what have you, or they may be realistic representations of rocks, tree trunks, or, when done on a small scale, distant buildings or hills. Flats and other modular units are often used as set pieces standing free, or in small groups against a cyclorama or drape background.

Theatrical scenery is generally made of muslin or light canvas on wood frames so it can be quickly moved about backstage or shipped along with a touring company. Since this degree of portability is not necessary in the television studio, most television scenery is considerably more substantial. (Motion-picture scenery is the other extreme; it is often built in place, and as solidly and carefully, in many cases, as the original that it represents.) Standard lumber-yard materials, such as striated plywood, peg board, Upson board, Masonite, and various simulated wood-grain textures are regularly used in building television scenery. Some studios have mounted sets of styrofoam on wooden frames.

Projected scenery involves transparent glass slides and a projector that throws the image either on a cyclorama from the front or upon a translucent screen from the reverse side. The latter is called a "process screen" in film studios and, more often, a "rear-projection screen" or "R.P. screen" in television studios. It is very versatile, permitting rapid changes and a wide variety of backgrounds, but it presents definite problems and has limitations, particularly in lighting and in the placement and movement of performers.

Some of the most effective television production, both dramatic and nondramatic, has been done without scenery at all. Of course, this is not strictly true, for if no scenery were used, studio walls and wiring would be visible; a cyclorama of some kind is employed. If this is a gray or light-colored cyc, the effect is generally known as "space staging." Action may be staged in foreground, middle distance, and background and there is much opportunity for creative lighting to play an effective role.

Settings, however, consist of more than scenic backgrounds. Furniture and properties, or "props," have been with us in show business since the days of the Greeks, and they are prominent in writings about the Elizabethan theatre. It may be helpful to think of props as "set props" and "hand props." Set props are items of furniture: chairs, tables, sofas, pianos, and benches which are generally required for the action of the program; a table for discussants or panelists would be a set prop. Hand props, as the name implies, are carried on by hand or are handled by the performers.

"Set dressings," on the other hand, are not called for by the writer or by the exigencies of the action. They are provided by the designer to give the setting completeness or atmosphere. Drapes, pictures, cushions, statuary, bric-a-brac, and incidental furniture which may never be sat upon would all constitute set dressing. Using the same neutral flats, for example, a skilled designer could add a field-stone fireplace, a rusty old harpoon and a fish net on the wall, fishing or lobster buoys in the corners, and thus create a Cape Cod fisherman's cottage. By decorating the same walls with an extremely modern and sophisticated batch of pictures and other ornaments, including lighting fixtures, he could suggest a swank New York apartment. Set dressings, in short, are not *used,* but *seen,* and thus add much to the illusion created by the scenery.

SPECIAL STUDIO EFFECTS

Within the means of most television studios are many effects that can enrich a production if they are used with discretion. Some of these effects can be achieved with the equipment on hand, without the need of extra gadgets and requisitions to the special-effects department. Other effects can be done optically with prisms, mirrors, or masks in front of the camera. Some effects are achieved electronically—by means of the electrical circuits within the camera or by the addition of further electronic equipment.

Many special effects derive directly from the theatre or from films—as, for example, rain, snow, cobwebs, and bursts of flame. Other effects are specifically born of television—as in the case of electronic effects. We may divide the subject into two classifications: "studio effects" (those produced in the studio by whatever means) and "electronic effects" (those involving the camera or control-room equipment). Another, more detailed method would be to classify special effects according to the means used in producing them. One such classification system would include optical, chemical, mechanical, and electronic effects. A few examples of each are provided below, with the by now familiar warning that a whole college semester could be spent in the study, design, and execution of special effects, and that a book the size of this one might well be devoted to them.

Optical Effects

As it is used here, the term "optical effects" includes simulations created by the employment of mirrors, prisms, or lenses. Such devices may involve glass that is silvered, polished, cut, or shaped to permit unusual reflection or refraction of light. Mirrors are used in a number of different ways in television, but most often to obtain an unusual angle and thus produce an illusion that either the camera or the subject occupies a physical position which would not in actuality be practicable. A pair of large mirrors, acting as a studio periscope, may make it possible for an ordinary studio camera to provide what seems to be an extreme low-angle shot, an extreme high-angle shot, or even a top shot from directly overhead.

A mirror may be used to turn an image upside down, and so may a prism, usually with greater convenience, since it may be mounted directly in front of the lens. In general, prisms are used to invert images, or to cant and roll them, as in the case of the rolling ship. A 90-degree cant produces the effect of the space man walking up the side wall of his space ship. Multiple-image prisms will repeat the same subject in several parts of the frame, as in the case of the harassed business executive's telephone which suddenly becomes three or four phones and which may even rotate madly about.

There are several types of prisms which can be affixed to the front of the camera lens to produce these various optical effects. The *image inverter* is perhaps the most commonly used. This may be a *dove prism* or a large *right-angle prism* placed on the lens in such a way that the camera looks directly through it in the longest dimension. It has the effect of reversing left and right in the same manner as a mirror. Then, if it is rotated, the left-right reversal will gradually become a top-bottom reversal, and the picture will turn upside down. Such a prism can be mounted in a free-turning mount controllable by means of a crank from the back of the camera so it can be rotated continuously if desired. Trick effects, such as building a set upside down and then reversing both set and actors so the actors seem to be dancing on the ceiling, have utilized this *image inverter*.

One of the famous *Garroway at Large* programs, in the late forties, really had fun with the inverted screen. Characters jumped about from floor to ceiling; Dave appeared first right side up, then upside down, in an attempt to keep up with them, and finally came back after titles for his usual closing gag, this time upside down and with his back to the camera. "Chicago," he said, "from you to came program this."

The *multiple-image prism,* used in front of the lens to produce a multiple image of the subject, is a piece of glass the back side of which is perfectly flat, but the front side is ground in several flat facets sloping slightly from the center to the outside. A two-facet prism will produce a double image, a three-facet prism a triple image, and so forth. A great variety of these prisms are available and have been used in the motion-picture field for years in the production of film trailers, commercials, and the like. Some of these prisms produce a central image of the subject surrounded by several more images around the border of the picture. Rotation of the prism will then rotate these border images in a ring around the central picture. (They stay vertical, it should be noted, instead of turning upside down.)

Chemical Effects

Chemical effects are used for flame and smoke, for the most part. Among the more common examples are the following:

Dry ice (frozen carbon dioxide). If this is combined with boiling water, the normal vapor evaporating from the water will condense into heavy clouds of real fog.

Titanium tetrachloride. This is a liquid which, when poured into a receptacle, will provide a dense white smoke from a relatively small quantity of fluid. This smoke is very effective visually and rises naturally, but is somewhat acrid and actors hate it.

Ammonium chloride, whether formed by passing the vapors of ammonium hydroxide over those of hydrochloric acid, or used in its solid form (a white powder) and heated, will provide a white, rising smoke, which is also quite acrid.

Magnesium powder, reacting to an electric current passed through fuse wire, will deliver a fine flash indeed, and mixing a little ammonium chloride in with it will add more smoke to the flash.

Sterno, or "Canned Heat," is a safe source of flame, whether in metal troughs between the asbestos logs of a fire or in a classic brazier in a Roman or Greek temple. Adding a little common table salt to the Sterno will make the ordinarily pale-blue flame burn with a bright-yellow color, more readily visible to the monochrome camera.

Mechanical Effects

Mechanical effects run a wide range. They may be as large and elaborate as the "snow sheets" or "cradles," which provide a blizzard on cue, or as small as a "rain drum." A spinning disc may be used for the transitional device known as the spiral, or whirligig. The disc may also be used for the mounting of a number of still photos which begin to whirl, first slowly, then more rapidly until they blur.

Snow falling through slits in a canvas "cradle" may be made of Pablum, of granules of styrofoam, or of white confetti salvaged from printing-shop waste. Styrofoam granules seem to provide the best "snow," while "rain" may drop from perforated pipes.

Electronic Effects

Probably the simplest effect to be created with the electronic equipment is the superimposure. In one respect this can be thought of as the mid-point of a dissolve, since there are two images on the screen at once. However, at the mid-point of a dissolve, both images are at half strength, a condition that is not always best for a superimposure. In the case of a super of white letters against a pictorial background, for instance, both cameras must usually be at full strength, so the super is made differently from a dissolve. Composition is important; it is usually best to arrange two pictures that are to be superimposed so that important areas of one fall upon dark areas of the other; light-toned or busy subjects tend to confuse or obscure each other when superimposed. The super can have decorative value, as in the case of a dancer superimposed over the strings or a harp or guitar. While it is tempting, especially to the new director, to use superimpositions frequently, these effects should be reserved until a real purpose or a real value can be achieved.

Two types of electronic reversal are possible with most camera equipment, at least with slight adaptation. *Reversal of polarity* changes blacks to white, and whites to black, resulting in a negative image on the screen. By the same token a negative will appear as positive. News programs frequently save time and money by shooting, and editing, in negative film, and using the negative on the air, reversing polarity for a positive image. All film-chain cameras are equipped with a switch for this purpose. Occasionally a weird effect, a "witch dance" for instance, will be produced in negative by reversing polarity in a studio camera. Color cameras do not provide the option of polarity reversal, but color saturation (distortion) can give a somewhat equivalent effect.

A picture can be reversed from left to right, or turned upside down, by the process known as *scanning reversal;* it is sometimes employed to correct the reversing effect of a single mirror or a prism. Extra wiring in the camera is required, but this can be installed in short order and provided with a switch with which the cameraman can reverse the camera's scanning.

The reader will remember that the television picture is produced by scanning an optical image on the face of the camera tube by means of a tiny beam of electrons. Sweeping back and forth, it analyzes the picture into 525 horizontal lines. All cameras, monitors, and home receivers synthesize a picture in the same manner, beginning in the upper left-hand corner. If, however, a camera is altered so it starts scanning from the upper right, for example, the monitors and receivers are not going to know this, and will continue to start from the left, placing whatever information the camera picks up from the right side of its screen on the left side of theirs. The picture will then be reversed in the horizontal dimension.

The beam control is located on the camera control unit and is adjusted by the video engineer. The television picture can be made to turn negative by decreasing the beam control very slightly below its proper setting. Moving the beam control can also give the impression of lightning, sudden bright lights, or explosions.

In keying or matting, the pictures from two sources are combined to make a composite picture that seems to derive from a single camera. In contrast to a superimposition, however, the first picture is electronically inserted into the second so they do not show through one another. When titles are "keyed in" to a closing scene, they are clearer and more opaque than when they are superimposed. When two cameras are combined in this fashion it is said that one is "keyed in" to the other. The second is thus called the "background" camera, although it may frequently contribute foreground elements of a scene, as when the keyed-in portion consists of the view through a window or the windshield of a car. It is the presence of certain keying tones, or colors, in the background shot that determines what areas will be keyed in. In blackand-white television the keying tone is black; any area of pure black anywhere in the shot will key in a corresponding area of the second picture. Thus contrasty lighting must be avoided or shadow areas will key in something unexpectedly. In color television, where the process is known as Chroma-Key, the color is blue. In CBS coverage of political conventions, for example, Walter Cronkite appeared to sit before a window that looked down on the convention hall. In actuality he sat in a studio before a blue screen, which keyed in a window-shaped area from the shot taken by a second camera placed high in the convention hall. Chroma-Key blue cannot, of course, be used in sets and costumes when keying is to be done; it must be limited only to the area to be keyed in.

SUMMARY

There is no part of television production that is more tempting to work with than special effects. While few of the possible effects are unique to television, many can be accomplished in other media only with much more trouble and expense. Special effects, moreover, can be the most technically challenging and stimulating part of production. Thus, they sometimes lead the young director or producer to overlook the much more basic and important challenge to his imagination and ingenuity provided by the problems of content and structure in a program.

Perhaps it will help if a beginning director who is about to use a special effect asks himself the following questions:

1. Will the use of this effect really enhance the production and make it more effective, or will it merely provide distracting trickery?

2. Will the gain in effectiveness be worth the sacrifice of time, both in advance preparation and in studio rehearsal, that the use of this effect will cost?

3. Am I sure that it will work?

Perhaps it will not help to ask these questions the first few times the opportunity to involve a special effect presents itself—after all, how is one to master these effects unless and until he tries them? But after the first urge to play with the new electric trains has passed, the haunting questions will arise, and have more than a ghost of a chance of preventing the director from using an effect just for its own sake.

13 / Television Producing

The term "television producer" can have a variety of meanings, depending on the size of the production organization involved. It is safe to say, however, that since a producer is necessary for a production of any kind, this is, therefore, one function that cannot be eliminated. Hence, when only one person is producing something, and doing everything himself, he will be called the producer. Sometimes the title may be producer-director in recognition of the key creative function that he also performs.

THE EXECUTIVE PRODUCER

The larger the production organization, the more division of responsibility is found. A single production is usually only one of a series, and several series may be in production simultaneously. The producer of the series thus becomes the executive producer, with producers of individual programs under him. Each of these producers may have the help of an administrative assistant called the associate producer. The nitty-gritty work of day-to-day operation of a production is often assigned to a third-level person called the unit manager or production manager. Most series are seen weekly, but it takes two weeks or more to put each production together. Thus the series may have two or more unit managers.

The executive producer will generally establish the basic policy for a series. He will plan the type of program it will be, based on analysis of audience acceptance and salability to a sponsor. He will define the kinds of stories which are to be used, the theme that will run through the series, the central characters and their basic characterization. On this basis, he will establish how many name stars are to be used in the cast of each production, and the approximate budget that such a series will require.

In a large production organization, whether it be a television network or a package producer's office, many people are involved. The producer, associate producer, story editor, and unit manager are generally free-lance people and are hired for the series, although some networks have unit or production managers on staff.

THE TELEVISION PRODUCER'S RESPONSIBILITIES

When a producer undertakes responsibility for a network series, he must start making decisions immediately. First he must hire a staff. This means he must engage a director for each of the programs he is doing, a story editor for the series, an associate producer if necessary, and a unit manager for each production.

The chances are that one or two scripts are ready at this point, since it may have been a script or a pilot program that inspired the series. An early move, however, is to contact several writers who are known to be capable of turning out the kind of stories that are required and get them started on some scripts. The script editor will take over this responsibility as soon as he is on the job, but the producer will still be closely involved in the evaluation, analysis, and doctoring of each script that comes in. Besides the artistic considerations of dramatic unity, believability, and plot construction, the script must be judged as to its suitability. Whereas suitability of the script for its intended audience may have been clearly established before it was written, suitability for the particular cast or star performers already engaged may require script changes.

The producer may take an active part in casting, may in some instances make most of the decisions in this matter, leaving only the selection of bit players and extras to a casting director. At the least, he will obtain the star performers, often going through a list of a dozen suitable players before finding one who is free to take the assignment.

The Budget Estimate

Then begins an important part of the producer's job: the detailed planning of the production. He must prepare a budget estimate, starting with the overall figure that he has been given and allocating a reasonable amount for each of the various expenses he knows he must face.

Budgets are generally divided into two major elements with a "line" drawn between. "Above-the-line" costs are the administrative and creative essentials: producer's and director's fees, costs of scripts, casting expenses, performers' fees, music. All other production expenses are "below-the-line" costs: they include such items as scenery, props, and studio facilities and engineering charges. A typical list of budget items follows.

Above-the-Line costs (55%)

Script	6%
Supervision and direction	16%
Music	2%
Cast (stars, actors, extras)	28%
(Also added here may be items for social security for the above, travel and entertainment, film to be integrated, etc.)	3%

Below-the-Line Costs (45%)

Scenery (often broken down into design, materials, labor, rental, painting)	11%
Props (broken down into labor, rental, purchase)	4%
Costumes (labor, rental, and purchase)	3%
Graphics	*
Make-up	*
Stagehands	5%
Transportation	*
Storage	*
TelePrompTer	*
Studio use (rehearsal without facilities—"non-fax"; and with facilities—"fax")	10%
Film studio	*
Rehearsal hall	*
Mobile unit	*
Audio prerecording	*
Sound effects	*
Extra camera	1%
Associate director	*
Floor (stage) manager	*
Script person	*
Mimeographing	1%
Video recording	1%
Post-production and editing	1%

* Less than 1%.

The percentages given above are derived from the budget of a typical one-hour dramatic program. However, they can only be considered a very rough indication of the relative size of the various budget items. Each production is in some way unique, and it is to be expected that shows depending heavily on film sequences or mobile on-location taping would budget "Film studio" or "Mobile unit" as major items.

The producer who works under an executive producer will often have the above-the-line items pretty well established for him by his superior, and he must allocate the remaining amount as best he can. During the course of the production it will be up to the unit (production) manager to keep an eye on all costs and inform the producer whenever any item seems to be going over budget. At this time the producer may decide to revise his budget estimate so he can take the necessary funds from another item. If this is not possible, he must decide whether it would do more harm in the long run to deny the director the extra rehearsal time or outside film shooting he is crying for, or to go to the executive producer for more funds. His superiors may have no source except company profits from which to provide the needed funds; certainly the sponsor will not increase his investment once the contracts have been drawn and signed. More often than not, a few hundred dollars may be denied, unfair as it may seem to the director, who has no detailed knowledge of the budget problems but sees only the amount he requested as a very tiny percentage of the entire budget.

This all adds up, then, to an administrative job on the executive level, requiring highly developed abilities in dealing with important people and the capacity to make important decisions through the exercise of taste and judgment. It calls for imagination and initiative of a very high order, on the one hand, and an organized mind on the other. A producer must be part genius and part accountant. His job is more important than that of the director, not merely because he is playing the role of business executive over him, but because it is he who must stick his neck out and decide just what the organization will do. To the director is left the psychologically less difficult task of simply doing it. But the director who has a producer over him is relieved of a thousand tedious business details, which, if he is a typical director, could not interest him less. He is free to devote his energy and thought to the creative and artistic problem of making the production as good as he possibly can.

As we have said, few television stations today can produce fully scripted shows of any great complexity. Dramatic productions, for example, are done only in the network-originating stations and in a few of the larger independent stations, but are beyond the scope of most of the smaller operations. This is primarily because of limited rehearsal time. It takes at least five hours of camera rehearsal to put a good half-hour dramatic show into camera shots, and the studio cannot be used for any other purpose for a few hours before and after a rehearsal and taping session because of the necessity of setting and striking sets and lights. The small station could never find a sponsor willing to pay for the large part of two days of studio use if his audience were limited to only the local viewers. Five hours of rehearsal for a half-hour program constitutes a rehearsal/air time ratio of 10 to 1. Much higher ratios than this, sometimes up to 30 to 1, are characteristic of major productions in European television studios.

The Producing Team

A word should be said here about the roles of the various members of the production staff. Several patterns of producing are common today —adaptations arising primarily because of the varying degrees of responsibility assigned to the director in the production situation.

The following are the most common staffing patterns.

1. *Producer alone.* This is the method used in most small stations, where one person (often called the producer-director) does the entire job of producing and directing the show. The only production assistance he will have during the rehearsal and running of the show is from the floor manager.

2. *Director and assistant director (A.D.).* Under some systems the A.D. (assistant or associate director) works with the director throughout the preparation and production of the show. In others he comes into the picture only when studio rehearsal begins. He takes over the chore of timing the program, he keeps the scripts, and he feeds cues to the director when necessary during the running of the show.

A commonly used method puts the A.D. on the intercom system with the director. The directing function is then divided between director and A.D., the latter giving all cues related to setting up camera shots or repositioning cameras. This then frees the director to call takes and concern himself with the camera that is on the program line.

3. *Director, assistant director, technical director (T.D.).* In studios where the "technical director system" is used, the T.D. takes over all responsibility for the placement and handling of cameras. The director does not work directly with the cameraman, but must relay all instructions through the T.D. The director still calls the shots but gives no camera directions during the show. Once very common, this method is now rarely used, at least in its pure form. Today, a T.D. generally performs only the switching function. This type of production-direction situation was discussed in detail in Chapter 10.

4. *Producer, director, A.D., T.D.* When the production of the show is more complex, a producer and a director will work on it together.

During the preparation of the show the director will be concerned with script and rehearsals, while the producer handles the business and legal aspects. In some productions such as broadcasts of football games (discussed in detail in Chapter 9), the producer will sit in the A.D. position during the telecast, determining placement and choice of commercials, determining what special effects will be used, and may also make some decisions on the shots that will be used.

5. *Producer, staging director, director, A.D., T.D.* The staging director is used only on complex dramatic shows, musicals, or dance shows (in which case he may be the choreographer). His responsibility is to cast and direct the performers, working out the action and rehearsing the performance. The two directors will work closely on preparation of the show, so that action, almost at the moment of conception, is adapted to camera. The television director is usually the only one of this pair who can handle cameras and plan their use, and during the studio rehearsal and air time he takes over entirely. The staging director then stands in the back of the control room, along with the producer in many cases, and maintains a critical and detached attitude so he can evaluate the effectiveness of the show. He may direct whatever changes in action must be made to fit the camera during rehearsal. Neither he nor the producer have any part in the show during air time or final taping, however.

6. *Producer, staging director, director, A.D., script person, T.D.* In this set-up the assistant's job in the control room has been subdivided, and two production assistants are used instead of one. The script person (also called the program assistant) may work at the director's elbow. She (or he) will take over the job of timing the rehearsals and during run-throughs will make notes of what the director or staging director want changed. The A.D. is then free to work with the director on the running of the show, taking off his shoulders the burden of anticipating the next cut or the next move. The director is then free to call the shots and to watch the program with a certain degree of critical detachment.

7. *Unit manager (production manager) added to above list.* This person's job is mostly involved with the preparation of the show rather than the actual rehearsal and airing of it. He is an assistant to the producer (he may even be called associate producer), and he carries the major load of the administrative details. The producer himself may take only a small part in the actual production of the program.

In addition to the six people among whom the functions otherwise vested in the television director are distributed, there may be assorted production assistants and secretaries on hand to run errands, make phone calls, bring coffee, and in general assist their bosses. The producer may have his secretary on the set, and so may the staging director or choreographer, and so may the director, unless he happens to be on the station staff. The production staff in the control room during rehearsal may comprise as many as ten people, each of whom has a part to play. This is a far cry from the small one-camera station which saves on personnel by doing without a director in the control room and having the cameraman and the talent handle the whole show. If there is no switching to be done, why have a director? Yet, in the small town, the same audience watches both the elaborately produced program and the one-camera show, sometimes one right after the other, and is sometimes equally entertained.

When a package-producing company or an advertising agency produces a show, the producer is a member of the producing company's staff. The staging director is either on staff or is hired on a free-lance basis for the individual production or the entire series. If a show is produced by a network (a house package), the producer is usually on the network staff, although network sports departments sometimes hire free-lance producers. The television director is usually on the staff of the network that carries the show, although he may also be from the producing company's staff or hired on a free-lance basis. In such cases the networks must approve the television director, and usually require that he have had experience working in their particular studios before they will accept him in lieu of one of their staff men. Assistant directors, program assistants, and script persons are usually on staff. The technical director always is.

PRODUCING THE COMPLEX PRODUCTION

There are many different methods and approaches to the producing and directing of television programs today. One thing upon which everyone agrees, however, is that there are a very great number of things that must be done to get the show ready and that someone must do them. How much of the work described on the following pages is done by the producer and the director together, and how much is done by the director alone or the producer alone, and how much is done by assistants, colleagues, or superiors, depends on the particular set-up governing any given station and sometimes any given program. In the remainder of this chapter, we will be discussing the preparation of the program (pre-production) before it is taped or transmitted.

For simplicity, a typical half-hour production has been used. A one-hour program requires twice as much rehearsal, but not always twice as much advance notice for such services as art, costumes, and the like.

Production of the half-hour show begins with a completed script placed in the hands of the director at least two weeks before the date of the show. The various production departments are then made aware of the particular needs and responsibilities in terms of bringing all production elements together on the day of the final rehearsal.

Script Clearance

Before a show can go into production, the script must be fully prepared, read, and revised to the satisfaction of the producer, director, script writer, the network's continuity acceptance department, and anyone else who may be concerned. The script editor, whose major concern is liaison with writers, will also, in many stations, pass judgment on the acceptability of script content. Each network maintains a staff for the purpose of continuity clearance, which is necessary in radio as well as television, and consists of investigating all the legal complications that might result from use of published material, quotation of phrases, discussion of controversial issues, or choice of fictitious names. For example, one script contained a nefarious character in the diplomatic service, for whom the writer had chosen a rather obscure name; a check by continuity clearance of the Washington phone book revealed two people with that name, either or both of whom might have been in diplomatic work; and another name was chosen.

Station policy in matters of good taste is also involved in continuity clearance. Scenes involving sex, gambling, and excessive drinking are very carefully examined. The general requirements of the Television Code of the National Association of Broadcasters are met, even though it may seem like a slavish adherence to the letter of a law, while the director is still able to convey as much of his dramatic meaning as he desires by the more powerful means of inference and innuendo. Since 1970, considerably greater latitude has been permitted in both visual and oral presentation.

Casting

The studio or the production organization will usually employ a casting director whose job it is to interview the tremendous flood of talent that always seems to be surging at the gates and to keep an active file on actors of all ages and qualifications. Some productions use "talent agencies" that supply performers from the many actors, singers, and dancers whom they represent.

A cast list to provide the casting director with the talent requirements of the program is prepared. Next to the name of each character are noted a few words of description: sex, age, type, and any special demands which the part will make on the actor. Often producers or directors will have in mind certain actors whom they have used before and with whose work they are familiar, and these choices may be listed in order of preference. The casting director will provide a choice of several possibilities for each role, and the proper actor will be chosen from among them after the producer or director has listened to them read sections of the script. The casting director will also be provided with a tentative schedule of rehearsal days and hours. An actor available for the day of the airing or taping is of little value to the production unless he can also attend the rehearsals that precede it. The rehearsal schedule may be somewhat altered later to adjust to the commitments of key personnel, but it is established in large part at the beginning of the production. "Conflicts" are permitted, occasionally, when the rehearsal schedule will not suffer.

During the first week of the production period, the producer or director will spend a certain portion of his preparation time interviewing performers in order to cast the show as rapidly as possible. The actors are given scenes from the script to read and the director takes careful notes of each applicant's general style, his ability to play the part, and whether he looks convincing in the role.

Since considerable memorization is necessary, it is desirable to make the final decisions on casting as early as possible and to get copies of the script into the hands of the cast a few days before the first reading. The actors will probably not have their lines down cold until a day or two after the rehearsals begin, but an early script gives them a head start and helps keep the production running smoothly and on schedule. The rehearsal schedule is usually attached to the script.

Production Services

The next step is a meeting with the production department, which includes persons having responsibility for sets, props, costumes, make-up, special effects, and artwork. The director will come prepared with a list of the requirements in each category, taken directly from the script. These lists will not be complete, because as the show develops, new ideas are formed and new requirements discovered. A basic list, however, should be in the hands of the production department as soon as possible, and additions to this may be made (apologetically) from time to time. Some production departments have composite forms, on which all of this information should be entered. By means of this list, the budget of the show is later charged with the expenses that have been incurred. On the basis of the first lists, the production department will estimate the probable cost, and the producer will have the opportunity to change his plans if the estimate does not fit his budget.

Independent agencies or producing organizations may use the facilities of the station or network's production department, or they may take care of each of these items themselves on the outside if they desire.

Settings

A production with sufficient budget is assigned a designer, who is either on the staff of the network or part of the production organization. At the smaller production centers there may be only one designer who does all the shows or even all artwork—sets, graphics, etc. The director and/or producer should confer with the designer about the sets for the show as early as possible, because most of the planning of camera shots and action will depend largely on the layout of the set. The director may come to this conference prepared with a rough sketch of what he wants in each set and how he thinks the various sets can be fitted into the studio. He will have certain key camera shots in mind. His mind is open, however, for the most part, and he often revises his earlier ideas completely in the light of ideas that the designer suggests.

A large budget will allow the construction of special scenery for the show. Usually, however, there are sets and set pieces stored from previous productions that can be repainted, assembled in a different manner, and used many times over. In such cases, the director will make his choice of existing sets either by visiting the warehouse and looking at them or by examining sketches or photographs which the design department keeps on file.

Whether the scenery is new or used, the director must establish the floor plan at an early stage of the production. Before he can start out-of-studio rehearsals (six days before the show) he must have accurate measurements of the studio sets, so he can lay them out on the floor of the rehearsal hall. As the scenery is being designed he will check frequently with the designer to make sure that he will be able to get the shots he is planning, or to become familiar with the set so he can expand his plans and take advantage of ideas contributed by the designer. Even with the greatest of care on the part of all concerned, the director is often surprised to find tables larger than he had expected, or hallways narrower than he had thought they would be; and slight adjustments in staging or camera work must often be made.

The director must not forget to inform his designer to leave room in the studio for musicians, if he is employing a live orchestra. Two portable dressing rooms are needed if there are quick costume changes, and space must be provided for them also. (This is not true, of course, if the program is being produced on videotape that is shot in segments and edited later.)

The designer must know not only the size of the studio for which he is planning sets, but the limitations of the elevators and corridors leading to that studio. In one case known to the authors, some of the finest scenery ever built for television could not be used because it was too big to fit into the service elevators leading to the studio.

When studio rehearsal begins, the director should provide the floor manager with several copies of the "set plot," which lists all activities involved with the scenery, such as the setting or striking of sets or set pieces during the show, and the moving of wild walls (flats not connected with the rest of the set).

Artwork

Artwork on the average production amounts to little more than opening and closing titles; although on some shows graphic materials of various sorts—still pictures, special props, which must be prepared by the art departments, maps, charts, graphs, and the like—will be required. As with every other department, the art department must have as much advance notice as possible, even though the entire list of credits is not available until casting has been completed. In submitting the list of titles and credits (either to the head of the production department or directly to the art department) the director must be sure to make clear the general mood of the show, and check back again after the title backgrounds have been sketched out, to make sure that their style is in keeping with the production.

Special Effects

When special effects of any kind are required for a show, additional problems often arise, most of which do not show up until the last stages of rehearsal. It is one thing to envision a beautiful effect, discuss it with the special-effects man and get his enthusiastic assurances that "it's a cinch, it's a breeze; we'll have it for every rehearsal"; and it is quite another thing to try to get the effect to work to the director's satisfaction in the studio. Certain effects are more or less standard, have been done on countless shows, and are entirely reliable. Snow, rain, optical effects, and many electronic effects are sure to work. However, the director must make the distinction between the sure thing and the experiment. Fog, for example, unless it is done optically by a filter in front of the lens, always seems to be somewhat of an experiment. Many special effects are things which have not been done before, at least not in exactly the same way, and ample rehearsal time must be allowed just for the effect, if it is important to the production. The director should have his plans all made and his alternate action decided on, in case he cannot use the effect at the last moment. If the effect is vital to the plot, however, and the entire show hinges on it, he should try it out on camera at some earlier time than the day of the studio rehearsal, to make sure it can be relied upon.

The special-effects man will exude self-confidence and assurance, and may even turn up at dress rehearsal with an effect which does satisfy the idea he had in mind; but if it is not what the *director and producer* had in mind, it may be cut from the show, much to the special-effects man's disappointment and disgust.

Costumes

Either the station production department or the show itself will have a wardrobe mistress (or costume designer) whose responsibility it is to plan and design costumes, see that they are rented or made and fitted, get them into the studio dressing rooms on time, see that the cast is properly dressed in them, and check them out again after the show. If there are costume changes during the show, she or he will take an active part in the production.

Actors must be sent for fittings almost as soon as they are cast, either to the rental company if the costumes are to be rented or to the wardrobe department for measurements if the costumes are to be specially made. Two days before the show the cast should be sent again for final fittings.

In making up the costume list, the director or the producer should be careful to include not only the number of costumes, their nationality and period, but also their quality and condition (rich, worn, tattered, and so forth). For color television, it is also very important to take into consideration the color of the sets, so the costumes will neither blend in and have no contrast, nor conflict with the colors of the set.

Props

The prop list should be made out and turned over to the production department two weeks before the show, to allow time for acquiring "hard to find" props or for constructing special props when necessary. The director will be able to list most of the hand props simply by going down the script. *Hand props* are small objects that are used in the hand, such as guns, handcuffs, and snuffboxes. After conferring with the designer, a list of *set props*, including furniture and other large items, as well as a great variety of small objects and bric-a-brac which the designer has in mind for atmospheric set dressing, will be drawn up. Each network keeps a large prop department in which most of the usual items can be found, but a staff of prop men at each network is constantly involved in traveling around town hunting up strange and unusual props. In some stations these people are called prop shoppers, in contrast to the prop men, who handle props in the studio.

It is wise to make a distinction between props that are absolutely required and those that are merely suggested and could be replaced with substitutes if necessary.

Hand props are frequently desirable at rehearsal, since the problem of how an actor will pick up a prop, and how he will dispose of it after he has used it, is very likely to be forgotten if the props are not actually in hand. A dancer rehearsed for a week with an imaginary bowl of fruit on her head during one part of a dance, and it was not until the dress rehearsal, when she was given a real bowl of fruit, that the director realized she had been picking it out of thin air in previous rehearsals and changing it back to thin air again each time after the action was over. The problem of where it was to come from and where it was to go had not been worked out. However, union rules in some cities require the presence of a prop man whenever actual props are used, and these make the expense of using anything but imaginary props or substitute props prohibitive for most programs.

The prop man must be sure to have on hand for rehearsal enough expendable props (edibles, cigarettes, etc.) so there are enough left by air time.

There should be a prop table on the set for the exclusive use of the prop man, on which all hand props are laid out so that everyone can know where the props are and where to return them after they have been used.

A prop plot should be prepared and two or three copies furnished to the floor manager when the studio rehearsals begin. This list should include all movable or hand props, indicating which are preset, which are carried into the scene, and by what actors, and by what entrances. The list should also indicate when props are to be struck during the show.

A misplaced prop can cause havoc in an otherwise smooth-running show. The story is told that Bill Gargan, playing one of television's earliest private eyes, Martin Kane, once was about to make an entrance and realized he did not have the gun that was essential to the scene. He looked frantically around, but could not even see the prop man, and his scene had already begun. However, he did see a gun, resting in the holster of a studio policeman. "Quick," he said. "Lend me your gun." The policeman was too dazed to resist. The scene went off as rehearsed. Gargan pointed the gun, a loud report was heard (from the sound-effects man), and Gargan returned the gun. The sweating policeman then opened it and showed Gargan a loaded magazine. Gargan had made a habit of never pulling the trigger of even a prop gun, and the habit had saved another actor's life.

Music

Every production uses music, if it is only for the opening and closing theme. Most of this is from tapes, records, or sound tracks laid down on videotape. Records and tapes are on file in the station's music department, although an occasional production will have enough budget to afford specially written music. Only a very skillful musicologist can choose recorded music that seems to be as well integrated with the production as a specially written score. It requires a wide familiarity with recorded music and almost a composer's taste and skill.

In preparing the various lists with which the director begins the production of the show, he must make out a music list with notes as to the duration of each piece of music and the mood that is to be conveyed. It is important to give the music department a copy of the script, often indicating segments that should be "backed up" or underscored. After a few days have elapsed the director or producer will again visit the music department, listen to the various possibilities that have been chosen for each need, and make the final choices.

Studio Facilities

The engineering department must know what equipment is required for the program almost as early as the production department must have the details of its requirements. When the program is first scheduled, the studio to be used will be assigned, but the director must let the engineering department know how many cameras are necessary, how many microphone booms, hanging mikes, floor monitors, and other special facilities, including special lenses. If additional personnel are needed (such as added mike-boom operators if more than one boom is to be used), this must be anticipated at an early date and ordered along with the studio facilities.

Advance Recording and Filming

Some productions call for the use of recorded voice for thought sequences or narration by a member of the cast. These audio recordings should be made early in the rehearsal week so that the tapes may be used as soon as possible for rehearsals.

When filmed or videotaped sequences are to be integrated with studio scenes, additional problems are involved. The process of film production is very slow in comparison with television—which means that there is even more reason for shooting these scenes as early as possible. Such filmed sequences are sometimes written as silent scenes to be accompanied by live narration in the studio or as an integral part of a drama. Shooting the film is a production operation in itself, requiring much the same preparation that a live show entails; hence the production of the film sections is often farmed out to a film-producing organization having its own staff and facilities. The television director should be sufficiently familiar with the basic techniques of film production so that he can supervise the preparation of the film footage that will be part of his program. Videotape inserts are much easier for the director to manage, but they also should be produced well ahead of time. They will involve additional scheduling of studio facilities and equipment or the use of portable recording equipment on location. If standard broadcast VTR equipment must be used, expensive mobile-unit equipment (remote trucks) will probably be required.

SUMMARY

Production involves many people, but is primarily in the hands of the producer. It is the responsibility of the producer to develop the original conception of the program and to oversee the implementation of that conception. In some situations, the producer's responsibilities with the actual production end when the script is placed in the hands of a director; in other situations, the producer is actually involved in the production through to the end. He is then producer-director. An executive producer is usually out of the actual production picture, but is deeply involved in the necessary financial and public relations activities.

Because there are so many people who must contribute to a complex television production, each of whom must plan his work carefully if he is to meet the inexorable deadlines of broadcasting, nothing can substitute for adequate advance notice. This means that almost all of the major production decisions, as well as detailed lists of requirements, must be made before the production is any more than a script on paper and a dream in the producer's mind.

14 / Non-Broadcast Television: The New Worlds of Video

The number of broadcasting stations has grown tenfold in the last quarter century, and so has the audience; there are now close to 100 million television sets in use. Throughout the world the total of broadcasting production centers probably amounts to three or four thousand. Television is now so commonplace and so much a part of our culture that it is completely taken for granted by people who do not know the first thing about it. Most of the television audience is unable to discriminate between a program that takes many man-months to produce and one that is so simple, or so standardized, that it can be produced with hardly any special preparation at all.

The once magical translation of visual reality into miniature size and its display on a flat surface became commonplace a hundred years ago. The once magical transformation of a flat picture into realistic motion has been commonplace for nearly eighty years. The once magical transmission of a moving image of reality in real time, across a distance, is rarely considered remarkable today. When the distance is very great, the broadcasters will call attention to it by superimposing their character-generated captions: "Live, via satellite." It is still mysterious, of course, to those who know the most about it. Only the real scientist knows how little is yet known about the most ordinary phenomena. No one really knows how electromagnetic waves (if they *are* waves) are carried. What is the medium? What moves?

Meanwhile, the television medium, commonplace and accepted, has gone on to develop and to expand far beyond broadcasting. It is natural for us to think of television as a mass broadcasting medium, devoted to entertainment, general information, and culture. The student of television production is naturally drawn by this image. He sees himself as the director of a future network program; seated behind the big glass window, with his assistants, his buttons, and his talk-back, he manages a team of over a hundred creative and attractive individuals, giving orders, making decisions, working against time.

This exists, of course, but there is also much more. The production of television programs for broadcast is now a small, perhaps a very small, part of the whole. Today there is private, non-broadcast television in industry, in government, in medical and health care, in education, and in community cable television centers throughout the nation. The total of non-broadcast television production centers in the United States may be, according to some estimates, ten times as great as the number of broadcast centers. Manufacturers and distributors of television production equipment will tell you that is where the big market lies. Although the student of television may see himself as a network director somewhere in his intended career, he will, whether he realizes it or not, probably find his first opportunities in other than broadcasting studios. But that is to be expected; television, whatever television is, covers a very wide field.

We must return to the question with which we started this book: what *is* television anyway?

Television may be classified, along with sound film and videotape, as a Class I* medium, since it is capable of communication via sound plus all the basic visual capabilities. Joining television in this class of media is a younger brother, the video telephone, which is used for two-way interaction rather than presentation, and usually in the individual (person-to-person) mode.

But aren't these last two strictly *tele*-media—transmitting their messages live, in real time—while other members of the same class, such as sound film and videotape, are *recording* media—storing a message for later playback? Is not videotape more closely related to film than to TV? Is production for videotape really television production at all? General usage applies the term "television" to anything that is finally seen on a television screen, whether it was produced live, on tape, kinerecorded, or on sound film. Hollywood film people who work on films intended only for television distribution generally say they are working in television. The only exception seems to be that the theatrical feature, when eventually released to television, is generally billed as a film.

With the advent of inexpensive portable television cameras and videotape recorders, coupled with the seemingly endless re-usability of videotape, many small groups of artistic or community-active individuals have formed production organizations. They rarely consider that they are in any way associated with television, however, except that they like to see their work played back over cable television systems. They prefer

---

* According to R. Bretz, *A Taxonomy of Communication Media* (Englewood Cliffs, N.J.: Educational Technology Publications, 1971).

to say they are working in "video." If by this they mean that their medium is videotape, a recording rather than a telecommunication medium, they are helping to limit the word "television" to the medium of live pick-up transmission and simultaneous reception.

But whatever television is, the techniques of television production described in this book will apply. It is fully possible to make films using live-television techniques, and traditional film methods have heavily influenced the production and editing of videotape. With the appearance of the mini-theatres, in which modern 16mm film is entirely acceptable, something close to 10 percent of Hollywood film production is probably being produced on videotape, then transferred to film for distribution and projection. A producer who prepares himself for one Class I medium will undoubtedly find himself before long working in others.

There is also a rapid development involving the use of television cameras, VTR machines, video cassettes, and the like in many fields and for many purposes that do not call for the production of programs. Yet many, perhaps most, of the skills (if not the techniques) of broadcast television must apply.

While the exact figures are not known, it is estimated that there may now be over 200,000 videotape machines (reel-to-reel and cassette) in use. Wherever there is a videotape recorder, except where it is used only to record and/or replay someone else's programs, there must also be a television camera, and someone who knows how to use it.

In education today, closed-circuit television is much more widely used than is generally believed. Its proponents have been disappointed at the slow progress and the small percentage of schools that originate their own programs. As a result, there has been little recent publicizing of educational television. Yet as early as 1970 almost a quarter of all elementary schools had videotape machines, and more than a third of all the high schools. (In Great Britain half of all secondary schools now have such equipment.)

In industry, television is widely used for training purposes. A recent survey identified at least 300 major firms with their own production centers and closed-circuit systems. It was estimated that this number might double during the next two years. Some of these organizations also use their private television systems to produce and distribute internal news and promotional features, the production techniques of which are often well above average broadcast quality.

Medical television, too, is an important and rapidly expanding field. Here again, instruction is a primary objective, while two-way systems for telediagnosis and teletherapy are making it possible to greatly extend the high quality of health care previously only available in large urban hospitals. So important is this field that several books have been written on the subject of telemedicine and hospital television.

The student of television production will find, when he attempts to enter the field, that opportunities lie not only in broadcasting but also in federal and local government, in community cable television, in mental institutions, in hospital and home care, in the operation of cable television services such as news and local events, as well as in the schools and industry in all aspects of education and training.

If a television producer-director can handle the media of Class I, which include all audio-visual means, he may readily adapt his talents to the media of the "lesser" classes, such as still pictures with sound, silent film, audio only, and others. With his television knowledge and skills he will find a wide field of possibilities open to him as he begins his production career.

Index

lantern slides, 125
laugh track, 109
lavalier microphone, 114–15, 118
lens, 25–7; focal length of, defined, 26
"let actor in, out" (director's cue), 74
"level, give me a" (audio cue), 76
lighting, 120–4; amount of, 120–1; balance, 123; in composition, 100–1; direction of, 123; for dominance, 101; high and low key, 124; instruments, 121–3; level, 120–1; quality of, 121; in production schedule, 178–9; in rehearsal schedule, 180–1
lighting director (man) (engineer) in rehearsal, 183
line (program) monitor, 10
lines of force in composition, 101
liveness, quality of, 109
log, 134
long lens, 26; perspective effect, 91: illustrated, 90
long shot (LS), defined, 27, 73
"loosen up" (cue to camera), 73
low angle shot, 30
low-key lighting, 124
luminance, 103

magnesium powder, 212
magnetic sound-on-film, 196
make-up, 204–5; as budget item, 218; in rehearsal schedule, 180–1; at taping rehearsal, 186
Marcus, Richard, 203
mask, 132
master control (MC) defined, 10n; crew in, 11; residue directing from, 133
master monitor, 10
master pot, 110
matte, 132
"matte" (cue), 78
matting, 214
medium shot (MS), defined, 73; medium long shot (MLS), 27; medium close-up (MCU), 27
microphone boom, 116–18
microphones, 111–18; method of transduction, 112; mounts and placement, 112–18; pick-up fields, 111–12, 113; types of, 112
mirrors, 210–11
mnemonics, television, 84–5
mobile unit truck, 158, 160; as budget item, 218
monitors, in directing, 63, 67

music, as budget item, 218; as cushion, 150; list, 229; in production schedule, 178–9; recorded, 229
musicians, in rehearsal schedule, 180–1; at taping rehearsal, 187

National Educational Television, 203
non-broadcast TV, 232
non-directional microphones, 112, 118

off-the-air monitor, 160
off-the-cuff directing, 142
omni-directional microphones, 112
one-shot (1-sh), 2-shot, etc., 29
optical effects, 210–12
optical sound, 196
outside rehearsal, 174, 176, 177; in production schedule, 178–9
overhead camera, 15
overhead shot (top shot), 34
over-the-shoulder shot, 33

pan card, 127
pan shot, defined, 34; pan left, pan right, 73
pancake make-up, 205
panel show, 152–3
panning, reasons for, 38
panoram dolly, 22–3
"pedestal up, down" (cue), 73
periscope, studio, 211
personnel, production, 12; program, 16–17
perspective in long and short lenses, 90–91
pictorial composition, 86–107; see also composition
picture area on TV graphic, 131
pilot program, 16
play-by-play announcer, 158
plumbicon tube, defined, 15n; compared with IO, 26; lenses for, 25–6; lighting for, 120
pocket shot, 29
polarity reversal, 213
poly-directional microphones, 112
Portapak, transitions with, 57
post-production, 201–3; as budget item, 218
potentiometer, 110
presentation (proposal), 16
preview monitor, 10
Prime Time Access Rule, 5n
prisms, 211–12
private line (PL), 138; in remote program, 160

ABOUT THE AUTHORS

EDWARD STASHEFF, Professor of Speech Communication and Theatre at the University of Michigan, has been involved in television since 1945. Before joining the Michigan faculty, he worked in New York for ABC, CBS, WPIX, and WNYE-TV. He has taken time off from his teaching duties to work with the National Educational Television Network; to serve as Director of Production for Israel's first television station; and to act as consultant to the Israeli Instructional Television Centre, to Everyman's University of Israel, and to numerous school systems and educational television stations in Hawaii, Ontario, and Winnipeg.

RUDY BRETZ is a communications media consultant. He has been a filmmaker and radio engineer, and in 1939 was a pioneer television cameraman. Mr. Bretz has produced or directed over one thousand television programs, taught television production courses at eighteen universities and colleges, and played a key role in establishing many educational television stations, as well as the Alabama Educational Television Network. He developed the Theater Arts Television curriculum and the first applications of educational television at the University of California at Los Angeles and has trained general and educational television broadcasters in eight foreign countries. Mr. Bretz was General Manager of WBIQ, Birmingham, Alabama; Producer-Director at CBS Television, New York; Production Manager at WPIX, New York; and for seven years a researcher at the Rand Corporation, where he now serves as a consultant.

JOHN GARTLEY is Assistant Professor in the Radio-Television-Film Department of Northwestern University's School of Speech. He previously taught at Montclair State College and the University of Michigan. In 1971 Mr. Gartley was awarded a Department of State lectureship in Ethiopia, where he had previously served as a Peace Corps volunteer (working in the Educational Radio and Television Section of Ethiopia's Ministry of Education). At present he is a media consultant for the J. Walter Thompson Company and advisor to WNUR-FM, the Northwestern University educational radio station.

LYNN GARTLEY, Assistant Professor in the Radio-Television-Film Department of Northwestern University's School of Speech, received her doctorate in 1972 from the University of Michigan, where she won several awards for outstanding achievement in television directing. Before coming to Northwestern, Ms. Gartley taught courses in radio, television, and film at the University of Wisconsin-Parkside, Eastern Michigan University, and Seton Hall University.

1508-1
5-27